ELECTRIC BRAE

'I think I have been waiting twenty-five years for this novel. *Electric Brae* is poetical, political and, thank God, post-Calvinist. It is a novel full of the geographical space of Scotland and the existential space of the twentieth century. A pan-Scottish novel with everything there, daringly conceived and beautifully written.'

The Orcadian

'For me it's a book about people who are convincingly portrayed as human beings, which is worth talking about because it's hard to do.

What I love about the book is the way it totally inverts the standard Calvinist approach to life. Here life is not a dismal pilgrimage across broken glass which is good for you because it's sore, and then you die and get a wee rest. No, here life is something to be approached with love, and that's the difficult kind of love which leaves us open to every experience, good and bad, which is our right.

So it's a warm, brave book which has serious implications for anyone who would use poverty, morality, sex or politics to limit their lives or anyone else's.

And it's a good read.'

A. L. Kennedy

'A creation which makes daring fusions of unlikely worlds of climbing and sculpture, of music and nautical engineering, of Orkney archaeology and Edinburgh bedsits . . . In addition there is the complexity and unpredictability of people.

I discussed last time Iain Banks' efforts to create a new kind of fusion of older Scottish and Renaissance landscape with modern alientation and urbanisation. It seems to me that Greig, importantly, goes even further in this respect. Powerfully he asserts that amidst random and confused contemporaneity we shouldn't forget our place as mortals of earth, landscape, weather.'

Books in Scotland

'A novel which does for mountain-climbing what Neil Gunn's *Silver Darlings* did for herring fishing. *Electric Brae* shimmers with the new light it sheds on Scottish preoccupations – and Scottish geography – seen from strikingly different angles . . .

The technical sophistication and narrative experiment with which it attempts to unearth the aching archaeology of memory makes it throb with moments of emotion which cleave to the reader like an ice-axe in a glacier. *Electric Brae* is proof that a thaw long-overdue in Scottish fiction may well be underway.'

The Scotsman

ELECTRIC BRAE

A Modern Romance

Andrew Greig

CANONGATE

First published in Great Britain in 1992 by Canongate Press.
This edition published in 1997 by Canongate Books,
14 High Street, Edinburgh EH1 1TE.

10 9 8 7 6 5 4 3 2

The author thankfully acknowledges the assistance of
a Scottish Arts Council Writers Bursary while writing
this book.

British Library Cataloguing-in-Publication Data
A catalogue record for this book is available on request
from the British Library.

ISBN 0 86241 740 6

Typeset by Hewer Text Composition Services, Edinburgh
Printed and bound in Great Britain by
Caledonian International Book Manufacturing Ltd,
Glasgow.

To the fisherman's daughter

'. . . The Electric (or Magnetic) Brae is one of the country's odder amenities. Approaching, the curious visitor sees only an unremarkable road rising steadily across the flank of a hill to vanish round the corner. But a lesson awaits:

For if on the Electric Brae a man slips his vehicle out of gear whilst going downhill, he will begin to slow, come to a halt, then start to roll backwards, finally disappearing around the bend (whereupon he must look to his steering). Whereas the woman cyclist at the bottom, leaning forward to better strive uphill, will find herself going faster and faster and need recourse to brakes to control her flight – for in reality she is going down!

(Whether approaching from the top or the bottom, both parties share the illusion, and will find it convincing – particularly if they continue to attend to the horizon.)

On fine weekends the Brae can be a populous spot, frequented by cyclists struggling downhill, open-mouthed motorists saving petrol whilst they coast uphill, and by those children who amuse themselves by stotting balls then watch them run away in the wrong direction.

It is a phenomenon some find disturbing, even to the point of mild nausea, for it disturbs certainties; for others such unexpectedness is a matter of elation, whilst children giggle and pursue their toys. All are astonished.

Well might the canny Fly Fisherman pause to reflect that here up is down and down is indeed up, depending on where one stands – and both are delusions! Thus the Electric Brae is both a location and a point of departure for those – native, incomer, visitor or armchair traveller – who wish to understand more of the true nature of this country and its inhabitants (and, of course, its fish) . . .'

from *A Fly Fisherman's Guide to Scotland*
H.O.N. MacCaig 1927

PART I

Kim's Game

ONE

THE BABY CRIES, the Scots pines whisper, I write for you by the light of the moon.

Ach, and I exaggerate already. She's a child not a baby, and she's not crying now, so don't you worry about her. But half an hour back she woke from a bad dream, so I carried her over to the window and showed her the moon and the harbour lights through the trees, and talked quietly till she slept again.

Nor do the Scots pines whisper. The wind is high tonight and they creak, groan and hiss against each other, anything but a whisper. Facts, my father grunts. Mind the facts, laddie.

The bairn murmurs and turns over on the divan under the eaves. She likes this room but still misses her mother.

And though this table is at the window and the moon is big, of course I'm not writing by its light alone. The oil-lamp is lit and every so often I have to lean forward to adjust the brass screw controlling the flame, to keep it at a safe level.

The child has fallen in love with the lamp at night. She calls it 'moon'. 'Please light the moon,' she says. So already she too exaggerates for effect. (Kim, walking down the Canongate in Edinburgh on a Spring morning years ago: 'All Art is exaggeration – that's the trouble with it.') Gets it from her mother, I suppose. Or her father. Or most likely all of us, as we were then.

(Kim was wearing her old green coat with the diamante brooch Lesley had just given her. Graeme was with us too. The sun glittered from her lapel and we were all arguing and laughing as we passed John Knox's house.)

The bairn snuffles, clenches at nothing then lets it go. Child, I say to her, you owe your existence to a diamante pussy-cat.

I watch her sleeping. Her thin fair hair lies over her eyes, her upturned palms mind me of tiny empty nests. Must she prefer a pretend moon to the real one?

This ache of watching, of wanting to protect while knowing I cannot, I know it from before.

So. The baby who is really a child is settled, the pines hiss like thousands of needles riding on the inner grooves of an old record, and I write to you by oil-lamp because it is time.

Do you remember 'Kim's Game'? My granny would bear in the big tray with its miscellany of household objects covered with a white cloth. She put it down on the table, paused while we sat round with our pencils and paper, eyes wide-open, straining. She flicked away the cloth. We had a minute, then she'd call 'Time up!' and remove the tray, and we'd start scribbling our lists, as if by hurrying we could overtake our fleeing memories.

This afternoon I played 'Kim's Game' with the child, and the remains are on the table here. Little everyday things I had around the place, such as a guitar plectrum, a plastic soldier, a packet of Rizla, a diamante brooch, and a mangled, rusty piton. Objects picked up at random – okay, I did orchestrate them just a bit – to play a memory game to amuse a child on a wet afternoon. And to begin to teach her what she'll need to know.

'Mind whit ye say, mind whit ye dae,' my granny said. 'For your words will go where your feet will never carry ye.'

So many voices in this quiet room. I pick up the mangled climbing piton, stare out at the night and wait for it to begin.

Piton

THE MAN ABOVE climbed in balance, standing well out from the rock, the way the naturals do. As he moved fluently up the slabs, just the odd soft exhalation drifted back down.

I'd done the few routes within my soloing grade, so rolled a cigarette and lay back to watch. It was late autumn, blue and auburn, bonnie and all. Bridget and I had finally separated three months back and I still felt like blown wool caught on a barbed fence. Most likely I was trying not to think how she felt.

His style wasn't mine. The Etive Slabs round the corner from Glencoe are mostly friction climbing that turns on marginal adhesion between hard rock and soft-soled boots. To do it well you have to trust rock, friction, and yourself. Definitely not my sort of climbing.

I watched him finish with none of my peasant lunging and grunting, then closed my eyes for a while.

'You climbing or just sight-seeing, pal?'

I looked up. The climber I'd been watching was standing in front of me. A compact youth in loose jeans and sweatshirt, nothing fancy.

I shrugged. Must these Glaswegians always be abrasive?

'Whatever I've a mind to, chum. I'm not competing.'

He almost smiled. His eyes were dark, his hair black in a curt pig-tail. Narrow nose, cheekbones, short and compact. A West Coast Celt at play.

'Fair enough,' he said. 'The crag's no yer capitalist market-place.'

He leaned back on a boulder, massaging his ankle.

'Smoke?' I held out the makings.

'Ta, no.'

My muscles were stiffening but I hadn't done enough to justify calling it a day.

'Gonna do some bouldering.'

He just nodded. I got up, stretched, then started a traverse across the lower slab. Useful practice, bouldering, a chance to

5

explore your limits in safety. If things go wrong you can always jump off. Separate yourself.

I smeared across the lower slab as far as an awkward corner, got half way round it then slithered to the ground.

Feeling a right stookie, I went back and worked my way along to the problem. Re-arranged my feet and stretched around the corner. Got my fingertips to a wee nobble on the rock, now the left foot round . . . My right boot skidded away and this time I fell back on my arse.

Maybe I'm not good enough. Or strong enough. Still no comment from behind.

I climbed up and across for the third time, looked at the problem and tried to think it through. I couldn't see any options other than packing it in or trying the same again and hoping it would somehow turn out better. Here goes –

'If you turned yer left foot the other way . . .' the voice said quietly.

I looked down at him. No sarcasm, no patronising, just helping out.

'Like this?'

'Na. This way.' I felt a hand quite gently swivel my foot round. 'Now do the same wi the other. Now stand right up on it when you stretch, that'll gie you the extra reach.'

It did. This time when I reached for the nobble I was still in balance. Got the left boot on a small wrinkle and swung round the corner no bother.

'Thanks.'

'No problem, pal. Somebody had to show me that and all. Amazing the difference a wee shift of stance makes.'

I carried on the traverse another twenty feet, then jumped down and walked back.

'Fancy doin a couple of routes?' he said. Casual, like.

'I'm not your standard.'

'You're no meant to say that.'

'I don't always say what I'm meant to.'

We looked directly at each other for a moment. Then he nodded somberly. He was no ray of sunshine. Jesus didn't want him for a sunbeam.

'No competing, then. We'll swap the leads as they come.'

'Bags me the easy ones.'

He paused then, gave me another of those hard glances. 'Have you no pride?'

6

'That I do. But I'm saving it for something more important.'

'Such as?'

'I'll let you know.'

Another wee grin. We buckled on our harnesses, got out the ropes and walked round to another route. I checked it out.

'Yon?'

'Aye. You first.'

I looked up. I'd not led a full route at that grade before. Didn't want to make a pillock of myself. Must have been kidding myself about that not competing.

'Hey, you can do it, man. The crux is a stretch but that should suit a lang streak like you.' He nodded at my shoulders. 'Been training?'

'No. Work on the rigs. North Sea.'

'Ah.'

We buckled on our harnesses and roped up.

'No affront, but you dinni speak like a navvy.'

'Och, we're full of surprises on the rigs. Some of us can even read and do joined-up writing. You?'

'Teacher training. History, like.'

'You speak like a navvy.'

'Urban proletariat, man. Get going.'

I led off. The sun was on my back, the rock was being warm and friendly. I felt more trusting and the rope was being paid out smoothly from below.

Twenty feet up I selected a No. 2 nut from my rack, diddled it into the crack on my right. It fitted and held first time. With my free hand I worked a sling through the loop of the nut and clipped the sling to the rope. Always reassuring to get your first protection in.

I looked down at the intent upturned face below.

'What's your name, youth?'

'Graeme, dad. With an "e".'

'Right. Jimmy Renilson, without a "d". Just wanted to say, Graeme, if you've ony suggestions, feel free. I'm here to learn.'

(Typical Scottish males, introducing themselves late across twenty feet. I can still picture it fine as I turn the piton in my hand tonight, can see his dark Celtic face looking up, feel the warm rock, feel the warmth of immediate and irrational liking. Temporary sunshine, long time ago.)

This time he grinned. When he did smile people felt good. Over the years I'd see folk do a lot to make that dour bugger smile.

'Okay. Uh, that karabiner could be the other way round for a start. The gate should face out, safer yon way.'

I re-clipped the krab through the green sling and the red rope. The sun glinted on the metal and it all felt very pleasing as I eased away from my protection.

It was the first extended E1 I'd led. I thugged the crux without style or grace, but made it. I banged in a piton and belayed him as he seconded up. He climbed well within himself, very certain. Maybe it could rub off on me.

'Piece of duff, eh pal?' as he eased up alongside me.

'No bad,' I said, which was Scottish for pretty wonderful.

He led the next pitch, wincing a bit from the ankle he'd broken six weeks before. For all his attack and control, Graeme would always be accident-prone. I kept paying out the red umbilical cord as he moved up, silent and meticulous.

He made it fine to the top and put me on belay. I slipped off at the crux but he had me straight away on tight rope. Good man. I apologised for climbing like an amputee. He shouted down the sequence of moves that unlocked the problem, and I made it up.

Two more good routes then we packed up our gear as the sun dropped behind the hills. In the West the sky drained to long pale lochs with cloudy shores, an illusion but one of my favourites. We sat on a while. Even then he talked politics and I talked feelings. He was outraged by what he saw as the Labour government's sell-out. Callaghan was a traitor and Heath represented the powers of darkness. Innocent times. I listened, argued a bit, appreciating his passion. I was short of a passion at the time.

I found myself beginning to talk about a failure and betrayal closer to home: me and Bridget. He listened, uneasily, but he listened. It felt strange but good. I hadn't had a man to talk to for ages, me and dad having packed it in years back.

We came at things from opposite sides. I liked that. I liked him. He put me in mind of the rock he leaned against – hard and close-grained, with unexpected shiny facets.

Eventually we got to our feet.

'Good, that,' he said casually.

'Aye.'

'You prefer soloing?'

'It's alright, but you can go further wi a partner.'

'Yup.'

Long pause. I smiled to myself. It was like sorting out a first date. Looked like it was down to me.

'Fancy next weekend, then? You got any commitments?'

'Nothing desperate. You?'

'Na.'

We picked up our sacks.

'We'll gie it a whirl,' he said and to my surprise held out his hand. 'You're richt, the crag is no place for hard men.' He grinned, and we shook on that.

I hesitate, balancing the piton across my knuckles. Old rust, old blows, so many of them. No way to tell now if it was his or mine. I put it away in the drawer and sit a while, listening to the puttering of the pretend moon.

TWO

Rizla

MUST HAVE BEEN six months later. Late March '79. Springtime, if you're an optimist.

She was small, young and edgy in a lunchtime Aberdeen bar packed with half-cut oilies, so I shifted and let her by.

She got her shout in: two vodkas, one Coke. Being careful with the money. I was vaguely aware of cropped black hair in a Fifties quiff. No rings on the short broad fingers tracing outlines on the bar. She sighed and I glanced again. No lines on her pale face but something about her created a slight warp, some disturbance in the smokey air.

She pulled out a pack of Golden Virginia. I looked away and returned to our crew's argument over Japanese against British bikes.

I was wabbit. My father's word, still popping up like an outcrop of enduring, harder rock. My arms felt over-stretched and my knuckles were skinned, but a lot of folding money in my pocket. I was just off the platform, free for two weeks. Anti-climax was hovering like the malts behind the bar, just out of reach.

A party political broadcast came on the telly, someone reached up and switched it off. That left Pink Floyd on the juke-box playing something I'd once thought significant but now sounded pompous.

I was thinking of the Old Man of Hoy seen from the chopper. I was drinking slowly because I still had to get to Stirling and no one would be waiting for me there. I wasn't looking for anything. I had many fears and no particular place to go.

I wasn't looking out.

The barman had got sidetracked at the far end of the bar. She muttered to herself and abruptly wiped out whatever she'd been drawing. She flicked back the dark quiff that kept springing forward over her eyes, put the skinny cigarette to her lips and looked around. She was trying very hard to be adult. That made two of us, but I had less excuse.

She must have seen me eyeing her tobacco. I'd given it up in disgust, along with a load of other things. She pushed the makings towards me and muttered something as she looked away again, so I never caught the first thing she said.

I took the tobacco and Rizla papers. Why kid yourself? You can't give up what you don't really want to.

Some day, I was thinking, I'll climb that Old Man. In Scotland there are several Old Men, but the Old Man of Hoy is the boss – 450 feet of sheer prick. A lonely, exposed and rapidly eroding one. To do that lonely route and finally stand on its summit, now that would be some kind of target. I wondered if my pal and partner Graeme would be interested. More in his league than mine, but I could train up to it.

I lit up my first since the Devolution vote. It was almost worth the wait. Deferred gratification, we love it. It lets us square Calvinism with hedonism. She held out her hand. I looked at it blankly, a perfectly ordinary slightly calloused hand, then noticed she still hadn't lit her roll-up. I passed her my lighter. Her disconcerting, would-be adult face relaxed and I was about to say something friendly and banal when the barman finally returned with her drinks.

She lit up hurriedly, nearly burned the tip off her nose and scorched the underside of her cigarette. She hadn't had much practice and her wrists were thin. She counted out exact money, picked up her order and was about to return to her friend in the corner.

I held out my hand.

She hesitated.

She put down the glasses and dug out my lighter from her jeans.

'So who are you then?' she demanded and for the first time she looked straight at me.

Some folks happen to have clear mid-blue eyes, but they just use them to see with. Only a very few seem to bear everything in their eyes, as though their eyes were the glass window of an aquarium and at moments you can look right inside. And like an aquarium you can see it all and you want to touch what's inside but you can't.

That apart, she had nice enough eyes and for a moment I looked back into them.

I shrugged, as though her question was too big for any better answer, gave her my name. She nodded. She had a touch of blue eyeshadow and a red spot on her chin and she was about to leave.

'So what do you do that's fantastic?' I blurted.

She gave me the Aquarium Look again and I glimpsed fragility, cold glass, withdrawn life.

'I don't know, yet.'

'But you will?'

'I will that,' she said.

(Easy now to see in our first exchange we had asked the definitive question of each other's lives. Who *are* you, Jimmy? What do *you* do that's fantastic, Miss?)

'Kim,' she said. 'My name's Kim Russell. Though it's really Ruslawska.' She spelt it out. 'We're waiting for the Orkney boat.'

The Pink Floyd chorus waddled towards another climax of meaning.

She said she was going to an archaelogical dig with her friend Joan. She'd quit school. Maybe art college later. What did I do? I was an oil-extracting technician. One of yer actual roughnecks. I had two weeks shore leave and was heading back to Stirling. Stirling? Did I know Plean? She lived there. Plean was a dump. We agreed there was nowhere dumpier, except possibly Hamilton. Blantyre, she said, that's worse. Go there and see why David Livingstone went to Africa. But did I know Orkney? It was . . . holy ground. A beautiful sane place.

'But would you be happy living there?'

She frowned at the worn linoleum. 'But happiness isn't the point.'

For the first time in months someone had my complete attention.

'So what is the point?'

She looked up at me. Her lower lip plumped slightly in a secretive mouth. She seemed to vibrate a little all the time, as if she didn't quite fit the space she found herself in.

'Dinnae ken,' she said. 'Do you? Is it being happy?'

As if I could tell her. She'd spoken urgently, almost pleadingly. I had my countrymen's terror of appearing pretentious, which so often keeps us from saying much. But among the babble of Scots, English, Swedish, and Italian, she deserved an answer.

'If we're here looking to be happy,' I said, trying to keep my voice casual, 'it would be like going to Skye for the hot dry weather. Sure it comes, but not very often, and it certainly doesna last.'

She laughed and I was pleased. An image of the Reefs of Pretention (deadly, rips the bottom out of any conversation) drifted by but I kept it to myself. Shouldn't have. We always understood each other best in images.

No, I hadn't been to Orkney but I was interested. Particularly in Hoy and the Old Man. She nodded. Ornithology? No, rock climbing.

She grimaced. 'Does life seem too long to you, then?'

I'd had this before, from Bridget among others.

'Too bloody short,' I said. 'That's why I do it, though that's kinda hard to explain.'

'So explain,' she said.

'Climbing reminds me how much I want to stay alive. It's the pleasure of soluble problems.'

'You mean solvable.'

'Na. Soluble, like aspirin. Dissolves pain and that.'

A quick smile from that tense mouth. A little flash of white like surf.

'Anyhow it's not that dangerous, just feels it sometimes. Maybe some of us need that.'

This was too serious for Scotland and lunchtime. Those reefs were perilously near the surface.

She regarded me steadily.

'Fair enough,' she said. She had no lines on her face but her eyes were older than they should be. She inhaled and glanced away, kicked the bar a few times like it was its fault.

'I hope danger isn't the only way to make it good,' she muttered.

A bunch of memories like supply boats docked then left again. People, faces, places. Despite everything, they left behind a warmth like the whisky in my hand.

'Christ, so do I.'

She didn't smile, just regarded me. We looked at each other across a decade or so but I'd met one of my kind. Very different, but *kin*.

She said she'd better get back to her pal who must be dying of thirst. A tall, gawky-looking lassie, dying more likely of curiousity or suppressed giggles. They'd be at the dig for the next three weeks, then Kim was staying on all summer. If I was up checking out the Old Man, why didn't I drop by? The digs were pretty relaxed and I could even do some low paid but interesting navvying . . . She was babbling a bit now.

'Aye, sure,' I said. 'Maybe some time.'

She looked at me doubtfully. 'It's near the Brough of Birsay,' she said. 'Anyone will tell you where we are. Island telegraph. Will you remember that?'

Brough of Birsay, aye.

Then she picked up her drinks and squeezed through the crowd. It must have been hot in the bar, I was sweating under my shirt.

'Who's the kid?' the barman asked.

'Someone,' I said. 'Definitely someone.' I handed him my empty glass and squeezed my knuckles, wondering if I was getting early rheumatism like my dad. 'Someone who looks neat in jeans.'

He pulled a face and sighed. On account of me, or her, or the trouble that starts with men and women, I don't know.

'You are not drinking, Jim?'

Olaf of course, though we usually cried him Tumshie (as in Turnip = Swede). Repartee was fair dazzling on our platform.

I rejoined them for a last quick round and the heated finale of the motorbike debate. Olaf, Swiss Frank, Ditran, Alex, Tumshie – looking round I admitted the company of men wasn't inspiring but it was simple. We shared jokes and rough work in filthy conditions on a platform shaking with heavy engineering. Bunked down at nights, it was like riding a monster that could break loose at any moment. I'd started as roustabout, lowest of the low on the scaffolding deck, recently graduated to roughneck. They were decent men, there for their own reasons, and I wasn't going to knock them. We worked well together but meant next to nothing to each other outside the job. Apparently that was normal.

We phoned for our taxis and left the bar to split for various corners of Europe. There was a space where she and her pal had been.

The train took ages and the heating was off. It gave me something external to dislike. Stirling station has a fine old *Brief Encounter* clock but no one was waiting beneath it.

It was dark when I got to the upstairs flat near Riverside. I could feel the damp rising off the Forth. For a moment I wished myself back with Bridget. Loving or angry, she was real to me. We'd known each other since childhood, maybe that was the problem. Or maybe I was just a daftie, not mature enough to accept the fun days were over and we shouldn't want more than an okay job and a reliable someone to keep the chill out.

Leaving her for this dump and then quitting Ferranti to navvy on the rigs, now that was daft. Some kind of atonement. How very Scottish.

Ah well.

I switched on every light and fire and drew the curtains to keep out the darkness. I hesitated then unplugged the phone. I felt a heel but a more secure one.

There was no justification for the unhappiness I'd caused. Nor the vows broken. But there'd long been that sense of something missed out on. I'd been comfortable, but something had never happened. Maybe if I drifted like this long enough, it would bump into me. Or maybe I'm a fool. So many maybes these days.

I popped a Fray Bentos pie in the oven and found some cereal to be going on with. The colour TV flickered on the floor. Apparently we were going to have a general election. I turned the sound down.

Unusual name, Kim, for a Scot. Something about that conjunction of jet black hair and blue eyes. Something disjointed, unsettling. Challenging.

Ach, too young and maybe a bittie strange.

Anyway, what would she want wi me?

I turned off the telly, poured a small whisky. Next weekend I'd cragging again with Graeme. At last a man to talk with, even if he found it hard to respond in kind. I unpacked my slippers and *The Alexandria Quartet*, my latest attempt to educate myself in things other than engineering and manual dexterity.

Old Man of Hoy. Brough of Birsay.

Well, maybe.

I pick up the Rizla and extract a paper. I could allow myself just one, a measured response to an acknowledged addiction.

Instead I adjust the lamp as it heats up and flares. Long nights here after long days' work, and the child still wakes, but I don't seem to need sleep so much.

Those meetings: Pink Floyd didn't miss a beat, but even at the time there was something, that slowing and sharpening you get when an accident is about to happen. When she turned her eyes on me, so vivid and demanding, it was like touching an electric fence as a child. Perhaps I invent the haze of blue, the whiff of something burning.

I reach for another piece, and try to see it her way.

THREE

Photo

IN 1977 A FAULT line broke across the decade. Even in Plean Kim didn't have to read about it to know that. On the far side was everything old and done with. On her side there was nothing yet. She hung on, waiting to be born.

Following her instincts and saying very little about them, in '78 she stopped dressing in black. She forced herself to part the hair that had hung around her eyes for years, and stared in the bathroom mirror. She saw a frightened Aubrey Beardsley. So she scowled, slicked back her hair and inspected the result. A truculent rabbit. With a big nose and not sure if it was a boy or a girl. Maybe no one would notice.

She decided she'd have to live with having dad's nose, and learned how to accentuate her eyes to bring up what she hoped was a Chagall blue. Then she completed her essential education with Dave, who already seemed too young, demanding and unreliable. She'd have to leave him soon, before he left her.

She felt like a seedling growing in secret under crazy paving, groping for a crack to emerge through.

In '79 she made a break for it. She saw a man in an Aberdeen bar and liked the look of him. She liked his long build, his old-fashioned clothes (old tweed jacket, shirt, cords, lace-up shoes, the man's so straight it's almost style. Almost). He looked scuffed and puzzled at the edge of his group, part but not part of it. *Adrift* was the word. Accepting, maybe. That would be a change. He was older and she liked his hands.

If he can talk as well, she thought, he'll do. So she'd blurted out 'So who are you, then?' and made her move.

She leant over the bow-rail with Joan, her last connection with the past and sworn to silence.

'Do you think he'll come? Not that I'm interested. There's better things to do.'

'Such as?'

'Come on, Joan! Anyway, I thought you were going to be a missionary.'

Joan smiled and looked down at her friend.

'First I want a boyfriend. Africa can wait.'

And he thinks in pictures too, Kim thought. He looked right into me. I hope he saw enough, but not everything.

They turned up the collars of their anoraks and stood together, leaning into the oncoming swell.

And he came. Not straight away, but one blowy afternoon she straightened up with an aching back to see him standing on the edge of the site in his old jacket. He crouched down to examine a section-trench, ran his hand lightly down the different layers of history, asked a question of the digger beside him.

A second life, she thought. She stuck the trowel point-down into the ground and walked casually over towards him and the Orkney summer began.

Orkney. I can close my eyes and go there anytime. The windy, stone-flagged streets of Kirkwall, the red and yellow sandstone Viking cathedral like a grounded Ark above that market town. The solitary tree in the main street, thin northern light, the cadences that still sound Welsh to my ear, rising at the end to make every statement an amused question. And the streets of Stromness, that peedie fishing town so like my own but fifty years back in time, the meandering street and houses heaped like grey ropes and creels below the brae. The sea everywhere, swan-sprinkled inland lochs, low stone walls, good farming land. Standing stones and burial cairns, brochs and slipways. Stone and grass and the ceaseless wind. Where so much seemed possible and open and enduring, though even then it wasn't as simple as that.

I showed the child the photos the other day and I've promised we'll go there soon. It's part of her birthright, part of what she inherits from the four of us.

This photo is her favourite. Mine too, I guess. She wants to know more, and she will.

She wore peach-coloured pajamas and a light cardigan. We lay on the heathery slopes above Waulkmill Bay. The dusk was warm and her feet were bare.

17

'Look,' she said, 'I started when I was fifteen. Dave was a year older. We loved each other and when he finally took me properly it was wonderful. On the escarpment above the North Third Reservoir, near Carronbridge, you know?'

I nodded. Up till now it had been one of my favourite places. Dad and I used to fish the North Third until I gradually became more interested in scrambling on the escarpment cliffs and left him to it. That old-fashioned 'took me properly' was very young.

'Afterwards everything felt and looked so wonderful and I felt part of it, and he was part of me, and for the first time since my dad – '

I lay still with my arms round her and said nothing. One false move and she'd go back inside herself again, draw blue curtains over the aquarium. She could disappear inside for hours on end.

I gazed down past her ear to the bay. The tide was high and ready to turn. The day had been long and hot and windless, unusual for Orkney. Now it was nearly midnight on the summer solstice and the air was mauve-grey, warm and soft as a mouse. The *simmerdim*, Shetlanders called it. In the gloaming two boats swung and clacked together at anchor. My hand was on her hip and I wanted to make up to her for everything.

'It was based on love and we had the right, whatever our age. I felt the whole world, even Plean, was beautiful and on my side. It would always be. Jimmy?'

I nodded. I remembered the feeling. It had worn off somewhere in my twenties, born away on a receding tide of hormones. Inevitable, Bridget had said, and I'd finally believed her. But lying now by Kim was like starting the first pitch of a new route, when the world is heart-thumping and every move upward will stretch the drop below.

'So it didn't last,' she chided. 'What does? I learned that when I was twelve. What you want to do, do now.'

She guided my hands. Her directness was a relief to someone who had always preferred Lady's Choice at school dances. This new generation took lady's choice for granted. We lay and watched the half-light refuse to die, and my world was the warmth of her breast in my palm and the sound of her voice.

'Maybe he was too young,' she said. 'Boys are younger, aren't they?'

'About ten years behind, I'm beginning to think.'

'That makes us about ages.'

'Near enough for an equal struggle, aye.'

She looked down. 'Right enough,' she said quietly.

She examined the heather for clues, then shook her head and continued. 'He did get awfy jealous and possessive. We'd argue and then fight – I mean physically fight – and he always won because he was stronger. The trouble was,' she finally looked up at me, 'it kinda turned me on. Maybe I get my own way too much.'

I shook my head. Didn't turn me on.

'I know,' she said, 'that's what's different. You're stronger than he is but it's all held back and that's exciting too.' She grinned. 'I don't just want you for your antique mind. Or just because you take me seriously.'

Like the cryptic tiny drawings she was always doing on the side, so much held back. Her hand moved lightly across my chest, her fingertips rough from weeks of trowelling. In the bay the shadows of the boats shifted at anchor. She was too young. I was too old, and scared of messing up again.

'I came up here to get away from him. He says if I let anyone else touch me he'll kill me. Or himself.' She laughed quietly. 'But he won't. I'm no fashed.'

I said nothing.

'Jimmy?'

'Huh?'

'Just because you loved somebody once doesnae mean you're responsible for them now.'

My hand was still and sweating on her breast. Between my fingers her nipple was like the hips and haws we used to pick and sell when children, as ripe and tempting.

'Look, I've been trying to tell you I'm no too young. I mean, my soul's got to be a thousand years old!'

A splash, and a flicker of light in the bay. An otter most likely, taking what it needed. I wondered who, after all the twists and hesitations are done with, does anything else? That seemed to be the new mood. Take and don't apologize.

She turned my face to look into hers, and I saw down through her eyes like through clear water.

'*Now*', she said. 'Before I pass out from lust.'

It was light when we tooled home on my Kawasaki, standard roughneck issue. I took my time on the dipping coastal road, smelling salt and hay and beasts in the early off-shore breeze. She wore my biking jacket, had wrapped the travelling rug round me. Her head pressed hard into my back. I hoped she would find what she did that was fantastic, something to unlock her from the world she'd made since a furniture van had swept her father and his Triumph out of this world.

It seemed odd she still got a kick out of bikes.

When we got to the diggers' camp she was shivering and her eyes were glazed.

'What's up?'

'Nothing,' she said. 'Doesn't matter now.'

Maybe it was just the cold morning air in her eyes.

'I love you.'

'I know.' She paused and whispered in my ear, 'I'm just daft about you.'

There's a moment in abseiling when you have to step backward off the cliff and *trust*.

'I think it's time I moved into your tent,' she said. 'Do you mind?'

'Right, right, right! Do you know how often you use that word?'

She dug in the pocket of her jacket and pulled out a stone.

'Call this the Past. Or Guilt. Right?'

She pressed it into my hand, it felt smooth and heavy, fitted well.

'Now chuck it over the cliff.'

I weighed it in my hand.

'I don't think it can be done,' I said. I didn't add 'But you're too young to know that.' Age was a touchy subject with us. Still I swung my arm back and lobbed the chuckie stane out into space. We watched it dwindle and disappear.

'Don't ask if we've a right to this. If you're not going back to her, that's what you've got to learn to do.'

She winked at me then rolled on her back on the turf at the cliff's edge. I kept looking over as an unwelcome notion rose from below like the gulls around us. It squawked that I made myself feel guilty so I could carry on doing what I was doing and still keep my good opinion of myself. It veered away and vanished for a few years.

I shook my head, lay on the cliffs of Hoy and studied the Old Man across the gulf. Four hundred and fifty feet of disintegrating red sandstone pillar. It looked very vertical and alone.

'Well, I think you're crazy,' she said, 'but I've got to admit it's got a certain something.'

Her laughter was warm in my ear. As I took out the binoculars her hands distracted me.

'Christ almighty, woman! This is a pure natural objective I'm studying.'

'So is this.' She struggled with the zip.

Her direct ways, with sex at least, were a liberation. Bridget and I had learned with each other in the era of Foreplay, Consideration and Responsibility for Orgasm. Pleasure became like work – intriguing and sometimes satisfying, but work and most of it up to me. At times I'd felt more like a mechanic than a lover. I had a brief image of my dad bent cursing over the starting handle on wintry mornings, and laughed.

'We didn't do it like this when I was a loon. Not in Eyemouth, anyhow.'

'I don't want to hear about it.'

She turned on her side and moodily prodded the turf.

I went back to studying the Old Man, tracing Bonington's route description slowly up the stack till I came to the two great split blocks on the top. I thought I could see the rusting cable round the blocks that was left from the televised ascent in the Sixties, my first image of rock-climbing.

I put down the glasses and glanced at her. I felt slightly dizzy and my pulse was raised. There'd been a few further ascents, but so far only by the better climbers of the day. I studied the crucial overhanging second pitch again. Maybe out of my league. But I wanted this one like few things before.

'Are you going to climb that on your tod?' she muttered.

'Christ no! My pal Graeme fancies it too. He can be kinda dour, but he's a good climber and we go well together.'

She ran her tongue round my ear, like a wee beastie at a salt-lick.

'What's he like?'

'Younger than me, bit older than you. He's teaching now, probation year. History. Paints a bit too. Wants to start the revolution from the school kids up.' I was checking out the final exposed pitch. It scared me. Recently I'd noticed how many things did. Maybe that was progress. 'Nice idea but no chance.'

'Jim, you're such a pessimistic old fart.'

I gestured to indicate the Old Man, the cliff top, her.

'Graeme's all conviction. I'm not certain of anything apart from this.'

'You've surely got to have convictions.'

I put down the glasses, I'd seen enough. I laughed. 'Aye, but I'm from the East Coast and I know my convictions are in the end only opinions. *Naething's proven, naething's provable.* He's from Glasgow and he thinks his are *true!*'

'But what does he look like?' Kim persisted.

'West Coast Scot, you know. Small, dark and muscular, lot of bone-structure. Ties his hair back when he's climbing, looks a bit like a gypsy.'

'Sounds a bit of alright.'

'*And* his girlfriend sounds interesting. Lesley instructs skiing, scuba-diving and karate. He says the only sport she won't touch is climbing, and that's the way they are. Dead contrary.'

She'd lost interest and was having a snack of my right ear.

'Anyway, you'll likely meet them sometime if we – '

'Are we?' she said. 'Will we?'

We looked at each other. She had too much still to do to stay with me long. I mustn't forget that.

She laughed and wriggled out of her jeans. Her moods changed quick as Orkney weather. She took what she wanted and she learned what she needed to. And if sometimes I felt a certain tenderness was lost in the fire, well that would come later.

'Come on,' she said, 'let's celebrate. No one here but the Old Man.'

We were In Love. I can scratch my hair, look out at the moon then the lamp, and say it was an idyll, an illusion, a fantasy. Graeme would have agreed and probably added the prefix *bourgeois* to that, which didn't mean much but made him feel better.

In Love – it sounds like a small kingdom you might stay in once. A wee tax haven, like Monaco, Lichtenstein, Jersey, Andorra. You can imagine the glossy soft-focus brochure:

Come to Love, for the holiday of a lifetime.

But no one can stay there forever.

You'll never forget it.

Aye, and that's the catch.

Come and stay a while in Love – it's FREE!

Like hell it is. The longer you stay, bigger the bill will be when you leave.

Everyone should go there once.

But who can afford to go there twice?

Yet my heart, that pump, still works. And the moon still looks good going down over the sea. I turn up the lamp a little, knowing the difference between them, though there was a time when I did not, and it was not such a bad time.

Say what you will, the rest is work and dailyness.

On my visits that summer, we went down through layers of civilisation, sweating and scrabbling towards the foundations.

Fast progress at first, marking out the site, peeling back the turf, digging out the top soil. Sweaty work powered by adrenalin and curiosity. Then the work slowed as more subtle outlines and patterns began to emerge. Slow unearthings, learning to register the faintest shifts of texture. It was doing a lot for her sketching, and I was absorbed in the mapping and projection work. We both liked accuracy, in our different ways.

Gradually each contact became more demanding. Then it was time for getting down on our knees, for finer and finer sifting, finer discrimination.

The site we worked on had gone through several phases: a religious sanctuary, a burial ground, a late Bronze Age workshop, and finally a fort. A short history of Humankind, I commented to Kim.

'It would be better in reverse,' she said, 'then it might be progress.'

(Years later she stepped on a southbound train and said 'Lovers should start with a parting and end by meeting.' Then waved goodbye for a while.)

Much of what we found was clearly understood and identified, but as many features were simply 'of ritual significance' – meaning no one really knows. That was our work by day. At night we dug deeper into the mythic roles: Queen, Prince, Virgin, Slut, Stranger, Pupil, Teacher. There was power there, and unease.

What happens, I wondered, once we've reached bedrock? Presumably then the dig's over. I had not known she would be so fierce, that she'd want to be taken primally, ritualistically, preferably in the dark.

'Primal,' she said one night, 'not primitive. Powerful, not angry. That's all I'm asking.' She crouched impatiently on the sleeping bags. 'Can't you feel the power in this site?'

Her eyes gleamed. Thinking of her mood shifts, her sudden mental absences, Joan's wary yet protective attitude towards her,

I sometimes wondered if she was a wee bit crazy, or maybe just being her age.

'Love can come before and after,' she said. 'During, I just want to burn, burn to ashes. And not talk about it after.'

That was incoherence to me. Why should there be anything not talked about between us?

She darted from the tent and began to dance, a rythmic shuffle in her pajamas in the drizzle. I watched but didn't join her, listened to her bare feet squelching in the mud. Childish, original, or nuts?

Margaret at the dig said she was just pretentious. Margaret didn't like people who weren't like Margaret. Joan shook her head when I told her.

'Na. Kim wouldnae bother doing anything for effect. That's what's worrying about her.' She looked down and squeezed the little cross at her throat. 'I've known her since St Mary's Primary, I should know.'

I was near asleep by the time she came back in. She tunnelled against me till the shivering stopped.

'Hold on to me,' I thought she muttered. 'Don't let me get too high.'

It was Kim who found it. Working away at her corner of the site she scraped against a hard, straight edge. She told no one but trowelled away silently all afternoon, leaning over her patch like a child protecting its exercise book. By the end of the day she had isolated the outline of a huge flat stone. Only then did she call the supervisor over.

She had hit on the lid of a large burial kist. In three days the whole structure was revealed: a box made up of four big stone slabs. The cap-stone was too heavy for even half a dozen diggers to lift in safety. It had never been opened or disturbed.

The JCB crane came on a close afternoon. Grey-green thunder clouds piled up over the hill behind us, Kim's green shirt was sweat-stuck to her body. As moisture tickled my neck I saw a brief clip from some low-grade film: pulling her clothes off and having her face-down in the sandy earth by the kist. I quickly censored it. Not nice. Crude. But when she glanced up at me across the cap-stone I had a feeling she'd seen much the same.

The air was thick as we gathered round a burial that had not been glimpsed for 3,000 years. Some boxes are made never to be opened. Even Roddy the group's clown had no jokes. Joan was looking my way as though there was something I was supposed to understand.

The crane's chains were fitted. Kim's hips shifted, the hairs lifted along my arms. The JCB revved and the cap-stane lifted and thunder broke over the ridge as we crowded round to look into the kist.

The skeleton was crouched foetally, on its side. The femurs had been broken to make it fit. The skull faced East as it had for three millennia, waiting for the light to come. Beside it was the red clay jar containing the dust of food and drink for the next world. It had fallen over and there was a jagged crack down one side. I heard Kim's inbreath. Her face was white and rigid under her black thatch, her fingers clamped round my wrist.

So this is the bedrock, I thought.

More thunder, then the rain whapped down in stair-rods as we quickly dragged plastic sheeting over the open grave.

'Wish tae God I'd never found it,' she muttered. She stomped off towards the beach in the rain and I let her be.

That night she did not blow out the lamp in our tent but stared intently into my face as she lowered herself onto me, and my heart hammered at my ribs like a man beating on the walls of the cage surrounding him.

Playing Kim's Game you discover what you remember and what you have forgotten. But more than that.

You confidently write *Red sealing wax* but when the tray is brought back at the end of the game you stare, baffled, because the sealing wax you so clearly pictured is not there. Instead there is a red lipstick container and a stamp. From these – both of which you'd left out – you invented sealing wax.

I pull out the shoe-box marked *Kim – Letters & Cards* and flick through for conflicting evidence. It's near the top of course, one of her last notes.

Sore knees, that's what I remember most! And sitting in the hut when it rained – drinking tea and rolling cigarettes while everyone talked and I felt very young – an ignorant tongue-tied wee lassie who'd been nowhere and done nothing. I resented that.

All those things you remember, well they may have happened. Passion – that damned kist. But I also remember those nights when you couldn't

*bear me to touch you – your silences – the long letters to and from Bridget
you didn't think I noticed – the mark where your ring had been. That hurt
me. All your guilt and second thoughts – how you still turned away from
me to sleep.*

*I thought my body was the best way of interesting you and I loved
being wanted so much.*

*But, yes, I spent a lot of that summer on my knees, and we got into
some pretty strange stuff. I'd rather you didn't think about it. Certainly
there were sunsets on the Brough, dances, conversations, times when we
were closer than I knew possible – ach, the earth moved sometimes and
that doesn't happen often. But it's all just water-skaters on the surface of
the Absolute and anyway I've lots of work to do (starting a commission in
Heidelberg next week if I'm well enough, and then the summer show).*

*I know I wobble sometimes – like the Earth on its axis! – and I'm so
grateful for those who help out then. My friends are dearer to me than
my hands.*

I was only learning, like you.

My love – Kim

'Passionate love: miracle or psychosis? Discuss,' I hear Ruth say,
and see her brown ironic eyes still waiting for an answer. But all
that comes later, in good time.

I look at the photo and remind myself: sealing wax.

She leaned her damp sweating precious head on my upper arm
as the world steadied again and our Gaz lamp hissed from the
ridgepole. I felt chuffed but curiously sad. Fatigue, I supposed.

She quietly slid away and looked at the ceiling, gone from
me again.

I propped myself on an elbow and studied her as she lay
naked on the sleeping bags. She was oddly prudish in some
ways, certainly didn't like being studied, naked or otherwise, but
at times like this she wouldn't even notice.

So I examined this little gas-lit enigma, wishing I could draw her
as she'd sketched me. Kim thought of herself as a mongrel, part
Pole, part Scot. Those short strong legs and full female hips had
kept her wee Pictish ancestors anchored to the ground in Scottish
gales. Then the narrow waist, little rounded stomach, small breasts
and thin shoulders and arms of an altogether more delicate people.
Her hair didn't match her eyes, and on that small, oval face her

father's nose was stuck on like an afterthought. Odd-looking, you might say.

But I was crazy about that mongrel body, its brief, burning need, her quickening breath at my ear. No denying that had been a big part of it at first. Nothing so unusual about that. She was young, vital, challenging, and she wanted me – that was adventure enough. She filled some kind of space in me I'd scarcely been aware of.

I did not yet know what to call whatever it was in her I still yearned for after we'd made love.

And now the summer was almost gone, the dig was winding up, and I was heading back off-shore again.

Suddenly she turned and looked me over. Hard and objectively. I felt myself being filed away for future work. That was okay, that's what she did.

'I've been very happy,' she said finally. 'Despite what I said about happiness. What should we do with it?'

And the image I had was from my now infrequent rugby games for the local Borders Thirds. Once in a while at full-back the ball will come spiralling out of nowhere and drop into your arms and you stand astonished for a moment by the serendipity of it. Then you look up and see all this ugly stuff coming your way.

'Then you think, Bloody hell, what am I going to do with this?'

She laughed. Images we always understood. 'So what do we do with this pointy ball of happiness?'

Pointy ball! I winced. Lacking a Borders upbringing, she did not know the place of rugby in the great scheme of things. Nor did Graeme who in his Glasgow chauvinism was convinced no one in Scotland played rugby except pseudo-English public school wankers.

'I mean,' she continued, 'what's in the future?'

In the Future. If Love was a tax-haven paradise not unlike Orkney but less windy, I pictured Future as being like Northern Canada – huge, wild, marginal, a place where people became lost.

'Would you like me to live with you?' she asked.

Two answers to that, one a resounding Yes.

'What do you want?'

'Everything, as always.'

She rolled over on her stomach. My hand re-traced the line of her back, the lovely slope down from her shoulders into the small

27

of her back and then rising again. The curve of the field above the house where I was born.

'Maybe I should stick with Archaeology. It stirs my imagination way down and I like the method too. Accuracy and imagination. Pay's rotten but that doesn't matter and I like the company.'

I didn't want to prompt her in any way. Well of course I did, but it wouldn't have been right and it would likely have made no odds.

She hesitated.

'Or go to Art College as expected. Drawing and painting's not really what I want, but it might help.'

She was still trying on possible lives for size. I waited.

'But after the dig Jeanette and Simon are going to rent a cottage in East Anglia and they've asked if I'd like to come. I'd sign on and have time to think and potter and try to find out what it is I'm good for.'

I listened to her voice, trying to hear behind the words what she wanted.

'That sounds good,' I said carefully.

She squeezed my arm tight.

'I was so worried,' she said. 'I thought you might be angry or hurt. I do love you like crazy and part of me wants everything with you, roses round the door, the lot. But I'm young – I can't stand you saying that but I can – and I *need* . . .'

I held her. 'So run with the ball and see how far we get,' I said.

Her face was hidden in my chest.

'But I don't want to lose this,' she said.

I spoke without thinking.

'The only way to "keep" someone like you is not to hold on to you.'

Soon she slept. I lay awake. I didn't expect to 'keep' her long. Maybe a month or two after she'd gone South.

Dig a little deeper, son, I thought.

Truth is, I like it like this. Two weeks on and two weeks off, all the heightened partings and reunions. Passionate uncommitment.

Now carefully, gently, trowel away another layer. Get down to the bedrock.

It's not love that scares me, I told myself, but its disappearance. The feeling as it trickles through your fingers like water.

The Gaz hissed. She slept in my arms, together with all the joys and fears she brought. I no longer felt there was something I'd

28

missed, this was it – this little space, this island, this one summer. I wanted to live with her forever but I had no faith in it.

I finally put out the lamp and turned away from her to sleep more soundly.

That summer in Orkney still replays as romantic fantasy, as a stick of sealing wax where none was. I still remember it like that.

Damn it, it was like that. Miracle or psychosis, passionate love did exist, does exist, from time to time. It would be easy and perhaps kinder to deny it. But inaccurate.

I look over at the bairn as she stirs restlessly. Her thin arms stick out of the Scotland Grand Slam T-shirt she wears as a nightie.

So naïve, so intense, so long ago.

I have the photo still, this one I took at Kirkwall airfield while the twin-engined Otter rocked on the runway and we could smell the mist off the sea and cut grass and I was about to leave for the last time. She is very young and looking into the sun. Behind her are the sloping pastures and huge blue sky of Orkney. Her hand is raised to shield her eyes from the light, at an angle that seems both a salute and a warding-off. Her other hand is at the back of her neck, holding her hair down in the wind. She stares out at me: defensive, questioning, vulnerable, direct.

In Orkney, in Love, in Simmerdim – been there, seen it, done that.

Na, it's too easy to be flip. And being hard's the softer option. Just say: lucky me, and wait to see if that feels true.

I put the photo away in the table drawer beside the piton, pick up the Rizla paper and slowly roll that cigarette. The child whiffles gently in her sleep as she's carried, dreaming, into an unknown future. I reach for the next piece, try to consider it objectively. And still Kim lingers, shading her eyes against the Orkney light.

FOUR

Bluebird

GRAEME HANDED BACK the photo of Kim in Orkney.

'Aye, verra nice. Whit happens when the wean grows up?'

'Get tae fuck.'

Graeme grinned, looked out at the mild, torrential autumn rain.

'Touchy subject, eh? Dinni hear you swear much these days.'

'She's no a child. Kim's only five years younger than you.'

'Her age, I was starting on the assembly line. Just a laddie, kent bugger all.'

Save the urban proletariat credentials, thought Jimmy. He concentrated grimly on the twists of the Loch Lomond road. Sod the bonnie bonnie banks, coming down in stair-rods – he could scarcely see the edge of the road let alone the water.

'As it happens I love her despite her age, not because of it.'

'Ah well.'

Graeme sounded uncomfortable. Jimmy pressed his advantage.

'And how come I never get to meet Lesley? You hiding her?'

'Nuh.'

Silence. Jimmy watched him struggle with the gag of his conditioning.

'You two fallen out again?'

'Nuh.' Then the words came quickly. 'It's jist she's been awa a lot – instructing, like – and this past while she's been having a . . . thing wi . . . somebody.'

Jimmy placed his hand briefly on his arm.

'Hey, I'm sorry.'

Graeme shrugged.

'Happens once in a while. Jist the way she is. No a big problem, no something you'd sling your hook fer.'

Jimmy raised his eyebrows. All too easy to typecast his friend.

'And you do the same?'

'Ither wimmen? Naw.'

'Why not?'

Graeme said nothing. He shoved The Clash's *London Calling* into the cassette player and cranked the volume up.

Jimmy sighed inwardly. Thrawn bugger. He'd get nothing more from him for an hour or so. Anything personal, words like love for instance, seemed to embarass him. Torrents of white rage sluiced from the stereo speakers.

He swung left at Tarbet and headed for the public loos in Arrochar, voted the best in the country by readers of the *Sunday Post*, who ought to know. It was one of his rituals when up this way to go in, have a decent wash and sniff the cut flowers. Graeme waited in the car. Sniffing flowers wasn't really his scene.

The rain had stopped, the cloud were rising smoking from the beautiful-ugly outline of The Cobbler across Loch Long as Jimmy emerged smiling from the super-loos. Graeme rolled down the window.

'Bonny girl but,' he said. It was almost an apology. 'Do I get to meet her?'

Jimmy nodded. 'I'd like you to. Better be before she goes South. Things are kinda open after that.'

Graeme laughed quietly, actually put his hand briefly on Jimmy's shoulder.

'Know whit you mean.'

'Sorry about Lesley.'

'No need. It's aa jist bourgeois crap anyhow. Twa million folk oot of work.'

He didn't elaborate. He's not an elaborator, except when he gets started on the new Government. They found the camp site, put up the tent then went to the pub to discuss the game-plan. It was all training, training for the Old Man. With Jimmy so much in Orkney over the summer, there'd been little climbing together. When they're ready they'll go up and knock the old bastard off.

'Come alang wi me on Sunday and you'll meet her,' Graeme said last thing.

'You're no going to the College and no takin the job at the travel agent?' her mum said.

'Nuh.'

'Why for no?'

'Don't want tae.'

Kim ducked into the cupboard under the stairs and tried to find the light switch. Amazing how quickly you forget a place you've outgrown.

'No enough for you, I suppose. It was guid enough for your sister.'

'Christ, mum, how bloody dull does a job have to be to satisfy you?'

'It's a job, hen. And don't use language.'

'Why don't they just lobotomise me and be done wi it?'

Silence from behind. She shouldn't have said that. She found the scuffed leather bag. The carving tools were inside, and his old brushes, scrupulously clean.

'Can I take this, mum? *Please.*'

Her mother looked at her, opened her mouth, then closed it again.

'Aye, sure. They're nae use here. Sell them if you've a mind tae.'

On her knees in the cupboard, Kim blew the dust off her father's folio.

'And this?'

'You were aye his favourite.'

Kim wondered what her mother saw when she looked at her like that. She hugged her awkwardly.

'Thanks, mum. I *will* write.'

'Ah'll be bound.' Her mother sniffed, almost smiled. 'These hooses were jerry-built after the war, only meant tae last twenty year. Aathing gets damp. Your dad's stuff will dae better oot o here. You too, maist like. It's no been a guid hoose.'

They faced each other in the dim passageway. It had been six years since they'd looked each other in the eye. Dust or something tickled in Kim's nose. They really ought to talk about it.

'Ah'll mak the tea, then,' her mother said and hurried away into the little kitchen. Kim looked after her then knelt and checked through her dad's carving tools. She willed her hands steady as she carefully tested their cutting edges, still sharp as they had always been.

Jimmy and Graeme stood in the corner of the gym, watching the two women fighting on the karate mat. Short, explosive movements, gasps, then the whack of fist and foot on the crisp robes. Parry, dummy, whack, spring back to prowl again. Jimmy noticed the smaller one's attention flickering between her opponent's hands and feet; the taller young woman just focused on the other's eyes.

'Which one?' he hissed.

'The tall wan, of course. The classy doll.'

Tall and poised in white, the long legs stalking her opponent round the mat, the black belt tight round her waist. The flash of her short red hair, the blur of movement as she parried twice, pivoted, kicked high, took the point. The other girl said something and she laughed. They finished, bowed to each other and left the mat.

'Meet Superwoman,' Graeme said. 'She swims like a kipper and could chop you up for kindling. A gallus broad.'

'He's full of Glasgow bull,' she said and held out her hand. 'Hello.'

Her grip was strong, her voice English upper with a tinge of something else, her slightly protruberant hazel eyes level with Jimmy's.

'You looked good. I mean, really controlled,' Jimmy said.

'So you are into control?'

'You obviously are,' he retorted. 'Pretty violent, too.'

She shrugged. 'Actually hit somebody and you're out on your ear. But it gets the aggression out.'

'I'm sure that's important.'

He wasn't sure what this sparring was about.

'With him around? Absolutely.'

Graeme grinned.

'Sod this,' he said, and went off to check out the climbing wall, leaving them together.

'So where did you get your accent?' Jimmy said eventually.

'England, where do you think? Then one of your posh boarding schools.'

'I mean, the other bit.'

'My father was American. I lived some time there. I thought it had been knocked out of me.'

'Not entirely. I can't imagine anyone knocking much out of you.'

'Not now, they wouldn't.'

They stood in silence, watching Graeme swing up the wall.

'He really likes you,' Lesley said suddenly. 'He looks up to you.'

'Well, I am four inches taller,' Jimmy laughed.

'Don't be facetious,' she said sharply. 'It's such a second-rate form of communication.'

Perhaps he resented feeling vetted. Certainly her clear voice, even with the American tinge, set his teeth on edge.

'That's a bit snotty, don't you think? You're not the boarding school prefect now.'

They stared each other out. Then she laughed.

'I'm so glad we're not going to just be polite. Anyway, I was expelled.'

'What for?'

'*Unspeakable crimes*,' she whispered.

'Sounds interesting.'

'They certainly were.'

She didn't elaborate. They stood in silence watching Graeme spidering on the wall. She bent forward to brush dirt from her knees and then he saw it, like a little blue bruise, high on her left shoulder.

'Like my tattoo?' she said without looking up.

'Very much. Swallow?'

'Bluebird,' she replied.

Curious, he lightly touched her sweating skin. A bluebird in flight, swooping up, apparently free.

'I'm facetious when I'm touched and don't know what to say,' he said. 'I'm glad, because he's my closest pal, even if he's hard to get to.'

She straightened up.

'Mine too,' she said, smiling. Why, he wondered, does that accent always go with perfect teeth? Is it something they put in the oats in those schools?

They watched Graeme straining at an awkward lay-back.

'He's not like he seems,' she added. 'He's not hard at all. Or at least he's struggling with it. I wouldn't waste my time if he didn't.'

Jimmy nodded. Graeme eased himself down, changed hands and went at it again. She spoke quietly, half to herself.

'He may seem sociable, one of the lads, but really he's on his own.' She glanced at Jimmy. 'I'd guess you're the other way round.'

'Possibly.'

'Do you mind me being personal?'

'It's not very English, but no.' In fact he now felt very free and easy with her. 'It's just very unlike someone I know.'

Again that clear stare.

'Is that the Kim I hear about?'

'Yup.'

'I'd like to meet her.'

'I'd like you to.'

'How about tonight?'

Jimmy explained Kim was in Plean at her mum's, packing to go to England. Did her mum have a phone? No, but the neighbours took messages. Then they could phone and drive over. Taken aback by such decisive ploy-making, Jimmy could think of no good reason why not. That was settled. Good.

They watched Graeme struggle where the lay-back crack whispered out into blank wall.

'And what are you like, then?'

Lesley ruffled her crew-cut.

'I like things simple, and I like to have fun.'

So it seems, Jimmy thought. If Graeme can take it, that's your business.

'Jolly super fun?' he mocked her accent.

'You takin the piss, pal?' she replied, mocking Graeme's.

'Yup. Is that allowed?'

At that point Graeme abruptly fell out of the crack. He thumped on the floor, got up slowly, shrugged and hirpled over towards them.

'So, what's doing?' he asked.

Lesley draped her arm round him. Her jacket collar drooped and Jimmy glimpsed the bluebird again. Pure flight.

'We're all going over to Kim's to take her out and get sloshed and exchange the sarcasms that pass for affection in this barbarous country. Then we'll maybe go dancing. Good idea, huh?'

'Ye've had worse,' Graeme said. 'Barbarous ma arse.'

I turn over the little ceramic bluebird pin. Lesley left it behind at my place after she came out of the hospital. Maybe she didn't feel so free any more.

I put the bluebird away in the drawer. Even considered carefully, objectively, it's gleaming with sweat and slippy-smooth, like her shoulder that first time.

FIVE

Plectrum

HE SHOULDN'T HAVE come to the Heriot Watt Christmas party. He shouldn't compete for an anxious moon-faced student he didn't even want. He knew who he wanted but they'd agreed when Kim had gone South: no commitment. Wait and see.

Now his opposition played his trump card.

'As it happens, a long time back I used to play with Eric Clapton. Country & Western! I was on piano, Eric played bass. We were terrible! One night when Eric and I were out of our skulls in Soho . . .'

Who can compete with that? thought Jimmy. Then again, who would want to?

A foregone conclusion, really, the Man Who Played With Eric Clapton being a senior lecturer, and Jimmy just a former engineering student wasting himself on the rigs. The victor gyrated away with his satellite hanging on his arm.

Jimmy leant his forehead on the window. Another ruddy winter of discontent. Bitter night shifts on the drill floor, Alex drying out up on the derrick, all of us bitching but terrified of losing our jobs. The cohesion's gone. And Kim's in an increasingly foreign country.

Noting the red face, fat lips, absence of recent publications and a subtle bloating around the mind and wrists, Jimmy identified The Man Who as a minor star in its late middle age phase, expanding even as its output dwindles. Then, he vaguely recalled, the star finally collapses in on itself and becomes very small, very dense, very dark.

A comforting thought, but he cannot rid himself of a sense of darkness encircling the country, the city, himself. Soon he'll have to leave to unroll his sleeping bag on a floor in Leith.

He leaned his head on the plate glass and looked into the dreich Edinburgh night. His visit to East Anglia had not been a success. Between bouts of bed he and Kim had irritated the hell out of each other.

Dinna wheenge, son, his old man says. Bloody Scottish stoicism.

What's it ever achieved beyond a tight mouth and a retentive arse?

He collared a bottle of particularly spiteful wine (the cutbacks have already begun) and offered it to a junior lecturer in Fluid Dynamics. She accepted, smiled, said her name was Alison.

It was enough that she was someone.

Kim sat on the pebble beach and looked up at the stars. Simon and Jeanette were kind enough but way over her head and anyway they had each other. They'd said they were Anarchists which sounded exciting, but seemed to mean no money, spinning out tobacco in ever thinner cigarettes, playing boring old music and discussing theorists whose names she couldn't pronounce properly.

Still, at least they cared about something other than just themselves. They had some kind of cause, like Jimmy's friend Graeme.

Whatever I'm meant to do, she thought, is not a theory. It's not about anger or politics. Better still, not about me.

Lately the world seemed so dismal and coarse, she couldn't bear it being dismal when it was trying so hard to be beautiful. I need to make, she said to her secret sharer, fragments of a world that doesn't quite exist, or one day I'll crack again.

She wrapped the duvet more tightly round herself and shivered. Lesley had hugged her so warm and friendly when she'd left, it felt funny but nice and reminded her what an inadequate being she herself was.

Lately she spent most of her time on the beaches. They seemed kin to her, open, desolate, re-forming. She was collecting stones, shells, driftwood, sea-smoothed glass, not very sure why.

The rest of the time she spent mostly in bed, imagining the songs of the birds on the peeling wallpaper. Once she'd tried herself on the broken glass of the phone box at the end of the road, twisting gently till red threads broke out on her wrists. Then she'd felt scared and faintly ridiculous, and from then on gave the phone box a wide berth.

Now she looked up, along the coast, and a rising moon, bloody and pink, caught her by the throat. The little voice she trusted beyond any other finally spoke.

When will I be complete?

The question had been waiting for her since she was twelve. She waited on. The reply seemed to whisper back across space.

Probably never.

Ah. She felt herself waver, as though she were nothing more than a ring blown from someone's cigarette. She waited for the little voice to tell her how she felt about this.

Fair enough.

She stomped thoughtfully back to the permafrost cottage. In her wee room she lit candles, sat cross-legged on the bed while through the wall Eric Clapton's guitar wailed for Layla. She looked at the random objects she'd gathered.

She considered their textures, their weight in her palm and their weight in her mind.

She allowed herself to think of the stone butterfly her father had made after his first breakdown. Then the carvings in bone, wood and pumice with which the former Cracow Art College teacher, then a semi-employed Scottish waiter, had whittled away the evenings of his exile. Intricate sentimental landscapes. Such workmanship. And such irrelevance, she thought angrily, all decoration like the guitar pyrotechnics coming through from the kichen.

She glanced at his carving tools in the corner, gathered half a dozen pieces of sea-glass onto the coverlet, picked up her notebook and let her mind go blank.

There was something here, something she could do. Something to hold in the hand and find life bearable.

Dad.

An incompleteness that would feel complete . . .

She opened her pad, stared at her little collection and began writing and drawing whatever came into her head. She worked steadily through the night, without preconception and almost without influence, till one candle then the other guttered out.

She woke at first light and continued, driven by an energy she'd not known before. And on the third day she finally picked up his carving tools, slowly turned them in her hands. She had so far to go, so much to learn.

('Everything I've ever made,' she said once in an interview, 'has been the development of a few basic notions worked out at the onset of the Eighties. I know what they are and I'm not telling, but I'll never get to the end of them.')

Jimmy is on the train back from East Anglia. He's wearing the hideous purple tammy Jeanette had knitted him. Kim's parting gift is in his pocket, cool and inscrutable.

Another inconclusive week of sex, laughter, sulks, metaphors, passion, fatigue. He and Kim have talked at length, at considerable length, about their passion for each other and their need for independence, for Space. Jimmy has lots of space in him, most of it empty. Kim is so dense and compacted at times she finds it hard to breathe.

It's best when she's enthusiastic and talking about her new work, her ideas, her toys as she calls them. But for much of the time there seemed little place for him.

'Wait on,' she'd said at the station. 'Everything's changing. Please wait and see what it becomes.'

Punk has become New Wave and unemployment is over two million and the Government still hasn't fallen. Graeme is enraged about everything – the new radical Right (who have eloped with one of his favourite words), the failure of the Left, the increasing use of bolts on his favourite crags.

But like he says, 'If you can't stand the skulls, pal, stay oot o the scullery.' So he's recently taken the plunge and left the Communist Party to join Labour and help ensure a radical manifesto for the next Election.

Yes, the Eighties have lurched in and they don't look good. From the train Newcastle looks like the grit left in the bottom of a dirty bath when someone's pulled the plug. And he's off to extract the oil that pays the giros and keeps the wheels grinding.

Everyone needs work, he reckons, but most of us just find employment. Many not even that. He has no talent like Kim's. So he needs the money, he needs that green grease across his palms.

Somewhere around Darlington the gaunt man in the seat opposite had struck up a conversation with the restless woman next to him. Two hours later, Jimmy is wishing he'd bought one of those new Walkman things. The subject now is godless science and the heresy of Darwinism. Jimmy tries to shut out the interminable monologue by recalling in order every room, hillside or bay where he and Kim have made love.

'. . . but before I was born again, I played in a band with, uh, Eric Clapton.'

Jimmy opens his eyes from radiant visions.

'Country music?' he asks.

'Goodness, no! Jazz. Eric was really into jazz. He played drums. We all knew he had the makings of genius. Of course, he's a very rich and very lonely man now, he has lost the way.'

He glances at Jimmy's guitar case on the luggage rack.
'And what kind of things do you play, friend?'
'Games, mostly. But I'm trying to give it up.'
Smart arse.

When Jeanette is bored she plays Seventies records and kneads dough with scowling concentration. Her dark eyebrows meet at the crease over her nose. Simon is struggling to re-read Max Stirner by the fire; the music makes it difficult. He carefully rolls another cigarette.

Kim is in her bedroom next door with her hands over her ears. She is trying to work out a technique for carving words that will appear to curve into the depths of the glass, as though slipping away, or emerging. Would she rather incise ferns on a stone, or simply the word *ferns*? Should she go to Art College, or study Philosophy, or apprentice herself to a craftsman?

She sighs. She will soon be twenty. Art, Life, Jimmy, Fame – she wants everything and she wants it now. She hopes she has a real talent and fears she's another irrelevant poser. It's so damn exciting, she writes in her notebook, the only game. I'm terrified – I'm loving it – art's a two-edged sword. *But there's so much to do.*

(She triple underlined that. You can see where she's nearly gone right through the paper.)

She goes through to the kitchen, can't find any real tea and has to settle for some fousty flower stuff. 'Fousty flower stuff', she mutters. Jeanette's eyebrows mate. 'What is?'

'That music. *Boring.*'

They argue. What Jeanette calls meaningful, she calls wallpaper. She says she'd left home to get away from wallpaper. Jeanette loathes Kim's few records: The Clash, the Banshees, Talking Heads. No tune, no rhythm, no talent. Noise.

'Neo-Fascism,' says Simon, looking up from some tricky dialectics.

'Freedom!' says Kim. 'Punk took a flame thrower to your precious herbaceous border. It's about being young and pissed off.'

'It's being retarded!' Jeanette shouts over 'Living On Tulsa Time'. 'There's too much ugliness as it is. Why add to it?'

'You and your bloody Sixties! That music is out-dated as your kind of anarchy. Two million unemployed and you're still arguing about the right *not* to work! Anyway, why don't we ever have any real tea? I'm tired of this herbal piss water.'

'"Real" is a social construct,' Simon observes.

'Oh go to hell! Christ!'

Kim slams out of the kitchen, bangs her bedroom door, sits on her bed and begins to cry. She hates being angry, she dislikes swearing, she despises loss of control. She wants Jimmy's arms around her even if he is an old Sixties fart with all Bob Dylan's albums.

'If that's the new generation,' seethes Jeanette, 'what are we coming to?'

'An end, probably', Simon giggles.

Jeanette hurls the ball of dough at his head. He ducks. It thuds against the wall and hangs there. Muffled sobs come through from next door. Simon gets up and carefully peels the flattened dough from the wall and solemnly carries it to her spread across his hands.

'Pizza, then?' he says.

The train approaches Berwick. Nice town, wrong side of the border. Its solid grey stone feels just right. He understands that defensive huddle.

He relaxes back in his seat as the train crosses the Tweed. Let me not die out of my country.

He takes out Kim's gift again, a chunk of hazey blue sea-smoothed glass. On the flat base there are tiny letters but he cannot decipher them. This is so like her.

'Hold it to the light,' she'd said.

He does so now, and turning it over notices a small moon-shaped clearing in the haze. And when he holds that to the window of the train he can see right through to the lettering on the other side. Mirror writing. Squinting, he can now read the tiny italic inscription.

The ultimate triumph of the moon.

Meaning?

'And don't ask what it means,' she'd said, 'just accept it.'

'Ta verra much, I'll call it *Inscrutable*.'

He'd got a giggle, followed soon by bed. It's not really her body he wants any more, but sometimes that's all that's on offer.

Somehow, for all her passion, he gets by-passed. It's not Jimmy she cries out to, but Male. It's not Kim who comes so urgently it sounds like pain, it is Female. He is beginning to realise he doesn't want Female, he wants Kim . . .

The train groans North, the gaunt evangelist drones on. Out the window, the North Sea stretches into shifting grey. The farm cottages hunkered down low out of the wind, the scrawny trees bent to the East, the fields sloping down to the cliff edge – a hard land, but his.

Unlike the West Coast, it is not lovely. It's salt-hardened, sceptical, resolutely non-fantastical. East Coasters, he thinks, attenders at the church of What Is.

Recently it's begun to seem too narrow a church. And that's something to do with Kim, the ways she's challenged and provoked him. Whatever, he no longer has the sense of something missed in his life. He's got all he can possibly handle.

Eyemouth is out of sight, but he knows it's there. The beach, the promenade, the old narrow harbour, the marine yard. He mentally says Hi to his mum and broods about his dad. The colossus is finally crumbling, and they're still not reconciled.

Jimmy squeezes Kim's offering in his palm. How is he to understand her heresies? Through the Seventies he was encouraged by women to be gentle, unforceful, to see sex as a kind of extreme friendliness. But Kim doesn't want that.

'I don't want gentle,' she'd said scornfully. 'I don't want forty-five chords and extended solos. And I certainly don't want to talk about it.'

He shifts in his seat, disturbed. The magazine he's been flicking through tells him men fear intimacy. It doesn't say we can yearn for it, he thinks, nor that some women . . .

He'd looked into her face, saw white specks radiated through her blue iris, saw the darkness of her pupils swell. He'd thought sex a conscious, cultivated pleasure, not this raw clash.

There is a gap of generation between them, and sparks crackle across it. But he will never forget the very few times she made love *with* him.

The ultimate triumph of the moon. So what's he supposed to do with that information?

He marks his place and puts away *Docherty*, an unexpected Christmas present Graeme had thrust into his hands. The train sighs into Waverley. Jimmy picks up his guitar and bags and nods goodbye to the other Man Who. Lot of strange folk around these days, not all of them in the Government.

At the top of the Waverley steps the wind slips between the buttons of his jacket like a dirk. There'll be snow and ice on the hills. Time to phone Graeme, flirt with Lesley and drag the lad away for some real climbing, winter climbing.

After all, there is more to life than one young woman. Such as? Such as controlling your fear and riding on its adrenalin climb steeper and better than ever before and finally top out on the Ben in winter and see the humps and curves of Scotland spread out glittering below like – well, like a beloved woman.

She has marked him forever, he knows that.

Into her bulging rucksack Kim zips the photo of Jim sitting on a winch looking disreputable and gorgeous. Can a would-be Great Artist want also to live with one man in a cottage with roses round the door?

In the past months she has been lonely and slightly loopy, survived it, read and talked and thought, and has the beginning of an inkling of what could – with dedication, application and the right circumstances – be her work. Time to move on. It'll be good to surprise Jimmy.

So why this sick and sorry feeling?

Jimmy has asked Alison to a party in Glasgow, held by some poets and musicians he used to play with, hitting the small time in Dumfries, Galashiels, North Berwick, Cambuslang and other hot spots.

He likes Alison. For one thing, she is scrutable. She grew up on his side of the '77 faultline. She is relaxed, ironic and informed, knows about a lot more than Fluid Mechanics. She refuses the Arts/Science split that he still feels like a Berlin Wall inside. She encourages him to read and think, to extend himself beyond the unhappy limits of Scottish Male. She says all that has got to change. Then she'll buy him a drink and propose a toast: *to the end of the broken whisky glass culture!* And she laughs and they drink to the friendship of men and women.

Kim can seem very young and insecure beside her.

Look, when it comes down to it, Alison is nice and Kim is not. Guess which one haunts him.

And Alison is an East Coaster too, Dundonian: sardonic, urban, but less relentless than the Glasgow style. He enjoys her company, they can even flirt a little. And he is not in love with her, so there is no anxiety.

Still, he is cheesed off to find her monopolised at the bash by a Recognised Scottish Writer who may be witty and charming (if you like that sort of thing) but whose work, Jimmy increasingly feels, is facile and self advertising. But the RSW has published three books, and Alison has read them.

Jimmy punishes the free wine while the over-rated hack outlines at length, at considerable length, his work in progress to an apparently enthralled Alison. So he shifts the conversation to Music, asserting its ultimate triumph over prose.

The obese fraud agrees. Though others have been kind enough to praise his work, he personally finds more satisfaction playing the flute with the Cecilia Chamber Ensemble. They have a concert next weekend. Perhaps Alison would accept a ticket with his compliments?

Alison, that free-loading sycophant, says if she's free, yes.

'And do you play an instrument, James?'

'Guitars, mostly. Rhythm and bass.'

'Oh, *Rock*,' sniffs the tone-deaf geriatric Lothario. 'Not what I'd call Music. Mere anarchy loosed upon a deafened world.'

Jimmy steps closer to Alison.

'Maybe it's a generational thing,' he says. 'When Punk came along, at first all I heard was noise – the way The Beatles must have sounded to my parents. Alison,' he adds casually, 'has a huge rock music collection, haven't you?'

Kim has said her goodbyes.

She pulls the front door shut and hears Simon stuff his old Afghan coat along the other side as a draft excluder. She will miss them in the rare moments when she permits herself to look back.

She steps into the night.

Jimmy elaborates.

'Rock music,' he continues, 'is a head-on collision of elementary order with elemental chaos. But it becomes elaborate, then decadent and controlled by the industry, and then a new movement like Punk has to come along with a scorched-earth policy. Then it starts all over again. Dialectical, ken . . .'

Jimmy has lost himself and, he suspects, Alison, in this piffle.

Which is why, when the Recognized Writer snickers and asks if he's played with anyone we might have heard of, Jimmy replies that years back he played briefly in a band with, uh, Eric Clapton.

Alison draws on her cigarette and examines him through the dispersing smoke.

'Now that is a coincidence,' says the sadistic writer swine, 'because there's someone else here tonight who definitely used to play with Clapton. I'll get him over – you must know people in common.'

He hurries off. Alison catches Jimmy's eye, he shrugs. The Liverpool Poet who is the occasion for this bash is brought over. He looks drunk and tired. Too many readings, hangers-on, free drinks and moments like this one. Jimmy offers him a cigarette; he accepts, glances at the fingers of Jimmy's left hand.

'So where did you play with Eric?' he asks. 'What was the band called then?'

The Inflated Ego grins. Alison stirs but stays silent.

'We had a residency in a pub off Gloucester Road, can't remember its name.'

'Maybe 'The Cock and Bull'' the mass murderer suggests.

'Jazz?' the Poet asks.

'No, straight Rhythm and Blues. We called ourselves . . . The Nth Degree.'

The Liverpool Poet examines his ancient winkle-pickers, pulls on his cigarette and waits for a beat. Poetry, it's all in the timing. He shakes his head slightly then looks up, smiling.

'Yeah, Nth Degree! Eric was always talking about that line-up. You must know Neil Weeks, the bass player.'

'Neil, aye. You know he works for Saatchi's now?'

'Really? A good man gone straight. Were you there on that famous night when . . .'

The defeated, pitiable, and really quite talented rival implodes and fades.

Kim walks carefully down the track to the road end. It's a starry night, fine for adventuring. The moon has gone down but it still pulls the tides, she knows that. Her sack clinks and clatters, weighed down with carved stones and shells and glass, sketch pads and her father's tools.

She breathes deeply, willing the nausea to subside. She can leave anywhere she wants to.

She waits at the road end, the future in her thumb.

Jimmy and Alison are making the long haul along Byres Road, side-stepping the young and guttered on the way to her sister's flat in Hillhead.

'Sure it's alright, me turning up to doss?'

Alison laughs, she seems to do that easily.

'Tess is in London at her girlfriend's.'

'Oh aye.'

'Family's no too chuffed – she finally came out last year. Tess tries to make a living from ceramics.'

'There must be something witty I could say about all that, but I'll no bother.'

They trudge on, side-stepping the odd regurgitated pie supper. He's a small town boy and finds Graeme's city profoundly alien and exciting. Lights, shop windows, music from pubs, unknown vivid energies in the street. It's . . . arousing.

'I suppose,' she says thoughtfully, 'a lot of people over the years must have played with Eric Clapton.'

'Lots,' he replies. 'Dozens, I should think. Mostly clapted-out.'

They walk on in silence, swaying slightly. Jimmy shifts his sleeping bag from one arm to the other as a snuffling sound comes from Alison. Then she is laughing, and he begins to laugh with her because once in a rare while life comes out tickety-boo.

'Men!' says Alison. 'Always sticking your neck out when you don't have to. And seldom when you should,' she adds and slips her arm through his.

Jimmy lies in his sleeping bag on the bedroom floor, listening to Alison's breathing slow and settle. He thinks Yes, we are many. Legion. Hundreds, thousands of us all over the world. We recognize each other instinctively when we meet. And we back each other up, because we're members of that vast orchestra of incomplete beings – the Men Who Played With Eric Clapton.

'Alison?'

'Yes?'

'What am I doing here and you there?'

She switches on the bedside light. Her smile is only slightly patronising.

'I was wondering when you'd ask.'

She will, he knows, make love in the old manner – unhurried, companionable, harmonious. The earth will not shake, the stars will not be torn down.

I get up from the table with aching eyes and look out at the clouded moon. Another girl, another planet. Another decade.

Kiss goodnight the sleeping bairn, her cheek hot next to mine.

How can anything be so unmarked, at least on the outside. Leave the door open in case she calls. Leave the rest of Kim's Game out for tomorrow night, part of the quiet, regular life we've had this past while, so healing to us both.

Turn down the lamp and blow.

SIX

Whisky cap

NO MOON TONIGHT, slight smirr of rain brushes the windows, the haar is spreading the harbour lights like margarine.

She took ages to go to sleep, she knows there's a change coming, but now the battered grey rabbit has slipped from her grasp and stares up at the ceiling. I stare out at nothing visible, wondering where we go from here.

I hesitate then select the whisky cap from the pieces on the table.

I came back from Glasgow after the party, opened my door and stopped dead.

'Thought I'd surprise you.'

'You did that.'

I dropped my sleeping bag by the door and looked at her. Sitting sketching at my kitchen table, she looked so right it made me nervous.

'I just let myself in and made myself at home,' she said, 'hope that's alright.'

'Tickety-boo,' I said. 'I spent the weekend at a pal's in Glasgow.'

Her old yellow rucksack was half unpacked in the corner. It looked deflated, let down. I could have said 'I'm not even divorced yet, I'm so crazy about you it scares me, and I've just spent the weekend sleeping with a good new friend – please live with me.'

'Good to see you,' I said and kissed her lightly, claiming nothing. 'Didn't know you were coming up for a visit.'

'I've left the cottage,' she said. 'Time for the next adventure.'

'Ah.'

I sat down at the table and glanced at her. I felt Alison's fingerprints visible all over me.

'I've decided what I want to do next.'

I gulped stewed tea and waited.

'Art's a dirty job but somebody's gotta do it. I've so many ideas now but I don't know nearly enough. I need technique and time and people around me who think it's all worthwhile.' She looked up. 'So I'm going to the Art College.'

'I'm glad,' I said and added neutrally as possible, 'Where are you thinking of staying?'

She fiddled with her pencil. Of course I longed to steer her. Sometimes love's not friendship turned up a bit. There was a lot of need in the air, and I thought it was probably mine so I sat back and waited.

'Joan and a pal have found a flat in Edinburgh, I could bide with them. It's in Bruntsfield, near the Art College. What d'you reckon?'

'Sounds right,' I said carefully. 'It sounds like what you want.'

'Fine,' she said and laid her work aside. 'That's that. As for you and me,' she added, 'we've survived this long. Can we see how it goes?'

I looked at her old rucksack on the floor. Kim on her next adventure. After all, I thought, if we lived together we'd probably get used to each other. If we lived together there'd be more to lose when we split up.

At the time I probably called this being realistic.

She dried the last glass and pinged it thoughtfully with her nail.

'Bed, please,' she said. 'You're back to that ruddy platform tomorrow and it's been *ages*.'

I'd had a bath before leaving Alison's, just as well, just as bad. We'd been good to each other, told the truth about our situations, shared the pleasure. Now I wondered if I'd be able again. Kim's lower lip swelled a fraction, her eyes became more brilliant. Pleasure and necessity are quite different. I didn't know how she did that, but I'd be able.

'Just one thing. We've a wedding down in Eyemouth when I'm next on-shore. The wee brother.'

'Your father doesn't approve of me. Am I invited?'

'You'd better be,' I said. 'I'm wi you.'

She put the glass down carefully, then wrapped her arms round my neck.

'Carry me, my lad,' she said. 'See if I can still do something else fantastic.'

The old man. I was aye feared of him as a laddie, feared of his hard hands, his voice, his judgement. You could say I took against him, yet the way I smoke this cigarette – holding it below my knuckles, looking down to exhale out the side of my mouth – that's him.

I carefully fill the cap with whisky, a small, measured dose, and watch the smoke uncoil. He persists in me like sections of old single track road running under the new one, just occasionally and unexpectedly popping into view.

I see the auld bugger shake his head. *Laddie, ye've a mooth I could post a haddock in.* But still I've inherited much more from him than a half share in a marine engineering business. And I can see I must broaden this story now, for there's more here to understand than a romance or two.

'Are you coming in on the yard or whit?' Alec demanded. 'Dad's no getting any younger.'

'Nor am I. I dinna ken, there's too many other things going on. Can it wait?'

'Not for ever.'

We were sitting in the long grass up at the Forts, looking down on Eyemouth harbour, the scuffy old beach, the clarty promenade, our childhood. From up here you could almost read the sign. *Renilson Marine Engineering.* Bridget and I used to come up here at night in our last year at school. At times it was tempting to come back full-circle. A very small circle.

Alec was talking about the yard. With North Sea oil and the fishing there was just enough business despite the recession but we needed to borrow to modernise and compete. The business should stay specialised and small and competitive. We'd had to lay off Sandy and Keith Watson. Interest rates were bloody but if the Government didn't go bust things would get better.

'Leaner and fitter,' I murmured, thinking of Graeme and his passionate anger.

'Whit am I meant tae dae?' Anger made Alec broader. 'I didnae vote for them, nivver would. You ken I'm SNP. You have your doubts, but the day'll come.' He cupped his chin in his hands in my dad's manner and squinted down at the yard. 'Point is, our yard employs eight folk – six now – and if we don't adapt, them and me will be oot of a job sooner or later.' He leaned back. 'You've got tae make the best of things as you find them.'

That was him. Then there was Graeme, Mr Angry. Graeme would rather spend his time struggling to eliminate nettles from the world than put on a pair of wellies and walk through them.

I wasn't either of them. I wondered where that left me. Kim's lover, I supposed.

'Death duties,' Alec said.

'Whit?'

'The old man's worried about them. That wee stroke gave him a turn. He needs to transfer the business.'

'I'll not be pressurised by him.'

'You don't have to fuck up your life to prove it.'

We looked at each other.

'What do you want?' I said finally.

'I want you to talk wi him. Let him know your plans. You'd be daft to stay on the rigs, it's no kind of life. What's the new girl-friend think of it?'

I shrugged. 'Suits her, mostly. And her name's Kim. She's young, she needs room.' I looked away, back down at the yard. 'It's not so bad in summer.'

'Sure, but temporary. You've turned thirty, Jim.' We stared at each other again. It was grand to see his hair thinning before mine. 'Why do you think I'm getting married? This is the real thing, no a rehearsal. I've had enough of temporary.'

I've aye underestimated you, I thought. I'm sorry.

'I'll talk to him,' I said.

I went to pick up Kim at Berwick station. She came off the train looking young and sullen and nervous. It had taken an ultimatum relayed through mum to have her invited to the wedding.

'It's a fiddler's bidding,' she announced. 'If anyone's rude to me, I'm leaving.'

'They'd better not be.'

'I shouldn't have come, I feel like an intruder.'

I'd booked us a room in the Ship hotel by the harbour. We made love there but neither of us felt any better. I gave her a guided tour of Eyemouth and my adolescence but couldn't raise a smile. Bridget hung around invisible and unmentionable at every street corner. We went round to the house for tea.

Dad stared at her then nodded curtly. My mum was cautious but welcoming, always the peacemaker. Uncle Bobby checked her out then winked at me.

'Ye'll be gettin plenty o Yon there, eh?'

'Ach, bile yer heid, Bob.'

My granny and the salty relatives, being bi-lingual like most of their generation, abandoned English for the tongue they used among their ain folk. I could follow their crack but it was difficult for her, and she wasn't very good in new company. Alec's Maggie was nearest her age; at the end of the meal she announced she and Kim were going out for a walk.

The relatives went to the pub. Mum and Alec were clearing up in the kitchen. Dad and I were left together in the wee sittingroom.

Neither of us were very good at this. When I was fifteen and fanatical about the guitar, I failed some prelims. He walked into my bedroom and smashed my guitar against the wall. A geriatric Pete Townshend couldn't have done it better. I'd been on my feet and measuring myself to go for the old bugger when my mum seperated us.

'You'll have a dram, Jim?'

'Thanks.'

I watched him at the sideboard. His hair was whispy, the stroke had left him with a limp and a slight hesitation in his speech. It confused me. My mum had taken him away before I slotted him. She must have given him a right telling because next week he'd handed back the guitar, done a right good repair job on it.

'Canna aa be good at the schuil,' he'd muttered.

From then on I'd practised guitar openly and worked secretly. Passed the exams just to show him. In that way I became an adequate guitar player and to everyone's surprise scraped into college. Being thrawn has its uses.

'Cheers.'

'Aye.'

Christ, Jimmy, say something. He's trying.

'Should be fun tomorrow,' I said. 'The wedding.'

He drank and looked at me. The bushy eyebrows that had scared me as a child were white now, his eyes were paler, misted. That swollen red-knuckled fisherman's hand had walloped me often enough. It had also taught me to use a rod, a rifle, a rugby ball, a soldering iron and an arc-welder. Everything else, anything of value, I'd learned from women.

'It's no richt,' he said suddenly. He leaned forward in the armchair and stared at me. 'And you know it. You mairrit her and you stick to it, else you're a waster. A clown.'

Mum slipped into the room and stood silently by the door. She disliked scenes, as I did through her. Doubtless her mum had been the peace-maker in turn.

I sat sweating, couldn't speak.

'In my day you made a promise and you stuck tae it.'

A promise sounded like a strip of flypaper.

'I ken that,' I said. 'I just can't do it anymore.'

'Of course ye can! What are you, feeble or something?'

My mum stirred by the door, said nothing.

'Okay, I don't want to. Not can't, don't want to.'

Dad waved his hand, his clouting hand, as though brushing away an irritating midge and muttered something that could have been 'pathetic'.

I was on my feet and looking down at him.

'Bridget's no a helpless wean fer Christ's sake! It's time she stopped running and whining to you. I'm fed up wi apologisin. Yes I made her a promise. Yes I couldna keep it. Think I'm proud of that?'

I paused. I was right angry. It felt strange, it felt great.

'John, he doesn't love her,' my mum said quietly.

Like Graeme, the word discomfitted him. Like a true Scot he was strong on duty and responsibility and the right hand.

He shook his head.

'It's no richt,' he repeated. 'Maybe I'm oota date. Ma time's gone.'

I sat down. He was an old man.

'Dad,' I said quietly, 'you're not wrong. But I'm not you. Canna be. I respect you but I don't agree. That's as far as I can go.'

Mum quietly poured what was for her a large sherry, trying not to chink the glass. He looked me over as if for the first time. I looked back at him.

'We'll agree tae differ, then,' he said finally.

'Aye.'

He picked up his glass, examined it suspiciously, drained it and poured another. At the end of a working life the old man was entitled to drink a bit, and he did.

'Bonny quine though. She minds me of the chemist's dochter in Brechin I proposed to when I wis seventeen.' He peered down through the years. 'Luckily she turned me doon.'

Mum sat on the arm of his chair and put her arm across his shoulder.

'Right,' she smiled, 'about tomorrow . . .'

Take my unease in posh hotels when I stay on business. The child loves it if I take her with me. She loves having the doorman, waiters, chambermaids, the receptionist as her audience and servants. (At this stage she is very confident, outgoing, happy it seems. Unmarked. Only once in a while do I catch in her something more lost and faraway, and wonder.)

But I can't relax, and the old man was aye the same on the rare occasions he stayed in a hotel.

'The better the hotel, the mair of a wean they mak you,' he'd say. 'The smairt ones treat you as though you were haunless then ask ye tae pay for the affront!'

'See yon commeesionaire' he said once, nodding towards the doorman, 'either he thinks I'm tae auld and knackered tae open a door for masel, or that I'm tae lazy. Noo, is that an insult or whit?'

That throaty East Coast voice, just for a moment I can hear it again, slow and emphatic, see his lang neb and creased cheeks, smell his sweat and tobacco, and I shiver.

The day was fine, I was fine, the wedding would be fine. Two quick whiskies with dad and no problem there. His remaining hairs were brushed back, he wore a grey morning suit and looked fair sprush. He even asked how my 'banjo playing' was going. He examined my knuckles and said they'd be rheumatic by forty if I didn't get off the rigs.

I glimpsed Bridget as we went up to the front of the church. The curly-headed chap must be her new fella. Young farmer, wants to marry her, gets a bit violent in drink. But at least he knows what he wants, she'd said. He knows what life's about. At thirty! Help ma boab.

Kim hung on to my arm in blue as she teetered insecurely in her sister's high-heeled shoes.

'You're looking dead cheerful,' she murmured.

'I'm not getting mairrit.'

We sat in the pews and waited. Up front, Alec looked suitably stalwart in my dress kilt. Dad sat straight up, hands spread on his knees. He was a staunch atheist and Church made him uneasy.

'He was almost friendly today,' she whispered. 'Did you two talk last night?'

'We openly disagreed. It was good.'

'That's good?'

'It is when you've never done it before.'

'Oh.' She looked down at her hands. 'I expect,' she said quietly, 'my dad and me would have fallen out lots as I got older.'

'Probably,' I said gently.

I took her arm as we stood up for the bride. My beloved was a terrible singer and her voice shook.

At the reception there was more whisky. Soon I was in my Clark Gable mood and didn't give a damn. We met Maggie's brothers who were down from Angus, clean and scrubbed for the wedding. They were large and friendly, had the look of men who'd grin and happily sell you a second-hand sheep. I saw Bridget coming from across the room. Kim muttered 'Sorry' and slipped away.

We said hello. We talked like acquaintances. I met the boyfriend, he seemed okay. He seemed the kind of man she'd wanted me to be, someone to be in charge and make all the big decisions. Remembering her temper, heaven help him if he got them wrong. We talked rugby while Bridget looked on. I talked a lot of shite and couldn't look at her. I finally palmed them off on Alec and went to find Kim to ease the tightness.

We'd been dancing Eightsome reels, Dashing White Sergeant, Strip The Willow. She looked flushed, I was sweating like a horse.

'Can we go outside?' she said.

I recognised her tone so picked up my jacket. It was warm late May dark in the garden. We were kissing behind the trees and I was terribly glad not to be married. There was music and coloured lights in the distance. Her mouth was light and caressing. I was glad not to be in charge, relieved not to know where we were heading any more than she did. If we failed to carry that pointy ball over the line, she wouldn't apologise and she wouldn't reproach. Her eyelids seemed incredibly precious.

'There's a grassy field over the fence,' she said.

I helped her over. We were lying in long grass. The earth smelled rich and near like childhood. I thought someone called my name.

'I may or may not be wearing knickers.' She was whispering in my ear. 'Don't you want to find out?'

'Here?'

'Why not? We're outlaws here.'

We were acting obscurely.

'What else are weddings about?' I said. She didn't reply but her hips rose to me like a furrow turned on the coulter blade.

*

We straightened our clothes, I picked up my jacket. Her dress tore on the fence, she wasn't pleased.

'If you must be an outlaw once in a while,' I said, 'you must expect to get a little ripped.'

'Oh, pooh!' she said. 'I've got to get to the loo. I'm dripping.'

She took my arm as we tacked back across the lawn.

'That's how I'd like to celebrate my wedding. Don't you think?'

'Absolutely. Better wait till I get divorced first.'

We were very drunk but we'd remember fine.

Dad was sitting by himself at a table on the patio. He waved me over. She squeezed my hand and left.

We were trying to talk about the business and my future. He'd produced a bottle of Black Label and we were far gone. I felt heavy, golden, soft inside from her. Our elbows kept slipping from the table as we leaned towards each other.

'How long are ye staying on the rigs, Jim?'

'I'm thinkin on it.'

He shook his head. My dad respected manual labour as the real thing. He'd worked with his hands for twenty years. He also saw manual labour as a dead end. His attitude to work was confused and Scottish and contradictory. Mine too.

'You've your mither's brains, son, you should use them. I'd like to see you working in the yard, yon hi-tech stuff – but that's up tae you, right enough.'

He winked. I grinned, acknowledged the invisible apology. He told me he'd made a decision: he was making over the business to the family. Alec would take over the day-to-day running of the yard and draw his salary.

'But if I was you, son, I'd get off the rigs. Get awa frae the sea.'

'But you were at sea for twenty years. The fishing, merchant navy during the war, back to the fishing again. Surely you liked it fine?'

'Like it? Like it?' He waggled a swollen, arthritic finger at me. 'I nivver liked it. Bloody cold miserable work, hellish in winter, long long hours in summer. Yeah, you'll ken that.'

His accent was moving in and out of focus like his finger. Who are we? I wondered. We don't even speak consistently. We'll say 'yes' and 'aye' and 'yeah' in the same conversation, alternate between 'know' and 'ken', 'bairn', 'wean' and 'child' and not even know why. Even the old man did it, and I've lost half his tongue, the better half. We're a small country with blurry boundaries.

56

'And awa frae hame maist of the time. It's no life, Jim, a richt scunner. Soon as I had a half-share in a boat I sold and got out. Stairtit the yaird.'

It had never occurred to me. I thought, if I'd thought at all, he'd enjoyed the fishing. Alec and I used to lie in bed and hear him coming and going at odd hours of the night. It seemed exciting and glamourous. We'd think of him at sea at night, playing cards, laughing, reading, standing in the wheelhouse somewhere off Iceland or the Faroes, putting in at Lerwick or Peterhead when the weather was bad. Seemed a great life, free.

'Want to know the reason? The real, real reason?' He lowered his voice conspiratorially. 'Only you and your mither know this.' I waited. 'When I was a laddie, at a fair an auld spey-wife read my palm. She told me a lot of rubbish then sudden-like said she saw I'd die in the sea.'

I grinned. My dad was a Scottish empiricist to the core. If you can't touch it, it's no real.

'I ken, I ken. Rubbish. But it stuck, here.' He tapped his skull. 'It gave me a richt gliff. Couldn't get it oot o my mind. I was shitting masel all through the Atlantic convoys. No, you'll not see me back on the water.'

But what about the loch fishing? We'd done a lot of that through my early teens. Alec had mostly stayed at home and worked on engines but loch by loch me and the old man had covered most of Scotland.

'Aye but, Jimmy, whit did the spey-wife say? In the sea.' He cackled and I wondered if he was getting slightly senile. 'She said I'd die in the sea. Lochs and burns are fine.' He laughed again. 'Lot of haivers, eh?'

We got up to go inside. He swayed and gripped my oxter. He still had a grip on him.

'Whit d'ye say? Shall we take a trip up North at the weekend before yon acid rain cleans oot the lochs?'

'I'd like to fine. But I'm committed to climbing that weekend, then off-shore. After that, eh?'

'Fine, son.' He suddenly looked tired and dishevelled. I thought his hand shook slightly, and my heart was shoogled too. 'Aye, in your own time.'

'We'll do it,' I said firmly.

He stopped and looked at me then held out his hand. We shook hands awkwardly. No soppy hugging for us. Even the handshake was rare. Normally we just nodded.

'Talk to yer mither,' he said vaguely. 'I'm just a good pair of hands, she's the clever wan.'

He peered at me through glazed and milky eyes.

'You're her child,' he pronounced.

He wandered inside and left me. I stood for a while on the patio with the bottle of Black Label cool and friendly in my hand and looked out at the dark clump of trees where Kim and I had gone. I thought of Alison, missing her as someone I could be easy with, but the wind had shifted and I could smell the big sea again. Inside, things had got to the 'Auld Lang Syne' stage. For once I agreed with Kim the past was better not brought to mind.

I waited till the singing was over before I went in. Few folk ken the right words anyhow.

I knock back the cap of whisky and carefully lob it at the waste-paper basket. It rattles across the floor. With a sigh, I get up and retrieve it. In those days there was so much I didn't want to be, it was hard to be anyone at all.

SEVEN

Kidney bean

WHEN I GOT to the yard today, I told Alec I was taking the afternoon off. He raised an eyebrow but didn't ask. I left the wean playing happily with his two, and drove aimlessly towards the Border, following belts of rain and sunshine as they succeeded each other out to sea without hesitation or regret.

I threw stones at the waves for a while, aimlessly then angrily. These days I find tears in my eyes only when watching soaps or old third-rate films. Not at the sad bits, but the moments when everything looks like it will turn out right. Or watching the child, sometimes.

I hesitated with a stone in my hand. *A hill of beans, Jim*, I heard him say. All the rocks I could throw in a lifetime would amount to no more. No point.

I kept the stone, a wee hard jagged one with a white quartz ripple through it. Worn out with games and company, the child sleeps tonight with it under her pillow, and I reach for the piece of Kim's Game I've had in mind all day and hold it carefully, at a distance.

Just like Graeme, Jimmy thinks, to be into Abstract Expressionism when there's a van load of Glasgow painters stacked with narrative paintings revving at the cultural traffic lights.

It's one of many evenings he's spent in Graeme's decaying tenement flat in darkest Govan. With Graeme's politics he should be painting social realism: desolate shipyards, empty factories, ghetto schemes, the crushed or heroic proletariat. Instead he paints abstracts. It doesn't square, Jimmy thinks. But then most folk don't square when looked into closely enough, and who wants squared people anyway.

'Swimming against the tide, man!' his friend says. 'It's the only way.'

He passes over a bottle of colouring and chemicals. Nice bottle, shame about the brew, Jimmy reckons, but accepts the Newcastle Brown.

Graeme puts on his favourite angry Elvis Costello, sits on a plastic milk crate and rolls another joint. He's in good trim, almost expansive. The end of '8o was shite, with Reagan elected and Lennon shot. Should have been arsey-versey. Sometimes he could despair, but he won't. Look where it got his mum. He stops for a minute, squinting down the barrel of the joint.

But now the Government are trailing hopelessly in the opinion polls; he's now on two of the crucial committees in the local Party; there are moments when the no-hopers he teaches seem capable of seizing the future; the painting is going well; Lesley's got regular supply-teaching – Outdoor Education in the Lothians and hasn't had a fling for ages. Can't ask more than that.

'In that order of priority?'

'Whit else? It's a hill of beans, man.'

'Whit?'

'Look tae the big picture!'

Graeme gestures expansively round the room, beyond the canvases, bottles, tools, Labour Party posters, piles of climbing magazines, books, fish-supper papers, paints, to include Glasgow and maybe Scotland in general. (Being Glaswegian, Jimmy reckons, he tends to equate the two.)

'A very big picture,' Jimmy says, looking at the canvas of the moment. It's a formidable corruscation of scratching, scouring, cross-hatching and gougeing through layers of paint, in Graeme's characteristic black and grey. 'But what the hell is it?'

(He looks, Graeme tells Lesley later, like a Border farmer faced with a llama at the county auction. It's the tweed jacket does it, thae brogue shoes. Whit a guy. You couldni say he was trendy. East Coast of course, just no with it.

And she in turn told me one very long night.)

'Paint on canvas, what d'you think? That's aa painting is. The rest is just – '

' – Bourgeois illusion!' Jimmy completes it for him.

'Gie the big fella a banana. Ma efforts tae impart the rudiments of contemporary art theory have no been in vain. It's paint-ing. Action, no representation. It *is*, not *about*. Ask Kim, it's wan thing we agree on.'

He examines the meticulously rolled joint, nods with approval, lights up.

'So what is it that it's not about?' Jimmy asks.

He enjoys these rituals. He is composed of questions just as Graeme is of assertions.

'The Aesthetics of Damage,' Graeme says briefly. 'Fuckin right!'

Kim feels strongly fucks should be kept for bed, and cunt is right out. Totally unacceptable. She'll not have it. 'But that's how the people speak,' Graeme had protested. 'Then they'd better stop if they're around me. Am I supposed to be impressed? It's disrespect to an act that's very important.' She'd been pale but very determined. Graeme had stared, then nodded. 'Aye, awright, when you're here. Whit d'you think Les?' And Lesley had sat back and laughed. 'Oh, she's fucking right!'

Jimmy has almost stopped swearing, though it's hard on the platform. She has pointed out how as a working-class Glaswegian intellectual, Graeme must conclude any intelligent statement with an expletive. As if to apologise for his articulacy. Clinging to the wreckage, she calls it.

Jimmy looks at the picture and wonders where to begin. Costello is singing 'This Year's Model'. He's not the New Man he's read about, the whole idea sounds phoney. But he can't live with the Old. Christ, there must be something he can feel good about in being a man.

'Look around ye! Look at the factories, the empty yards, faces in the street, graffiti on the bus-shelters. My stairwell, the faces of old folk, my old man – '

'What about your old man?'

Graeme hesitates.

'Bye and bye,' he says. 'But what d'you see? *The Aesthetics of Damage*. Scars and scores, lines, cuts and scratches, snakes an fuckin ladders. It starts with the wee nicks on yer knee when you were a bairn.'

'All bairns compare scars,' says Jimmy, accepting the smoke. 'Biggest wins.'

'Right! Badges o experience. Like Lesley's broken nose from karate, my crocked ankle, or yon scars across Kim's wrist.'

'You spotted them?'

'Oh aye.'

Jimmy finally exhales, feeling the sweet smoke seep like honey into his clammy cells.

'Divorce,' he says. 'Bairns are no the only wans. There'll aye be a mark there. I hurt someone right bad and I'll never trust myself the same. Why d'you think I don't live with Kim? I'm feart.'

Graeme nods uneasily. I've plenty ither mates, he tells Lesley later, but all we do is banter and talk football and politics. But Jim aye wants to get into the squishy stuff.

61

'You gonna Bogart that joint, pal?'

Jimmy grins, passes over the smoking fuse. As the honey spreads through his brain, he examines the painting again.

He used to think Abstraction a joke or a con. But Graeme must be dead serious when after teaching all day he comes back and puts hours of work into these canvases. Very occasionally one actually sells, but like the things Kim is working on, like climbing for that matter, that's not the point.

And whatever's done neither for money nor applause, fascinates Jimmy, as if there's an answer for him there.

And the more time he spends in front of Graeme's paintings, the clearer they become, like Punk suddenly heard as music. There are foregrounds and backgrounds, layers of history like he's been excavating the canvas, digging away at the foundations with a palette knife instead of a trowel. A kind of naked archaeology.

Naked archaeology ma arse, he hears his father say.

Giggling he accepts back the smouldering roach.

'I still like that one best. Bit of colour.'

He nods at the only coloured canvas, propped on the window-ledge. Pale orange background painted roughly over in blue, then scratched back to unearth three rows of orange curves that loop and crow like dancers across the canvas, then exit into the wings.

'Ach, too pretty,' Graeme mutters. 'That was when I first met Les, before the '79 Election. We were, like, "in love".'

'You dinna have to apologise about it,' Jimmy says, 'the "in love" or the picture.'

'*Bonnie.*' Graeme shakes his head. They consider the painting. He clears his throat. 'Daft, isn't it, "love". I canni talk about it like you. I canni explain how it is wi me and Les. Maybe that's why the paintings. Wankin in the dark, man.'

'Could be.'

'She drives me nuts sometimes,' he says. Jimmy catches a rare note of desperation and leans forward. 'Up the flamin wall. You know the cool way she can be, yon pan loaf boarding school accent, like you're nuthin. Snooty bitch.'

'That's no a right way to speak,' Jimmy says sharply.

Graeme looks at him. Jimmy stares him out.

'Ach, well. Okay.' He frowns at the floor. 'She's ma best friend and tells me everything, only sometimes I'd rather no know.'

'But she's not with anyone else.'

Graeme stares at him, opens his mouth, closes it again.

'Okay, maybe she's discreet,' Jimmy says. 'But she's honest.'

'Honest! Sometimes wonder if there's more I don't know.'

Jimmy laughs. He likes Lesley, her tall, powerful body, her jaunty crew-cut the red of wet autumn bracken, her laughter, her vitality, her lack of fear. Likes her a lot.

Graeme looks up at him.

'She hasni – '

'Don't be bloody daft.'

They look at the big picture for a while.

'She's the most important person in the world for me.'

It comes out in a rush. Jimmy nods. This he understands.

'Of course.'

'But it's still jist a hill of beans. The big picture is the one that counts.'

'What's with these beans?'

Graeme sighs. Not only is his pal a bourgeois individualist, he's also sometimes slow on the hip references.

He opens two more bottles of chemical waste and caramel, passes one over.

'In *Casablanca*,' he drawls. 'It's easy to see without looking too far that the troubles of three little people don't amount to a hill of beans in this lousy world.'

'Huh,' says Jimmy. 'The importance of a hill of beans depends on how hungry you are.'

Graeme hesitates then extends the bottle.

'*Bon appetit* then, pal.'

EIGHT

Ticket

WAY OUT BEYOND the harbour, two red lights slowly approach each other as if drawn by invisible strings.

A 'relationship'. It sounded like there was her and me and between us we were lumbered with a third party – a cumbersome but fragile concrete baby which could break up, disintegrate, be re-cast, dropped, improved or simply inadvertently lost.

We shortened it to 'ship. As in long ship, short ship, tight or sinking, happy or unlucky ship.

The red lights briefly meet, one above the other, then move on. I sit and watch our ship with two captains and no crew move hesitantly into the open sea.

At the end of her first year at the art college, despite a few cross-currents (Alison, Kim's interest in some of the more talented lads, her lack of interest in much of the syllabus), to our surprise we were still in the same ship and she'd passed her exams.

Time to celebrate. I decided to blow some of Scotland's Oil, wangled extra leave and we went abroad that summer. Graeme was a bit cheesed because the Old Man had been pencilled in for his holidays, but like I said, it wasn't going to fall down yet. He and Lesley would meet us later in the Calanques for some rock-climbing.

We went first to Paris. It was high summer and the city was sultry, clinging. She was raised and restless, like a candle near the draught. I remember sore feet and a blur of galleries and a second sexual honeymoon. She was fascinated by the prostitutes of the red light district and our nights often ended walking through there before she dragged me back to Swiss Frank's flat.

'It's a masquerade,' she said. 'Can't you feel the tug of it? To wear these disguises and be someone else. To let go all this heaviness . . .'

I raised my eyebrows at a particularly surreal pair of thigh-length boots that kinda reminded me of dad's fisherman's waders. She whistled at us from the doorway, I grinned as we walked by. I had all I could possibly handle, and the reality would be sordid. Still, the gleam from that unknown woman's eyes stayed with me the length of the street.

'I can feel it,' I admitted. 'But I'd still rather just be me.'

'Oh, Jim,' she said and punched my arm, fairly lightly. 'When you find out who that is.'

'I'm working on it.'

'Let's find some music at least. I feel like a birl.'

By then I was light-headed with fatigue, but in periods like this she scarcely needed sleep nor was capable of rest. I woke round dawn in the ruins of a storm-tossed bed and saw her still curled up in a chair working steadily on her notebooks. She seemed to draw energy from being out of Scotland.

In fact she'd dozed off then woken in a panic sweat. She'd quietly got up and made herself coffee though she knew she shouldn't, and stood looking out the narrow window at the lights of Paris. She was aware her hands had a slight tremble but she rolled a cigarette anyway.

She picked up the notebook. Make the problem the topic, she thought, it usually works.

She glanced at the bed where Jimmy slept oblivious.

I'd like to be two, she wrote. *One for serious, one for forgetfulness.*

She hesitated, left a space.

Except in sex, I cannot give myself away. There's times I'd like to, but I can't.

I should be sold without choice like the girls in Saint Denis.

A space, some doodling, a sketch of some ear-rings, then a tiny person dangling from a huge shell.

Blethers! Japanese belief: two souls – one mortal and pleasure-seeking (pain-finding), the other dispassionate, eternal, undisturbed below the storm. Two kinds of carving.

Drawings of little ships becoming ducks, a bath drawn round the lot. In brown crayon, a man looking down at the bath, blowing. A big strong nose. Unhappy.

Another page.

In two minds, as they say. It's not safe. I hope he understands and doesn't expect any more. Maybe in my own time – tell him, let him see. He is very loyal and I suspect he does love me.

Whatever that word means.

Space, coffee-stained thumbprint, then tiny, rapid letters:
I love him and, I love him but

I flick through the pages of her notebook, then replace it on the shelf among the others, methodical to the end. It might have made a difference if she'd told me then, but I was asleep and she felt it wasn't safe and so we bobbed on.

The galleries had been a relief to her, she'd scarcely seen anything she liked. At least, nothing that was *her*. I did find her looking depressed in front of the Rembrandt self-portaits.

'I'm wasting everybody's time,' she muttered. 'I should be a nurse or a nun and do some good in this world.'

She was silent in a dwam before some Chagalls and then bought large prints of his stained glass windows. (Two are here still, above the divan where the child snores quietly in her sleep, the others are in the pale rectangles of their absence.)

Most of the sculpture was dull, dull, or not what she was after. It was quite encouraging. She stared at the figure of a dancer that had been dressed. It reminded her of a circus dog wearing clothes.

'Yeuch!'

The curator looked scandalised.

'*Mais, M'selle, c'est Dégas.*'

'*Ca ne fait rien,*' she said firmly in Higher French. '*C'est dégoutant.*'

'The flat's full tonight,' she said as we hesitated outside the Metro. 'Can we go somewhere else?'

Through her dress I stroked the curved groove down the inner side of her pelvic bone, imagining the groove as a route, say a hundred feet high. It would be the ultimate curved edge, even better than the Old Man.

'Isn't there somewhere we can go?'

She faced me. Black spray of hair, eyes in shadow but I recognised that tone by now.

'Let's try something,' I said. 'Just look like you belong.'

I selected the snazziest hotel on the riverfront. We walked across a glittering lobby and into the lift.

'We can't afford this.'

'Wait and see.'

Sometimes I liked to keep her guessing. She was quivering with impatience.

We got out at the top floor. At the far end of the corridor I found the Emergency Exit. The main staircase went down, but a narrow one spiralled up. She followed me. The unmarked door at the top was not locked and we emerged onto a flat roof, among the heating vents and aerials.

I took off my jacket and spread it on the roof.

'M'selle?'

She lay down in the darkness. I heard her hitch up her dress, saw the pale gleam of her legs.

'You've bought me for an hour,' she said.

And it was later on that rooftop that she talked about her dad. Her voice was careful, like someone hauling a bucket up from a well trying not to spill a drop.

'Same nose is same mind,' he'd often said. She took after him, was his child. Not like her sister. This she must understand. He spoke with a heavy accent which embarrassed her as a child and which she became proud of in the year before he . . . died.

She remembered the length of his fingers and the yellow streak of nicotine like an old wound as he silently drew butterflies at the kitchen table. The smell and feel of his old tweed jacket, his free arm gently round her as she watched. A soft, strange, familiar smokey hairiness that was dad.

She spoke very low, so I had to strain to follow her; she remembered finding him in the garden hut, staring at the fork in his hand like he didn't know what it was. He shook his head when she spoke and wouldn't look at her and she was frightened. He pushed little piles of sugar round his saucer for a whole Sunday and spoke to people she couldn't see. He went away for a while after that . . .

She remembered his pride, his temper, his gentleness. They went for walks, he told her stories about the country where people like him came from. It was the saddest country in the world and he couldn't go there any more. Almost everyone was dead. She was so like him, he said, and the eyes of his mother, but she must grow up not to be sad. She must do all the things he couldn't because he was . . . alien.

And he told her how she got her name, from a book he'd carried through the war. And though her surname had been changed to help her fit in this new country, both of them would always know what her real name was.

From the beginning she signed her works *K. Ruslawska.*

I lay on my back beside her, as still as possible. I didn't know what had brought this on and I guessed it wouldn't happen often.

Eventually she continued.

Her earliest memory is of lying in long grass near some Scots pine trees, way high up on a ridge. Probably the escarpment above North Third Reservoir.

'But wasn't that where you and Dave first – ?'

I felt rather than saw her irritable shrug.

'Do you want to hear this or not?'

'Yes. Yes, Kim.'

Her dad's there. She is very young, the grass is high as trees. It's a secret world. The wind's making sea in the trees. She is lying on her side, head on the ground, watching a bug struggling up the huge trunks of grass. She sends her fingers down the deep green tunnel and suddenly her father's face is there at the end, hanging like a moon, loving and unhappy and enormous . . .

She trailed off into silence. A light wind had got up and I shivered, wondering whether to press her. Then she got briskly to her feet and dusted herself down.

'I've finished that Kipling book,' she said. 'I think my namesake was working for the wrong side. My father was as sentimental and fallible as anyone else, and had some very strange ideas. Maybe I'm not so like him after all.'

She laughed quietly. She was silhouetted against the chimneys so I couldn't see into her any more.

'So thanks, sailor,' she said. 'What now?'

'Home, please,' I said, and dusted myself down. We seemed to be covered in soot. 'But first we have to walk out of here with our heads high.'

'I love it,' Kim said as we crossed the lobby looking like extras from a Black and White Minstrel show, 'when you surprise me. What gave you the idea for that one?'

'Must have read it in a book somewhere,' I said vaguely. It didn't seem like a good time to talk about Bridget.

'Amazing what you can get off with if you believe enough,' she murmured. 'Maybe we'll be alright,' and out in the street she took my arm and went on tip-toe to rub her sooty nose on my sooty cheek.

*   *   *

I roll and unroll the ticket between my fingers. *Paris-Marseille*. I found it between the pages of her notebook. It remains some sort of evidence.

Sex is tangible evidence, something solid and undeniable. Maybe that's why the memory picks on it so, like a scab.

It exaggerates, or at least misleads. She never took her body that seriously, she wore it like a cloak thrown on as a necessity to go about the world in. And sex alone could have brought me to her, but not held me so long.

Memory fastens on sex as evidence that two people meant something to each other in ways you cannot always recall. Like shifts of soil colour, the outlines of a hearth, fragments of pottery and bone, it's evidence something bigger and more complex went on here. The subtler, softer meanings – a glance across the kitchen, the cup of coffee silently left at the working elbow, a glance picked up, the easy sharing of meals and mountains and washing up, indeed of all the unmemorable days and afternoons, evenings and nights of your life together – they leave few traces.

But once, as the train slowed approaching Marseille, we were standing shoulder to shoulder in the crowded corridor. We hadn't spoken for minutes, nothing particular to say. A crowded, sweaty train, everyone impatiently patient to get off. She was on my left, had on a blue headscarf, our rucksacks were at our feet. For no reason I'll ever know, she turned and looked up at me.

'I love you,' she said with equal and exact emphasis on each word, and opened her eyes as wide as eyes can be.

Other times, other light and subtle moments pass again briefly, like a silk scarf drawn across the palm. Grip, and the sensation is gone. Almost unspeakable, but real just the same.

As I walked along the clifftop path, the future seemed warm and light and full of ploys. Like this week's climbing and hanging out in the Calanques with my closest friends. When the four of us sat round the table together at night, our warmth and laughter, the trust and sarcasm that rose between us, seemed like a campfire holding off the darkness back home.

I saw her from the top of the cliff. She was crouched near the water's edge in a blue one-piece swimsuit, her back to me. (She believed bikinis were vulgar and didn't suit her, she was right.) She was drawing something secret on the sand with a stick. (Working with sand had interesting possibilities, she noted. At least it's very cheap and there's plenty of it. She could spray the end result rigid.)

She thought herself alone. I meant to shout but missed the moment. Instead I sat down at the top of the cliff and watched her being alone with herself.

She straightened up and threw the stick into the water with that lovely, awkward woman's gesture of throwing. The afternoon grew bright and still as hallucination. Then she threw her arms out wide as though tossing an invisible beach-ball big as the world, out to sea.

She was twenty and still had moments of unexamined joy. At such moments she believed the world would always hold her up, wherever she went, whoever she loved.

The sea was blue, the sky was blue, her swimsuit too, and she stood ankle-deep in the centre of her world. A gull she didn't see went gliding way above her head, drew a smooth white line like chalk and disappeared.

For the first time I saw her for herself, not as what she was for me.

Finally she dropped her arms, casually turned and saw me. She waved, I waved. The spiney grass was sweet and hot as I went down to the beach. As I approached her, desire, hope, fear, resumed normal service, but it was too late. Something had moved across my chest and drawn a line between everything up to that point and whatever would come after.

I saw the danger yet I walked towards her, carefully, as though that could make any difference.

And later on that first trip abroad, the four of us went on down to Tarifa on the tip of Spain. We were sitting on a restaurant balcony while a German group played *Viva L'Espana*, looking across the straits at the lights on the African coast. None of us was sober. Kim was leaning over the balcony out of earshot while Graeme and Lesley made plans to explore Morocco someday, maybe after the next election was won. Want to come, Jim?

'Sure, but it's more interesting to fall in love than go to Africa.'

Graeme shook his head sorrowfully.

'Aye, and the sun shines straight oot o her mooth.'

'Two years on and he still thinks she's wonderful,' Les added. 'Sweet, really.'

'As it happens, I love Kim because she's her, not because I think she's wonderful.'

Lesley looked me over thoughtfully.

'This is new,' she said.

Kim came back to the table.

'You buggers talking about me again?'

'Na, it's just paranoia, kid,' Graeme said.

Kim sighed.

'Self-importance by another name,' she said.

Lesley put her hand on Kim's thin forearm.

'We were just saying how wonderful you were.'

'God help us,' she said, 'the obituaries already. I'm no dead yet so you don't have to tell lies about me.'

We sat on in silence, watching a tug boat coming our way, its yellow searchlight like a moon in the blue dusk.

Tonight somewhere we're in that moment still, so clearly can I see us sitting round the table. Kim has just fallen silent after making that crack about obituaries. Her dark hair is moist as she leans on my shoulder. Leslie's hand is on her wrist, Graeme is facing me, idly turning his beer. We sit, balanced, briefly at rest.

'What's up, old 'un?' she murmured.

'It's kinda melancholy. Looking at the end of Europe.'

The lighthouse blinked yellow on the last promontory.

And she laughed and put her hand on mine.

'I look out and see Africa beginning,' she said. 'That's the difference between us.'

I screw up the ticket and lob it casually at the waste-paper basket. It goes in, the way things do when you don't try too hard.

NINE

Plastic soldier

WHEN THE EARLY-WARNING buzzer cut in over the swish-bang of fighter planes and frigate anti-aircraft fire from the TV in the corner, I put down my spray can and waited.

'Mick, can you no disconnect that ruddy system?' Kim muttered. 'It's driving me doo-lalli.'

Mick rolled back from the TV in his army fatigues and turned his mild, bull-like head her way.

'The Resistance will disconnect the whole ruddy System,' he announced, 'Because it's driving us all nuts. But we need the early warning, They may bust early, orders from the DA. Check?'

'Wish someone would disconnect the war,' Joan said. 'My cousin's out there.'

Kim grunted and went back to inscribing titles with silver ink on black card. She'd been told at the last minute she had to give her pieces titles, otherwise they wouldn't be taken seriously. She grumbled but did it. The exhibition was quite a big deal for someone still at college and she was ambitious in her way. She was ambitious for her work, she wanted it to go beyond her.

The eyes of the idol above the fireplace lit up blue, meaning friends were calling, ones who knew about Mick's second signal beam. Strangers cut the other infra-red beam and set off flashing red lights. Then the ordinary door bell whirred.

Joan stopped sandpapering Kim's *Personal Beach* and went to answer. Mick Deterre and his urban guerilla trip might be completely out to breakfast, lunch and tea, but he also kept the flat supplied with tall stories, soft drugs and a sense of drama. Joan seemed happier, and he'd taught Kim infra-red photography, lighting and relay systems, primitive microdots. She'd use it all some day.

I set up black card behind the three plastic soldiers and gave the can a shake.

'Like this?'

Kim looked up.

'Yeah, but get in close.'

'Is it the silhouettes or silver squaddies you're after?'

She grinned. 'God only knows.'

I lined up the can and gave the soldiers a good blast. One fell over, his wee plastic bayonet stuck up in the air, dripping silver. Sod it, I'd have to stick them down.

'Of course I enjoy spending my Saturday nights being a handmaid to genius,' I said.

'Ach, you're only in it for the fixatives,' she said and threw a green frogman at me. Their flat was full of half-finished cereal packets. I caught it as Graeme and Lesley followed Joan in.

'Hi, pal. Hi young 'un. Hope you pay your workers well.'

'In kind,' I answered.

'She sprays you silver?' Les asked. 'Weird. We must try that some time.'

Graeme grinned. Their reunion must have gone well.

'More or less,' I said.

Kim kept writing but raised her other hand in acknowledgement.

'Be wi you in a sec.'

Lesley gave me a big hug.

'How was the diving trip, doll?' I asked when I could breathe again.

'*Deep*, mannequin. Didn't want to leave. It's so peaceful down there, not like this nut-house. I'll take you down some day.'

I put an arm round Graeme's shoulders, we could do that now. He handed me a can and looked round the flat's big communal room.

'How's the war going, Mick?'

He tossed him a beer.

'Cheers, brother. I think England are winning. The Resistance could do with this hardware.'

Graeme grunted. The war had wrong-footed him. It would have been simpler if Argentina were a peace-loving socialist democracy.

'A plague on baith their hooses. Hey, is this the Warhol Factory or whit?'

I could see what he meant. Kim writing and folding title cards. Joan sanding and sealing the driftwood sculptures and paintings. Me making with the spray can. Alison couldn't come that night, but her sister Tess was Letrasetting in the corner. Lesley went over and crouched beside her. Mick DeTerre polishing a glass maze. The TV on and the stereo knocking out R&B. Kim seemed happiest working like this, on an island of concentration washed round by chaos, alone but not alone.

I set up the soldiers again, turned the card over and gave them another blast with the spray, studied the result with Graeme.

'Bit of a rush on,' I explained. 'We've been enlisted. I think the silhouettes work better. What d'you think?'

He squatted down beside me, looked at the card and the various pieces piled along the window seat.

'I think – ' He hesitated then continued quietly. 'I think when she's finished fooling around she may do something uncommon. No ma scene, but she's got it. And she works. No jist anither middle-class wanker. Dinni say I said so.'

He lit a small cigar and prowled round the room, can in hand. The war had been followed by adverts but would be back after the break. He put his hand on Lesley's shoulder and knelt to talk with Tess, which was more than I was able to do. Tess and I were polite, no more. I assumed she disapproved of men in general and me in particular for sleeping with Alison, though that was a long time back now.

Tess caught me staring, pushed her glasses up her nose and looked away. She and Kim had spent a lot of time together the last months, putting their heads together over ceramics. It made me uneasy because she could so easily tell Kim about me and Alison if she chose. She'd said often enough women artists had to systematically free themselves of all male influence.

I also wondered to what degree Kim's sexuality was as unresolved as her dress sense. She and Tess had been giving each other a wide berth all evening and I wasn't sure why.

Lesley winked at me, said something to Graeme then bent to help Tess with the Letrasetting. Graeme casually got up and wandered over to Kim.

'No bad stuff, kid.'

'Less of the kid, cheeky-breeks.'

He grinned.

'Ye'll no be wanting a hand, then.'

'Please,' she said. 'It's gotta be finished and dry by the morn.' She looked around. 'See yon Eric Clapton carving? Lousy, ain't it.'

Graeme fingered the mis-shapen dimensions, another of her customised driftwood pieces. He put his finger through the hole in its head.

'Seen worse.'

'It's empty,' she said, 'but the committee want it. Find a non-inflammable corner, use yon blow-torch and rough it up a bit. Carbonise the guitar and the heart, but lay off the hands, I like them.'

'Ma pleesure.'

I set up some new card and lined up the soldiers for another blast.

'Got something for you, Kim,' I over-heard Lesley say. 'You always said you wanted a cat but couldn't keep one in the city.'

She put down a small package and Kim unwrapped the diamante pussy-cat and sat with it winking in her silver-streaked hand.

The Bruntsfield flat. A time of gifts and shambles, of callers passing through, of work and talk, indolence and pleasure, of lives tried out for size, searching for the one that fits. I remember parties, panics, carry-outs, hearing long confessions in the kitchen from troubled souls who seemed to think I was safely past it all. For a while Kim's hair changed red, yellow, green, like traffic lights. Then it reverted to a short, upward spray of black, which gave her an air of permanent surprise or mild shock.

Once in a while in a tenement flat I still catch a whiff of it, that smell compounded of cigarette smoke, paint and white spirit, incense, glue, coffee, hashish, dust, fish suppers, old rubbish bags no one had got it together to put out on time, and for a moment the wings brush by me.

I feel the cracked brown leather armchairs and lumpy concave mattresses, see those high-corniced ceilings, the Chagall and Kandinsky posters, the chaotic bookshelves propped on bricks, hear the music of that time – Costello, Aztec Camera, Tom Waits, Talking Heads, Kim's favourite Laurie Anderson, even Dylan when I could get him on. And echoes of the voices that thought nothing was irrevocable.

I hate nostalgia, unless it's my own. The wings brush by me and are gone.

The blow-torch roared, Graeme crouched and gave Clapton the treatment. Kim pinned the brooch to her work-shirt and knelt beside me.

'The silhouettes are fine,' she said. 'I'll use it as a back-drop for the light-box. But the soldiers themselves are a disappointment.'

'Sure are,' Graeme said. 'But they're real, you canni ignore them.'

'This is my game and Reality is what I make it,' Kim said. Les winked at me. This was a long-running argument. 'No soldiers, no economics, no political theory'.

'Christ, it's no a theory!' He turned down the blowtorch. 'You know as well as me whit's happening in this country. You see it in the streets, the factories, down at the DHSS, the schools, hospitals, every thing you might once have been proud of about this country is being cut. And England's gone off its heid wi this war.' He stared at her, at us, blowtorch in hand, impassioned and desperately sincere, almost pleading for our agreement. 'It doesni take a theory to see this is aa terribly wrong.'

Kim looked down. 'I ken that,' she said quietly. She vaguely stroked the brooch then looked up at him again. 'But I ken this too. You have to work where your passion is, and mine's not there.'

She hesitated. Tess had stopped work, Joan wasn't sanding, the rest of us were round her and she was always uneasy to be the centre of attention.

'Aye, but – '

'No, Graeme,' she said, then grinned to take the edge off it. 'We'll agree to differ.' She reached out, squeezed his arm, and I saw then how much she'd come into her own this last while.

'You see,' she added, 'I'd only be playing their game, making them think power and money is the only one. God save me from Relevance.'

'Amen,' Joan said, and yawned. Like Mick she mostly wore fatigues these days, but the crucifix was still underneath. 'Looks like it's going to be an all-nighter.'

Tess frowned and went back to work, the slightly uneasy circle broke up. Graeme puffed his cigar and used it to re-light the torch.

'She looks well,' Lesley murmured. 'How's she been keeping?'

'No bad at all. She's a bit raised now but that's natural. Ach, I probably exaggerate where Kim's concerned, her mood swings and that. It's very important to her that she's an ordinary, happy young woman, and whatever talent she has is tacked onto that – like an outboard motor.'

Lesley nodded. 'My American sisters say men compartmentalize themselves and women don't. But she's the most compartmentali- sed person I've ever met. Kind of like the Titanic.' She swigged from her can, ran her hand through bright hair. 'Still, you can't help but love her, can you?'

'Talking of which.' I glanced towards the corner where Tess was working.

Lesley sat back on her heels and looked at me. 'Mm. Could be,' she said neutrally.

'But what d'you think?'

'I think that *Personal Beach* there says enough about our Kim.'

I looked over where Joan was finishing sanding it. We'd found that big pale charred log on the beach at Aberlady Bay and Kim had insisted we lugged it home. Eventually she began to carve a beach into it with little outcrops, shrubs, even a heron, sprinkled with real sand. Then she added a tiny fire and a figure standing by it, her mouth wide open as though calling on someone not there. The figure was pointing at a log by her feet and that log was the whole log in miniature.

'I'll lay you a hundred to one without looking any closer,' Lesley said, 'that miniature log doesn't have even a hint of another beach and person carved on it in turn. And that dead end is what'll make it special.'

'How did you know that?'

'Because of something I learned tonight. Because she needs to call a halt somewhere, and that's what hooks you. So am I right?'

Mick switched off the TV. 'The English army have just won the war,' he announced. He blinked and adjusted his wire-rim specs. 'But the Resistance has just begun. Speed, anyone?'

It was light by the time we finished. Joan pulled back the curtains, opened the windows, and all of us except Kim went to crash for a couple of hours. By that time the British troops had secured a beachhead on a piece of land that looked like a Shetland bog only less appealing. I half woke when Kim slipped in and I saw the curtains billow and the light ripple across the ceiling, felt the breeze pass over my skin. She lay restlessly beside me, her face flushed and taut on the pillow, near as the width of my hand yet far away as any star. Lesley had been right, of course, the world inside a world of *Personal Beach* came to a dead end. I thought of men preparing to take or hold ground, frightened or exhilarated, waiting amphetamined to the gills.

'But all Art is exaggeration – that's the trouble wi it!' Kim protested, and we were laughing as she and Graeme argued the toss while we passed John Knox' house, the four of us heading down the High Street on the way to the gallery next morning. Mick had gone on ahead, carrying her exhibits in his camoflauged jeep – about the most conspicuous vehicle on the streets of Edinburgh. Double-bluff, he said. If he displayed Urban Guerilla, They would assume he was harmless. As we did.

Early Sunday morning in the ancient empty street, cool wind and a gritty feeling round the eyes, empty-headed and light-hearted. The sunshine on Leith clutched at her diamante brooch for a moment as we turned into the dimness of the close.

I stood in the empty gallery while she had a last look round. We'd been setting up all day, now everyone else had gone home or to the pub.

I picked up *Incomplete* as she'd titled it, held it to the light and looked into the sea glass again. *The ultimate triumph of the moon.* Her earliest present to me, a warning, a promise, whatever.

I remembered what she'd told me in Paris. The child in the tall grass, inventing and exploring private worlds. Then parting the towering stalks to see her father's face watching her like a loving, unhappy god. Looking round now at her miniature worlds of glass, wood, perspex and bone, where the fragments of words and meanings emerged and slipped away, everything seemed to refer back to that moment.

I knew her works were intriguing and ingenious, but only now, seeing them all together, did I realise they were also unexpectedly moving. They were self-complete, they were . . . lonely. I looked through the moon-shaped clear patch again, feeling oddly tearful.

She was standing beside me.

'Don't worry,' she said cheerfully, 'you'll get it back when the show's over.'

I put the glass down carefully. It's what you can't quite put your finger on that makes you so want to touch.

'Ach, all that moon and womb stuff,' Kim muttered, looking around. 'I was just doing what I was supposed to do. Tess says I shouldn't be working in glass. Says it's too male – hard and brittle.'

'Tess uses "male" like Graeme uses "bourgeois". It beats thinking.'

She sighed. '*Female Works*, for Christ's sake, what kind of title for an exhibition is that? I'll not have my work ghetto-ised by anyone, not even women – especially not women – they should know better. By the way, I've decided I'm no a lesbian.'

'Oh, jolly good,' I said.

'Not even bisexual. Life's complicated enough. Anyway, I've learned lots about ceramics from her, and we'll still be friends.'

A long speech for her. She didn't like talking about Art or what she did. She felt that anything out in the open would evaporate, like perfume.

She zipped up her old yellow jacket. She was edgy and excited about the exhibition, though she wouldn't say so.

'Let's go to the Fiddlers,' she said. 'I'm afraid you're buying. I may have my sodding Art but you've got a job.'

She locked up and we stepped into the drizzling Edinburgh night. We smelled the breweries, heard a train rumble through the Gardens, a cry of seagulls on the night wind. Soldiers were lying shaking on wet heathery slopes in the fire-lit dark, but the streetlights spread yellow on the cobbles as we walked through the Grassmarket towards the Fiddlers Arms to meet our friends, and with our jackets zipped up to the throat, we were happy. I offered her an arm and she took it. It was all in front of us.

TEN

Shell case

I STRETCH AT the window and look down at Dunbar's narrow harbour. Lights are moving out there, someone else is waking yet. So many ships, so many harbours – Port Stanley, Eyemouth, Stromness, Lerwick . . . Why should these old campaigns be recalled?

I know the answer, but on nights like these I sometimes miss my oldest friends.

Kim's kettle finally whistles, the child stirs. I do the necessary and sit back at the table, studying the pieces that remain. The plastic soldier dripping silver and this shiny brass shell, how suddenly a joke can cease to be.

The only thing we knew for sure about Mick DeTerre was his name wasn't Mick DeTerre. He'd appeared one day with Joan. He wasn't particularly tall, but barrel-chested, and his close-shaved head was unusually large, with tiny wire-rimmed glasses. He shook hands quite formally, his voice came from deep in his chest. He looked like a minotaur dressed in military fatigues.

Then he casually announced he was an Urban Guerilla and he needed a safe house. He'd check the phone and set up an alarm system on the stair tomorrow. Check?

Then they went into her room and didn't emerge much for a while.

After that Joan was less obliging but laughed more. She started cutting Marine Biology classes, the dishes were left and the rubbish wasn't always put out. The flat lost its conscience but there were more high jinks.

They disappeared on 'training exercise', which seemed to involve sea-canoeing, orienteering and elaborate drop-offs in caves, under cairns and behind waterfalls. She never knew what, if anything, was in the packages he picked up and left. Occasionally there was 'heavy business, man' and on those occasions she didn't go with him.

Let's say we humoured him, though we drew the line at early morning Escape Drills out the back window and down the rope that he kept under Joan's bed.

'So what's the Resistance resisting, Mick?'

He put a finger to his lips and grinned.

'Those who know, know,' he replied.

I thought he was an ice-screw short of the whole rack.

'Deterrence,' he said, 'that's our role. Deterrence and rumour. They know we exist but not where or how many. Like the Sendero Luminoso in Peru. Check? That's deterrence.'

That's when we began to call him DeTerre. It wasn't his name. Nor, I think, was Mick. We never could place his accent, and he didn't let on.

He was preparing for the day when tanks rolled down Morningside Road and Sauchiehall Street. We were never exactly sure whose tanks, but at least the Resistance would be ready. Once after a few beers he mentioned the Scottish HQ was in the remote Rough Bounds of Knoydart, south from Loch Hourn. His local branch hideout was a cave in the Lammermuir Hills, where he claimed to keep six months' provisions, an Armalite, handguns and explosives he'd liberated from his days as a quarryman. Not even Joan was allowed to see it. Security, he said. What you don't know you can't be made to tell. We understood?

We nodded, trying to keep a straight face. Well, we all have our fantasies. I think even then Kim and I dimly recognized that.

'You've got to admit,' Kim said, 'he's different. Maybe he gets carried away, but he wouldnae hurt a flea. And Joan's happy. Call it a kind of missionary work.'

'She's lost weight.'

'So would you if you spent weekends crawling round the Pentlands living on beef jerky, shadowing the T.A. He's definitely no frae Plean. That's in his favour.'

He was a good joke and kept us all fairly stoned till that day shortly after the exhibition.

Kim and I were lying in. She'd been hyper for days before and throughout the exhibition, out-lasted everyone at the celebration party, and was still prowling round the flat when I went to bed. When I woke in the night, she wasn't there. I finally got up to look for her. The lights were all on, a record was clicking on the stereo but she'd disappeared. I heard an odd tearing sound under the table.

'Kim?'

She was crouched beneath the table, slowly and with great concentration tearing up her pack of Tarot cards. Beside her was a carton of milk and a bottle of Quiet Life tablets.

'Kim?'

She tore another card.

I bent down to talk to her, not sure where to start.

'What you doing there?'

She finally turned her head. She looked like a child at play, a wee wary-eyed beastie in a cage.

'Trying to slow down,' she'd muttered. 'Don't think that speed's good for me. Never again.'

'Good,' I said. 'What's with the cards?'

'Too much significance.'

'Ah.'

I got her out from under there. She brightened up and decided to go for a run. Followed by an enthusiastic amateur massage from me. Gradually her jaw relaxed, her back muscles softened. Followed by equally enthusiastic sex with distinctly personal overtones. (Have I mentioned that good sex is wonderful, a human joy, even in Scotland? This cannot be said often enough in this country, at these times.)

And at last she'd slept, heavily, not waking till late afternoon. Just as well, I was knackered and aware I was definitely in my thirties.

I'd gone out for all the papers, and now we were lying reading about the capture of Port Stanley and the reviews of the exhibition.

'You're on your way,' I said. 'I'm fair chuffed for you.'

'Ach, I wish they wouldnae go on about my age. I resent being filed under teeny-bopper sculptor, female, Scottish. I'm no even a sculptor, my technique's pathetic, my gender's irrelevant. If I have to compete, I want it to be in the big arena.'

'Dinna fash yersel,' I said. 'You've sold some and it beats working.'

'It does that,' she admitted. 'But this is just apprentice stuff at best.' She frowned. 'I've so far to go and I'll never get there.'

'Ach, I've got less far to go but likely I'll not arrive either.'

She looked at me curiously.

'Have you? I always think of you as so solid while I run around in wee circles.'

'Keep your illusions,' I replied, and wondered at my voice. 'Anyway, your so-called toys move me for one.'

'Really?'

She seemed astonished.

'They're an addition to the world. Something that wasn't there before. Like children, and that's got to be worthwhile.'

She spread her hands and looked down at them.

'I dinnae want kids,' she said. 'We've been through that one.'

A short silence. What they call an angel passing.

'Kim, I do need something of my own.'

'Like children?' she said quickly.

'The Old Man, for starters.'

'That Old Man,' she laughed. 'You two are obsessed.'

She lay back and looked up at me.

'We'll see,' she said gently. 'Give me time.'

I nodded. Our closest moments were like that, brief, oblique, well understood.

And then the thump on the door and Mick burst in.

'The heat's on, troops,' he announced. 'Been a couple of arrests. Joan and me got to split. Will you hide these for me, just this once?'

He dumped a carrier bag on the bed. It was heavy and clunked. We should have stopped him there.

'What is it?' Kim asked sleepily.

'Guns,' he said. 'Guns and ammo.'

'Whit?'

He was gone.

We looked at each other.

'He's harmless,' she said. 'A fantasist. It makes his life more exciting.'

'Surely. Like some folk fall in love instead.'

'Is that a fantasy?'

'What do you think?'

'I think we should have a look in the bag.'

We did. In it were three packages wrapped in oil-cloth. We opened them onto the duvet. Two hand guns and a box of assorted ammunition. I picked up one of the guns. It was surprisingly heavy.

'It's a model, isn't it?' she said. 'A replica?'

I kept my finger well away from the trigger and examined it carefully. My dad had taught me to use a rifle but I'd never held a hand gun. I sniffed it, found the safety catch, clicked it off then on again.

'I'm not sure that it is,' I said.

'If this is real, I'll kill him.'

'Who's being paranoid, them or us?'

We silently considered the possibility. That there was indeed a loose organisation of people like DeTerre. That they had stashes and hideouts and letter-drops. That John Lennon's shooting was indeed a command implanted in Chapman by the CIA. That one day the tanks – British? American? Russian? – would roll down Morningside Road in a military coup. That the problems we'd been having with the phone lately weren't just bad lines. That there would be no more Elections, even bum ones.

'He does have two passports,' Kim said. 'I saw them once in the bottom of his kit-bag. The other's Irish and in another name.'

'He showed me two spare sets of licence plates for the jeep.'

We looked at the guns. My sense of reality began to slide like a fried egg in an over-oiled pan.

She shivered. 'I hate guns,' she said, 'whoever's got them. This has got to be a joke.'

Her voice wavered. She swallowed. I thought she was going to throw up.

'The Red Brigade wasn't. Nor the IRA. Nor the UDA.'

'Nor the SRA?'

'Na. They were a joke.' She giggled as I'd hoped, relaxed a bit. 'Poor bloody country, we don't even make good terrorists.'

'But we're not occupied. Are we?'

We looked at each other.

'*Are we?*'

The alarm buzzer went off in the hall. We lay rigid. Then the door bell clanged. There was no one else in the flat and we were sitting in bed with two very real-looking guns.

'What do we do?'

'You answer it, but slowly. Give me time to hide these.'

She nodded, shouted she was coming. I fumbled the guns and ammo and cloths back into the carrier bag. She put on her dressing-gown. The bell kept ringing. She went out the room. Where to hide the fuckers? Her bean bag. I unzipped it, stuffed the bag inside, dumped some clothes on top as she answered the door.

I jumped back into bed and lay naked and sweating.

A murmur of voices. Male voices. Fuck's sake, Special Branch. I'd seen this movie. But it happened on the News too. Arms busts. That Irish passport. They'd find the guns in minutes. They'd think we were terrorists, IRA probably. Or did they know about the Resistance, was there a Resistance – ?'

The front door closed. I heard the extra bolts thud. Silence. She opened the bedroom door and stood there.

'Couple of guys said they were looking for Lizzy,' she said, 'whoever she is. They went away. I think it's okay.'

I lay back on the pillows. The noise in my ears subsided.

'Where do you think I hid them?'

She glanced round the room.

'In the bean bag, of course.'

'Fuck.'

When we'd stopped laughing she said, 'This is all very exciting but it's got to stop. He's abused my trust. I'm bloody angry.'

'It's not grand,' I said.

'I'll stick his Bowie knife up his arse and twist,' she said.

I winced. She never talked like that. She looked at the reviews strewn across the bed.

'Fantasies can get rough,' she muttered.

DeTerre and Joan came back three days later. Walked in as we were just finishing breakfast.

'About the firearms,' Mick said.

'Under the bed in Joan's room,' I said. 'Felt it was your problem.'

Mick ran his hands through his hair like he'd forgotten something.

'Yeah yeah. Thanks for looking after them.'

Kim's chair scraped back across the floor.

'I should fucking well think so,' she said.

She stood up and leaned across the table towards him. Whatever she did with her eyes, she'd done it again, and her hands were trembling. Her voice came out creaky.

'Are they real, Mick?'

He shrugged. 'Real as anything.'

'D'you realise what you've done? Christ, I feel . . . *outraged*.' She waved her arm. Waves were coming from her like from a rocking boat. 'Used. Abused. You used our friendship! I could kill you.'

DeTerre shook his big bull's head.

'It was essential to the Struggle, Kim. You understood, right? Anyway, I'm leaving now. My cover's blown, gotta go.'

'Bastard. You fuckin smirkin shite-faced – '

Her voice started hoarse, swooped up through two registers and just before it broke her mug of coffee blurred across the kitchen. The mug missed, the coffee spread across his fatigues.

Joan squealed, the mug bounced from the wall, the handle flew off.

'There are no civilians in the Struggle,' Mick said.

She told him what to do with the Struggle, his paranoid fantasies and his fucking toy guns. Then she threw the second mug. It missed completely and smashed on the cast-iron stove.

'Hey, take it easy, babe.'

Joan was crying in the doorway. I was on my feet but not moving. It was Kim's fight unless he went for her. She was quivering like an engine bolted to the test-bench with the throttle wide open.

'I'd better go now but thanks,' he said. 'And sorry.'

He turned away.

She was so fast. I heard the smack, saw his glasses whirl and land on the settee, saw Joan automatically pick them up. Kim's hand went back again. She was utterly unafraid. I thought he was going to belt her one back and I stepped forward.

He caught her arm, shook his head wearily, snatched her other arm as it went up for his eyes and held her away from him. What was coming from her mouth was more spittle than speech.

'Get the carrier bag, Joan,' he said over his shoulder. 'We're offski.'

Joan ran out. Kim's ears went bright red as she struggled to get at him.

'Ready,' Joan shouted.

'Bye, Jim. Sorry, Kim.'

What Kim was saying sounded like *Don't don't don't*.

He pushed her back at me. I caught her, held her. She twisted free and swooped on the heavy glass fruit-bowl on the table.

But he was out the door and away. I heard their steps clattering down the tenement stair.

'Kim!'

She spun and threw the fruit-bowl at the window. I saw the pane burst outward, the bowl slide through. A long pause then I heard the smash on the concrete slabs below. And as I held her kneeling gasping on the floor she sobbed *They all leave me* and then she threw up over the old green linoleum and I thought but no one's ever left Kim, and only later remembered.

'She completely lost the place after you two left.'

'You've not seen her yon way before?' Joan asked.

We were conferring in the kitchen. Joan had come back after three days, alone. I didn't ask.

I shook my head. I'd carried Kim to bed afterwards, limp and unprotesting as a glove-puppet, then cleaned up the mess and wondered what to do for the best. She'd lain there for two days, only getting up to pee. She wouldn't speak to me, just slept or lay with her eyes open. The next morning she got up as normal, packed her bag for the college. I asked something about Mick and she'd replied, 'Can I borrow a fiver for materials?' and stared back at me. I looked back into her eyes, into that baffling aquarium, and all the warning signs were up. *Do not attempt to feed the fishes.*

'Not on that scale, Joan. I'm a peaceable type and don't provoke her.'

'She's never gone for you?'

'A couple of times she's been pissed off and had a swipe at me, but it wasn't anything.'

'Yes, well,' said Joan, 'that's the one advantage of being female with a decent fella. We can lash out and not do much damage.'

I looked up at her. She'd changed over the last few months. Friends used to say she was 'sweet'.

'I cannae handle argie-bargie and anger,' I said. 'It reminds me too much of my dad. I don't like feeling my old man in me.'

'And why do you think she chose you?'

It had never occurred to me I'd been 'chosen'. I thought we had just happened. I accepted that as something between a miracle and happy coincidence.

'What's up, Joan?'

She hesitated.

'Please,' I said.' I've a right.'

'Davy, her first boyfriend, she told you about him? I suppose she said he used to knock her about?'

I nodded. I'd never met Davy Johnson but it had been a long ambition of mine to twist his head off.

'Well, that wasn't exactly true. As Plean lads go, he was a decent one. You should have seen him after one of their rammies.'

'Uh?'

She looked steadily back at me.

'Cut and scratched and bruised. Big bruises, not made with the fist. He'd walked away from her at a dance once. She just went bananas. Lost the place completely.'

'He must have provoked her pretty badly.'

Joan shrugged.

'You'd have to have been there. Like the other day, a completely different person. Scary.'

I got up and put the kettle on. The brown tape across the broken window bulged in the breeze. A little grue ran down me. Kim was normally the most self-contained, self-controlled person I'd met. She made me seem spontaneous. It was like she'd had a fit.

'Any more?' I asked casually.

'In school once, beginning of 5th Year. Our French teacher.'

I laughed. 'She never did like French.'

'You want to know about this or not?'

'Sorry.' She had changed.

'He was a right sadist – you know, teasing, sarcasm, showing people up. Good looking too. They took a scunner to each other from the start. He got her standing out in front of the class, gave her a bawling out for day-dreaming, said maybe she should share them with us. Some of the kids laughed – she was a bit of an outsider and it's true she was a right dreamer. Distant, you know.'

I nodded. I knew.

'She went that funny way. The teacher said she'd never amount to anything, just like her father, then he waved her away and turned back to the board and she went for him, completely ape-shit, like she was possessed. She smashed one of those cassette-players over the back of his head. He collapsed and she crunched him again. It was really horrible.'

'Sounds like you should have sent for the exorcist,' I said.

'Jimmy. I'm trying to tell you something.'

'I know. It's just that, well, that's not *her*. Kim's not – '

'It *is* her,' Joan insisted. 'Part of her. It was a big scandal at the school, had the police in and everything. I mean, she'd fractured his skull. It was only because of her dad, you know, that she got off with it.'

I put down Joan's coffee.

'Look, you're not kidding me? Kim got really upset when I squashed an ant once. She wouldn't speak to me for ages.'

Joan looked at me across the table.

'I'm her friend,' she said, 'but I wouldn't cross her.'

'But she hates violence. She flinches at it even on TV. She feels sick at it in films.'

'Is that so surprising?'

I looked out the window, trying to square this Kim with the one I'd known. Or created. Created between us.

'Tell me about her old man,' I said finally.

'He was . . . nice. Very gentle, strong, good-looking. He painted lovely sets for the school plays.'

'Come on, Joan.'

I looked down at the concrete slabs where the bowl had broken into shards and powder. I waited.

'He was unhappy. Solitary, you'd see him always with her or on his tod. We lived next door but one. I really did like him, even as a wean. I felt sorry for him.'

'And?'

Shards and powder. I wanted to understand.

'Well, he did get in a couple of fights in Plean. He thought he'd been insulted. The second time he went for our local hard man wi a shovel and got charged with GBH. He may even have been inside for a wee bit, or maybe it was one of his breakdowns. He wasn't very stable. Look, how much has she told you?'

'A bit', I said. 'You know what she's like.'

'Then after that he died but you'll know about that.'

'Yes,' I said. 'She told me, just once.'

'Once is enough. Sometimes I don't know how the world . . .'

We looked at each other, each with our own picture in the head.

'She hated our trying to be kind. It was very hard being her friend. She just wouldn't talk about it.'

'Hasn't changed that much. Trying to get Kim to say how she feels is like trying to open an oyster wi a credit card.'

'There's another thing. About knives.'

She hesitated.

'You might as well tell me. She won't.'

I sat down opposite her, chin on my fists and waited.

'The last big bust-up she had wi Dave. He told her he wanted to finish. It got out of hand . . .'

'Well?'

What had my psychopathic darling done now?

'She ran into our place with blood down her sleeve. She'd stuck her dad's pen-knife through the back of Dave Johnson's hand. Right through, Jim'.

I winced. 'She hates knives,' I protested. 'They give her the creeps.'

'And does that surprise you?'

I thought about it.

'That was when we went to Orkney to let things blow over. You were just what she needed.'

'To stick a knife in?'

'Because you're older and together and don't over-react. She trusts you.'

'Oh me, I'm a latent heid-banger wi one foot in the grave.'

'Sure,' she said, 'I've noticed. She felt she needed protection, that's what she said to me.'

'What, from him?'

'Not from him.'

'Ah.'

She eyed me over her coffee. Thick honey-blonde hair and the little crucifix at her throat again. She was ten years younger and I felt pretty dumb.

'You think you know somebody,' I said quietly.

'You've done alright.' She grinned. 'Never asked yourself why she hasn't gone off with one of the young dudes at college?'

'Yes. It's a mystery to me. Maybe it's because us geriatrics are better lovers.'

She laughed, shook her head then focused on me again.

'Would you sleep with me?' she said suddenly. 'If I asked.'

'You asking?'

'I'm asking.'

I stared at her.

'No,' I said.

'And if she had a wee fling with someone else?'

I hesitated.

'It would put me right off my Shreddies.'

'But you wouldn't go doo-lalli. You wouldn't knock her about or threaten to do yourself in? Or walk away?'

'Na. I'd hate it but I don't own her.'

'There you are then. Pity,' she added, 'it might have been fun.'

'Awa wi you.'

We grinned at each other.

'I'm her friend,' Joan said quietly. 'She helped me through – well, something difficult. But I'll tell you this. Don't rile her too bad and if you ever walk away don't turn your back. That's the trigger.'

She looked hard at me. I nodded.

'Don't worry,' she added, 'it'll probably no happen again.'

'So my beloved is the mad hatchet-woman of Plean? Sure, I'm no fashed. What about Mick?'

'I'll tell you someday,' she said. 'Anyway, you'll no be seeing him again.'

But I did, of course, further down the line, and things were very different then.

'All that introspection, it's no good for you,' Kim said vehemently. 'It's an indulgence and I'm not interested!'

I looked at her, pale and angry, and at the new pane of glass in the kitchen window, the fresh, unpainted putty.

'Kim, I'm fed up wi it. You've hidden too much. Not just about last week, but when you were at school, your dad, all that rubbish you told me about Dave, knives . . .'

Something flared in her eyes like a blue match struck.

'Joan. I'll kill her. She had no right!'

'She's your friend. If you won't talk about it – '

'No!'

'Hide-and-seek,' I said. 'Except with you it's nearly all hide. For years, Kim. Ships! We're no even on the same boat.'

'You know what to do then.'

We glared at each other across the ultimatum.

'Aye, alright. I've had it wi you. I'm off.'

Her face was white, the little scar was livid on her lip. I wondered if she'd really got it in a childhood fall. I didn't trust anything about her.

I picked up my jacket from the back of the chair and I meant it.

'Jimmy.'

'Yes?'

She stepped back towards the window, hugging herself to herself.

'Alright,' she said. 'The truth, if you must have it.'

Her voice was hoarse, she wouldn't look at me.

'My dad's accident. It wasnae quite like that. I told you about the bike, and the truck on the wrong side . . .'

She was pale as death.

'I didn't tell you I was with him.'

She said it quickly, so quickly I wasn't sure I'd picked her up right. She looked up at me, oddly defiant.

'I was with him. I was thrown off – lighter, I guess. I was with him in the ambulance. I saw everything. His chest, his head . . . Everything. I went a bit – crazy for a while.'

Jesus God.

'Will that do?' she said, and then she was dry-heaving and dry-crying and I was trying to shelter her from herself.

'I have these . . . terrible . . . *pictures*,' she said.

She started to greit like the end of the world. I held her, I believed her.

I drove back to Stirling late that night to go off-shore next day. It was after midnight on the near-empty motorway, just John Lee Hooker and Jason and the Scorchers on the cassette player for company. At that time I seemed always on the road from somewhere to somewhere, between Aberdeen and Stirling, Stirling to Edinburgh or Glasgow, or heading West with Graeme silent beside me as we wound down from Rannoch Moor past the Buchaille into Glencoe, or the four of us South to the Lakes or Wales or Chamonix. I was glad now I'd kept on my base in Stirling. Kim and I had come within an ace of parting. I reminded myself she'd surely go some day, despite what Joan had said.

Someone overtook me, going very fast, speeding into the future like a silver-tipped bullet. But I was thinking over what had happened, the things she'd said. I pictured the scenes I'd never witnessed and felt sick and endlessly sorry for her. She had her reasons, we all did. I resolved to let her be.

The turn-offs approached and receded untaken. To be warm and alone in the dark going home past the flare-stacks of the Grangemouth refinery, that was the best. I loved her but like the man in an old Hollywood clinch still tried to keep one foot on the floor. My headlights were a white knife levelled at Stirling and a wee voice somewhere whispered *No one knows how close to home I am.*

ELEVEN

Orange

WE HAVEN'T FINISHED with the fathers yet. Nor how men feel, which is like trying to take a keek at the dark side of the moon.

The other day the child found the ring-binders containing Graeme's climbing records. Mostly factual, of course, descriptions of the route, conditions, the odd sketch of the crux or even of me pillocking about. And just once in a while, a star, an exclamation.

To her they were just paper for colouring in. By the time I noticed what she was up to, there wasn't much point stopping her. Looking at her energetic vandalistic scrawls and squiggles, I think he'd have appreciated it.

So I can flip through the pages and find it. Late March '83, his school holidays. A few routes in Glencoe, then drawings of some secret crags we'd been checking out in Kintyre. That must have been what brought us, homeward bound, to the top of Rest and Be Thankful.

I turned sharp right onto the single-track road to Lochgoilhead.

'Here, where you goin? Ah'm needing a fish supper pronto.'

'Just want to check out something.'

I pulled in at the second lay-by and got out of the car. A cool afternoon, smell of moor and bog myrtle, a damp light bent over Ben Ime and The Cobbler. I stood at the fence and looked down the long emptiness where the glaciers had once ground down like ancient grudges.

'See the single-track road jooking up?' I said. 'That's built on the original drove road. My father said in the Thirties from the bottom you could see plumes of steam from the boiling radiators at the top.'

You can be haunted by a picture you've never seen.

'Aye, verra picturesque. Now what say we wheich down the new road?'

'All these leftover bits of old road mind me of my dad.'

'Don't expect he'd appreciate that,' Graeme said. 'What are we looking for here? Christ it's freezin.'

'Nothing,' I said. 'I just like to stop here once in a while. You could say I love it.'

(Even now I hear the yellow valve radio of my childhood warning of snow and ice on the Devil's Elbow and Rest and Be Thankful. In the stillness of this room I glimpse so many roads, and hear the litany of names like an article of faith: the Hills of Kishorn, the Electric Brae, Kylesku Ferry, the Summer Isles, Inchnadamph, Romanno Bridge, the Howe of Fife . . . Some places, like some people, you love before you've ever met.)

'Christ but you're a sentimentalist,' Graeme muttered.

'Someone said sentimentality is the expenditure of emotion on an unworthy object. Do you think this country's unworthy? Eh?'

Sometimes he greatly pissed me off.

'I wouldni know,' he said. 'I'm no a great wan for scenery.'

'Scenery! It's not bloody scenery. It's part of you.' I wondered what shape Hamilton, Paisley, Leeds and Shotts had hollowed out in Graeme. 'Well, part of me, anyway. Shame about the bloody conifers.'

'Trees or no trees, it's aa wan tae me.'

'Time you broadened your politics, man. You used to say feminism was a fringe issue.'

'Aye, that was till Lesley beat me up a few times.'

'So who's going to convince you Ecology isn't about pretty pictures?'

Graeme was silent. I'm not sure what we were being edgy about. Maybe Kim and Lesley being away, and another Election beckoning.

'Weel! Ah'm just wan o yer urban troglodytes.' He took a long look down the glen. 'Aye, no bad,' he said finally. 'Sure it's bonnie. When I look at this I see absentee landlords. I see deer and sheep displacing people, generations cleared off the land by English landowners – and by the Glasgow polis. I see our hills, which for sure are an ecological disaster in themselves, fenced off by tax-dodge private forestry. And let's not forget the nuclear sub base at Faslane – thanks verra much, guys – the missile tracking station round the corner, the NATO arms depot, the torpedo testing range, the Coulport oil terminal . . . I don't see your beautiful country, I see a tragedy.'

He'd forgotten to swear.

'No disputing that,' I said. 'Just the same, this place comforts me. It'll outlast anything we do.'

'Not if Reagan and Thatcher blow it. Things are fuckin edgy right now. Wi nuclear weapons, you canni take even this for granted. We've got tae win this Election.'

It was darkening now, just a last few pools of saffron light to the West. I thought of Kim and Lesley getting rained on at the women's anti-nuclear demo. We hadn't been allowed to go.

'Think aboot it,' he said.

'I have. I doubt there's much hope.' I took a deep breath while it was still there to be taken. 'Anither century at most. Sure, the world's fucked and we've done it and we'll keep on doing it no matter what political system because we're maistly greedy short-sighted self-deluding bastards when it comes to it. The women may make a difference but we're living in a banana republic that disnae even have its ain government to be corrupted. That's my politics and I keep them tae masel cos they're too bloody depressing to broadcast.'

I looked down from Rest and Be Thankful at the last light sinking into the ground. There was turquoise there, and a fugitive green.

'And still the world goes on being bloody beautiful.'

He looked at me curiously.

'Oh man,' he said softly and put his hand on my shoulder. 'Thocht I was the pessimist. You mustni think that way. We'll win.'

'Aye,' I said, 'dangerous times. Sure.'

We went back to my car. I put it into neutral at the top of Rest and Be Thankful and we gathered speed all the way down the new road. We were touching on 70 coming up to the sharp left turn at the stone bridge. I hit the brakes, spun the wheel and we missed the parapet by a coat of paint. I put the car back into gear. That was closer than I'd expected.

'Point taken,' Graeme said, 'whitever it wis. Mind if I drive?'

We changed over at Arrochar.

'Wanna show you something,' he said.

We went straight through Glasgow on the Great Western Road without even a fish supper.

'Can I ask where we're going?'

'Aye.'

Pause.

He ejected Archie Fisher, inserted Dr Feelgood into the cassette player, cranked it way up as we bombed through the guts of

Glasgow. It was a sudden dislocation from high silence of Rest and Be Thankful and I thought, this is part of us too – the fast roads, the driving music, jeans and tower blocks and women's hands reaching for the steering wheel. But still under the motorways the old roads persist and like our fathers lay out where we go, if not the style we go in.

'Well?' I said finally.

'Shotts, where else?'

'Christ, that's the end of the world.'

'You're telling me?'

He'd mentioned it once or twice before. Like Kim, he wasn't expansive about the past.

'So, a family visit?'

'Couple of things to drop off. See the auld fella.'

Even Lesley hadn't been there. I was flattered and very curious. We drove on, he didn't say much. He said bugger all.

Shotts is one of the bleakest villages in Scotand, and there's some tough competition. Featureless moor and grassland above the motorway, a few low scraggy trees bent to the East. Then a grim, isolated church, and its graveyard. The transmission masts blink little red eyes not so far away. The village is a few lines of grey houses. It's hard to imagine what terrible things one must have done in a past life to be living there now.

'Aye,' Graeme muttered, 'Irn-Bru in the soul alright.'

We turned off the motorway, stopped outside one of the council houses. It was, of course, raining heavily.

We sat in the car for a minute.

'The woman you'll meet is dad's sister,' he said.

'Ah.'

He looked at me.

'My mum topped herself some years back.'

There was nothing I could say that wasn't banal or ridiculous. I went straight to the ridiculous.

'Why?'

He took the keys from the ignition and frowned at them. Birled the key-ring round his finger a few times and seemed to give the matter serious consideration.

'She wisni happy,' he said and dropped the keys into my hand.

His aunt was warm and solid, like she'd made and put away a few scones in her time. She fussed over us in the hallway, exclaimed at his thinness and it was a pity he hadn't had time to shave. We'd missed tea, we should have said we were coming. She'd fry up something, faither was in the sitting room, no tae badly. We went through. It was very warm.

Bastard might have told me.

His dad was in a wheelchair facing the telly. He looked up and nodded.

'How's it goin, son?'

'Fine. Yersel?'

'Ach.'

Graeme squeezed his shoulder. One leg was missing, the other looked pretty useless. He was sitting at a funny angle, something wrong with his hips.

'This is my pal Jimmy Renilson. Tellt ya aboot him.'

'Ma pleasure.'

We shook hands. He was Graeme's husk. The boney face was scored with lines, his eyes were dark and alert.

'You're the laddie wha drags him up the crags, eh? Mind ye look after him.'

'He drags me up like a sack of tatties,' I said.

He chuckled and started a coughing fit.

'Aye, he's no bad. Damn sight better than we were in my day. Mind you, nae rock boots then. Oor belaying was old style, nae proper harness nor all yon ironmongery. Primitive we were.' He repeated it with relish. 'Primitive.'

I began to take in the climbing photos on the walls, along the mantelpiece, on top of the dresser. Old black and white, young men grinning from old faces.

'Aye, I used tae climb, son. Afore the laddie wis born.'

I couldn't place his accent. It wasn't pure Glasgow – a non-urban lilt came and went. Graeme had it too, but more faintly.

'And after,' Graeme said quietly.

'Good times but. Used tae cry me the Ayrshire Eagle in thae days. Dinna dae much noo.'

He laughed and set off another coughing bout. He pulled a cigarette from the pack on his lap. Graeme was there with the lighter. He sat back.

'Aa by wi noo,' he said casually. 'Graeme tell you about ma Accident?'

'No.'

Course he hadn't.

'At the Plant. Fuckin hoist cam doon on me. Ma fault.'

'That's whit they said,' Graeme muttered. 'Bastards. You were entitled to mair.'

'I wis careless,' he insisted. 'Takin short-cuts as usual, just wisni thinkin. That's aa it takes, wan second. You mind that.'

Graeme nodded. For all his assertive climbing style, he was the most meticulous climber I knew. Very organised, almost obsessive with his rack and rope-work. I tended to be casual sometimes, drift off for a few seconds. He always rapped me hard for that, we'd had fights about it. We wouldn't again.

Graeme produced a wallet of photos and they started going over them.

I looked round the room. Wasn't too keen on the orange wallpaper. Come to look at it, there was a lot of Orange Lodge regalia around. A dictionary, the Bible, Burns, an old set of Walter Scott. I glanced inside – school prize. Two early rock climbing guides with neat notes in the margins. That was it for books. Big record collection though.

'Hae a good look, son. Interested in jazz?'

'A bit.'

Lot of Louis Armstrong, Basie, Monk, Beiderbecke. I was surprised to find Roland Kirk's *Inflated Tear* but it didn't looked played much. I turned over the sleeve. *From Graeme.*

Aunt May delivered the mega fry-up. His old man was tiring, came to life briefly when he talked about jazz or climbing or the Lodge.

'Yer no a Pape, son?'

'Nuh.' Didn't seem much point in bringing up agnostic Scoto-Pantheism at this point.

No talk of politics. Graeme seemed embarrassed and edgy, kept glancing across the table for my reaction. Didn't see why, his dad was an interesting man and very like his son. It's the last thing we recognise.

His aunt May pointed out a wee landscape painting on the wall. I agreed her nephew was talented, passed over her regrets he only painted thae modern scrawls nowadays. I'd never seen anything pictorial of his before. I got up and looked at it more closely. It was the wee loch and low hillside across the motorway – bleak and lowering and oppressive except where a tentative shaft of light hit on a patch of moor that glowed like a ruby. No much of a one for scenery, my arse.

'Ancient history,' he muttered. 'Pass the brown sauce, youth.'

*

'You understand it?' he said back in the car. 'Without political understanding there is only pain.'

He looked weary, slumped fidgeting in the passenger seat.

'Seems quite a lot with it.'

'I can manage.'

'Sure.'

We sat listening to the rain stotting off the roof.

'Edinburgh, Glasgow or Stirling?'

'Christ, no the provinces. Glasgow. Some of us hae to work tomorrow. Let's get oot o here.'

Neither of us said much on the way. The cassette player was knocking out 'Another girl, another planet' by The Only Ones. Coded heroin music, heavy but ecstatic, black streaked with silver. Funny too, in an end-of-the-world kinda way. It seemed to suit our brooding.

The way life was sometimes, heroin had its rationale. Since Mick's departure, Joan put most of her spare time into voluntary work with young addicts in the housing schemes, but then she had her faith to sustain her. Young Kim had her Art though she seldom called it that. Graeme had political faith to mobilise his anger. Lesley, well she had fun and her flings and her own quirky feminism. But I was just Jimmy Ordinary and all I had was perishable landscape and a passion for Kim and neither came with guarantees.

Then the guitar solo and the cry that preceded it, a high yell like a man going over a cliff. It made the black beautiful so I turned it up louder, desperately missing Kim and her sudden gentleness on those rare occasions when the floor disappeared and I fell through. Say what you will, when faced with pain she was very gentle.

The track ended, and I stopped it there. Beauty's brief as sunsets though there's more of it about than could reasonably be expected. We entered the city of eternal night. Near his flat I stopped at the off-license and bought a few Belhavens and a bottle of Grouse.

We dumped our gear on the sittingroom floor. He prowled round clearing up while I sat on the speaker, wondering where to begin.

'Thanks for taking me along,' I said.

'I had to drop by anyway.' He hesitated with a pile of albums in his arms. 'Naw, thanks for coming. Should have told you about the auld boy, that wis bad jive.'

'About your mum,' I said.

'No!' He looked down at the records. 'It's aa by wi, Jim. As a friend, eh?'

So I opened two bottles, passed him one. Pain was coming off him in waves. What do we owe our friends? I picked up the Grouse, unscrewed the cap and lobbed it into the bin.

'Let's get rat-arsed,' I said.

He put on *Highway 61 Revisited* for old times' sake, and we began. I took off my jacket, seeing it looked like I was staying. He shook his head as he hung it on the door.

'Tweed jaikit and Paki black – man, you're a walking dislocation!'

I passed over the smoke.

'Yup, haggis and cocaine. Why not? Jimmy Shand and the Velvet Underground. Frae scenes like this . . .'

My head was floating large and rolling as the Orkney ferry.

'It's all R & B Thankful tae me,' I concluded.

He liked that. He giggled and poured another whisky. He wasn't heavily into drink and I wasn't big on incoherence myself, but that night we needed the anaesthetic.

We talked about painting and politics, fathers and sons. He even talked about Lesley, and used the word love without irony.

And we planned a hit on the Old Man, as we had so often before. This coming Summer, *definitely*. We'd go up to Orkney as a foursome, have a great holiday and finally knock the bastard off.

I felt closer to him than any other man. I had this notion, could have been delusion, that we compensated each other like corrective lenses. So many of our defences came down, brain cells were dying in their millions but it was worth it. Two hours later my heart was so big I could scarcely get it through the door when I went to the loo.

'I still like the wee coloured one best, the dancers,' I gibbered, looking at it in the corner. 'The one you did for Lesley.'

'There's anither,' he mumbled and started dragging canvases out of the cupboard.

'You wee beauty. Heh, could I buy that?'

It was like the other, but stronger, more joyful. Gorgeous. I was proud of him.

'It's no for sale.'

'Sorry.'

'Know why? Because it's yours, pal.'

He was grinning all over his face. His two faces.

'You sure?'

'Ain't I sure about everything?'

We started laughing, that stoned laughter that loses its object and spins out beyond it. He reached over to hand me the painting, stumbled on a pile of records and grabbed the easel to steady himself. It toppled and they fell together in slow motion till he was on his back with the 'big picture' – he'd never finish that one - over his chest.

I stood up with difficulty and held out my hand to help him up. He shut his eyes, opened them again.

'I love you, man.'

'I know,' I said. 'Me too.'

'That's aa right, then. Niver let ye down.'

He closed his eyes, still smiling.

I put some blankets over him then drank a lot of water. Switched off the stereo, set the alarm for his work in the morning. Brushed my teeth and made faces at the faces in the bathroom mirror. I got into my sleeping bag after a lengthy tussle and swirled down into the dark like water going down the plughole.

We never mentioned it again, but it was always there, said and understood.

I roll the orange round in my palm awhile, remembering. Then start to peel and eat it. After all, that's what it's for.

TWELVE

Skimmy stone

THIS HAD TAKEN us four years, but now the Old Man of Hoy was just a hundred yards away from the rolling ferry. Between it and the shore-cliffs we could see the rubble of the land-bridge that had connected it to the mainland of Hoy, not so long ago. Now it was right out on its own, crumbling and crooked but still standing.

'Big lonesome bastard,' Graeme commented. 'You sure your knee's up tae this?'

'I've lost a bit of extension, that's all,' I said. 'It'll go.' The drill floor is a dangerous place when you've something else on your mind, and a derrickman still hungover from his on-shore binge. I'd always limp a little now, and Alex wouldn't work again on the rigs.

'Lucky you didn't lose your ruddy leg, pal.'

'I'm dead jammy. Don't fash yourself, we can do this.'

Looking at it now, I felt confident enough. I'd be happy to let Graeme lead the crux, the overhanging second pitch, but E1 5b didn't seem so awesome a prospect now. Nor did living with Kim. We were ready.

'Nae guarantees,' he said softly. Unlike him not to be more confident.

He leaned on the rail and looked again through the binocs. The wind exposed his first grey streaks though he wasn't thirty yet. The pony-tail had gone, sacrificed to the Election campaigning. Well, his man had got in but that was about all. Another wipe-out. We'd sat round the TV watching the results come in. In football terms: Scotland 1, England 5. That same sinking, sickening feeling. 'Scotland the brave and impotent,' Lesley had commented. 'Don't see what more you can do, Graeme.' He'd bowed his head, but there were tears in his eyes.

He grimaced and handed me the binocs.

'You tell me, dad.'

I took a good long look. The time would come when I'd finally chimney up between the two great summit blocks, pushing them apart like Samson and his pillars only these ones would hold and I'd go up, up the last pitch, and when we carefully stood up on that four-foot by three-foot platform four hundred and fifty feet above the sea, at that moment we'd have cracked it. Whatever it was.

'We can do this,' I said, 'but it's gonna be wild. I hate maximum exposure.'

Further along the deck-rail, Les pushed her hand back through her bright crew-cut and turned her face up to the sun. Kim looked wee beside her. She must have said something because the two women hugged and started laughing.

He turned and looked at me straight.

'I get the wobblies too, Jim-boy.'

We looked at the women, still flushed in some private joke.

'Are they taking the piss?'

'Probably,' I said.

'Lot of memories for you two here.'

'The best.'

We leaned over the rail in silence as the Old Man dwindled behind us. (I can hear and see us very clearly. Memory is like binoculars, makes everything bigger and clearer. It exaggerates.)

'Les said she might be instructing in the States again,' I said, casual-like.

He grimaced.

'Aye.' Pause. He spoke fast. 'Maybe I should get on wi my ain life. Find someone else. Seeing you twa thegither . . .'

'I'd be sorry,' I said, 'but maybe you should.'

He took his eyes away from Kim and Lesley and looked at me.

'Think so?'

'She can't help it.'

'Course she can help it. We can all choose.'

'We choose to be ourselves. It's not quite the same.'

He spat over the rail.

'Fuckin liberals,' he muttered. 'You think naebody's to blame.'

'And you Calvinists think everything exists to be judged.'

'Ah'm no a Calvinist!'

'It's in the culture, man. And ex-Calvinists are the worst.'

He gave a quick grin and looked over at Kim and Lesley jostling each other at the rail.

'So if you want something, you should jist take it? Lot of that about these days.'

'Wouldna go that far. But in the end we have to be as we are. Unfortunately.'

He scratched his neck and looked down.

'Like my old dear,' he said quietly. 'Maybe no one could hae stopped her.'

Not much I could say to that but stand there beside him.

'Point is,' I said eventually, 'is there anyone you want more than her? Les, I mean.'

He kicked the life-raft a couple of times but it wasn't its fault. 'Nuh.'

He stared back the Old Man and added, 'She's still the most important person in the world tae me.'

Then she and Kim began to sing we were all going on a summer holiday, though it was autumn already. She was sitting on a life-raft with her feet up on the rails, beating time on her knees as Kim jived in front of her. So undaunted a woman, direct as a clean-struck pick.

Les caught my eye and grinned, ruefully, like some sort of apology. I shook my head slightly to say it was understood. Over the years between us had grown a mutual recognition, though I couldn't have said exactly what it was that was understood.

The ship stopped rolling and we sailed into Stromness, lying tight and douce under Brinkie's Brae. Roddy and Margaret from the old Birsay dig were waiting and waving on the pier, he had a baby on his back. No more worries for a week or two. Perhaps only Lesley knew better, and she sang and joked so much that day, slapping time hard on her thighs as we drove off the ferry onto the promised island.

I woke early, rig-time, and lay beside a curled-up foetal Kim and watched the dawn light shimmer over the ceiling like tidal water over sand. It looked like a good day, but no hurry to rush over to Hoy. No hurry for anything at all. Living on Orkney time.

I looked at Kim dozing. The first bloom of youth was leaving her skin, or maybe it was just the way I saw her now – less spell-bound, more truly. She'd graduated from more than Art College. If we argued now, we argued as equals and I had to hold back less. In time the ten years between us would erode.

I watched her asleep, counted the white stitch-marks across the underside of her arm. Like me she'd been lucky, it could have been the artery not the vein. She'd promised never to do anything fancy with plate glass again. The blood poisoning hadn't helped. With each passing year we were getting more like one of Graeme's paintings.

Her roughened fingers twitched and I wondered at the ache inside till I decided love could do with more practical action and less aspiration and slipped out of bed to kick-start the Aga and brew tea for two.

The flagstone floors were cool on my feet. With the white walls and pale straw matting, the bare kitchen was full of light. I sat on the windowseat, waiting for the kettle to boil and watched the day shift over Scapa Flow and the wind flow over the rough pasture, ruffling the manes of the ponies that leant over the fence. Every quarter mile or so was another cottage like our own – long and low, a chimney at either end and one in the middle, the massive stone slabs on the roof which even Orkney winds couldn't blow away. The involuntary shutter clicked. I see that kitchen yet.

I went through to the bedroom with her tea. She was lying in the same position but her eyes were now open, unblinking, like someone just set down in another country.

'Is it tomorrow yet?'

Sea-smoothed, glittery-grey, the darker concentric circles vanishing towards the centre, this stone lies in my palm, ordinary and unique as any lover. I just happened to pick this one up, or it found me. And once I'd done so, I felt responsible – ridiculous, sure, but I couldn't just chuck it away. Perhaps it would be better if we never brought such things home, and just left them on the stony beach amidst their secret lives.

'So you're finally going for it?' Les said casually.

'Yup. Time for the cohabitation waltz.'

I'd been sitting in the lee of the cottage gable, trying to work out 'The Northern Lights' and 'Desolation Row' on my Uncle Bob's concertina. Kim and Graeme were off exploring the burial mound at Maeshowe. Les had spent the morning pottering along the shore-line like a long-shanked, red-crested wader.

'Aye, we're ready now. My accident and Kim's illness had been a lot to do with it. Her looking after me, then me helping her. Maybe even the Election, in a contrary way.'

Les nodded. 'The cult of self-sufficiency has gone far enough. How's Kim feel about it?'

I laughed. 'You know what she's like with a new enthusiasm. Are you going off again? What's the attraction in the States?'

Lesley smiled briefly. 'I'll keep you posted. There's a lot more room for me there. Things can be . . . narrow here.'

'Is your father still there?'

'Yes, but that's not why I'm going.'

She didn't elaborate. She sat up and squinted down at Scapa Flow. It was quivering like a dark liquid mirror. They'd thought the ships were safe there.

Lesley sat up and stared out at it.

'My American sisters still say men compartmentalise themselves and women don't, but that's balls.'

I laughed.

'Aye, like the line that most swearing puts down women's bodies. As in load of balls, cock-up, stupid prick, cobblers. What a wheen o blethers!'

'Watch it, Jim,' she said. 'I can knock the Movement, but you can't.'

She rolled over. With her being English, it was sometimes hard to tell if she was being ironic. Scots prefer the bludgeon of sarcasm. She picked and frowned at the grass.

'You see, I can't just put aside what men have done to women historically. It's like the way you take against people with accents like mine, and for a similar reason. History of oppression and that. But it's a form of racism. You should watch it.'

'Like Tess's sexism?'

'Something like that. It's time to grow beyond it.'

'Yes ma'am.'

I knew what she was on about, but not why.

'Sod off. Understand, I feel the same instinctive ugh when I first meet most men as you do with south of England accents. Then one or two become your pals, and after a while you cease to notice gender or accent. Some you may even end up loving . . .'

She grinned and twinned her long fingers round mine.

'Kim needs a base,' she said decisively. 'For her that means a place and a man.'

'Doesn't it for you?'

She looked at me. Her eyes were hazel and slightly protuberant and I'd always liked her. It was a time of confidences.

'First thing I remember,' she said, 'was my mother sitting at the piano, crying. Because she loved my father, she said. Divorce is a disgusting habit, don't you think? I decided I'd never cry for any man, and I never have.'

She broke off a long green reed and began to wind it carefully round and round her right hand.

'I do love Graeme,' she said quietly. 'He's a smashing man, he's big enough to give me room and he never kow-tows to me. It's just . . .'

She tucked in the loose end of the reed, broke off another and began to pleat it in, not looking at me.

'I wonder if she knows what to do now she's found it,' she continued. 'A base, I mean. It's one thing to want something, another when you get it.'

'She's wanted us to live together for years,' I said. 'It's me that's been blate. Scared of getting it wrong again.'

She nodded, as if confirming something to herself.

'I keep forgetting. You don't let on much about your marriage, do you?'

'No,' I said. 'Like you said, a disgusting habit.'

We sat and looked at nothing much happening on the water.

'Surely it's time you got off the rigs,' she said. 'Two more chopper crashes, and that awful fire.'

I nodded. Forties Delta had shaken everyone on the rigs. I never fancied being incinerated.

'They're cutting corners tighter every year. The Inspectorate's a joke. Just anither year to straighten out my finances. I'll look out.'

She plucked a fourth reed and pleated it round her hand.

'It's just that I worry what you're doing with yourself. Why is that, Jimmy?'

Odd, suddenly I was sweating.

'Listen,' I said. 'I'm a person of no particular talent, not one of those big redeeming ones. Not like Kim's. Nor a cause like Graeme's. But I need a meaning and none of those things I've done in the past were it.'

'So what is?'

The question went on and on sinking like the *Royal Oak* out in Scapa. I watched the cloud-shadow move over the water above the men who had died there when they thought they were safe.

The tightness passed.

'Kim, I suppose. And climbing the Old Man,' I added casually.

She breathed out heavily, as though letting something go.

'And they say men don't invest in relationships.'

'Generalisations are generally balls – except this one. I suppose I want to care for her, let her grow. Be near her. Look after her, not that she needs it.'

'Yes,' Les said quietly, 'she has that effect on people. And she does need it. You believe that story about the plate glass breaking on her?'

She carefully tightened the reed bandage wrapped round her knuckles.

'Yes, she's a funny one, Jim. Funniest thing is she thinks she understands me. She even thinks she's like me.'

She clenched her fist hard. The tendons rose and whitened on her wrist and then the reeds snapped.

'So let's talk about something else,' she said.

Kim and Graeme arrived back for tea and my Bean Stew *Surprise*. It tastes good, that's the surprise. They were full of talk about the Maeshowe burial mound. Graeme had sketched the runes the Vikings had left when they broke in seven hundred years back. Vandalism made historic, he liked that.

Kim seemed raised, re-charged. She said standing in the tomb was like returning to the centre of herself. Which seemed odd coming from someone in her twenties, given that that centre was a burial, a place of death. But on the midwinter solstice the sun struck right down the shaft, hit the far wall and lit up a tomb older than the Pyramids.

Death and resurrection and working models of redemption, I think that was always what she was after.

'I could cast these runes like free-standing signposts,' she said. 'Indicating the Absolute, ken.'

'Whit's that when it's at hame?' Graeme, of course.

'It's always at home,' I said and opened a bottle to prove it. Second sweetest sound in the world, gloop, gloop. 'I think that's the point.'

Kim nodded forcefully. Whether her plate glass story was true or not, now she looked vital and alive, fully recovered a shaky summer. Stress, she'd said, overwork and blood poisoning. Nothing to worry about. She just got a bit hyper sometimes. Now she leant over the table like happiness itself, quietly scratching sand from her hair.

'We dinni need metaphysics after the last Election,' Graeme

grunted, 'we need an alphabet of vandalism. It's fight or go under.'

He seemed tired and brooding.

Kim laughed. 'We'll never agree,' she said. She turned to us. 'He's aye on about the big picture, but his isn't big enough. He's on about politics and power and social justice, and I keep banging on about death and meaning and the Absolute. Do you think they can connect?'

'I doubt it,' Lesley said, absently flexing her fist. 'But you might try.'

Graeme and Lesley had gone to bed. We were standing outside in the dark, smelling the salt wind and watching the flare-stack on Flotta glow on the underside of the clouds.

'Whatever happened to our Modern Open Relationship?' I said.

She laughed.

'It sank, I guess. And been replaced by a self-righting one.'

When in her last year at Art College she'd announced she needed more Space, to be freer, it hadn't been so funny. Nor unexpected.

'It seemed like a good idea, but every Open Ship I've ever seen has been busy sinking.'

'Monogamy is so much simpler,' she said. 'Now I can get on with the rest of my life.'

It had also been quite exciting, the Open Ship, once I'd got used to the idea. I'd rather enjoyed being free to go out and about and flirt again. I loved her but she wasn't the only attractive and interesting woman in Central Scotland. But still the green-eyed monster did come and perch on my headboard at night and show his hateful little movies. One of them had been running when the pipes lurched free on the drill floor and smashed into my knee. I didn't care to think about the pain before the needle went in.

She rolled a cigarette and passed me the makings.

'What was his name anyway?'

She laughed.

'A spotty youth of no account,' she said. 'A passing fancy. We soon discovered I thought he was boring and he thought I was pretentious. We were both right! You must admit, it hasn't happened often.' She lit up and wrote her initials across Scapa with the glowing tip. 'You?'

As she stretched, her sweater moved up her arm and I glimpsed the pale crease of her scar.

'Och, remarkably constant,' I said. 'On the whole,' I added, to keep her guessing. She needed to be sure of me but not so sure it was oppressive.

'It's going to be great. Having my own studio space at last. The big attic will be perfect. And I reckon the landlord's a soft touch.'

'Don't push your luck.'

'Just tell me when I do.' She brushed against me. 'You know I like that.'

We finished our cigarettes. The fence creaked as the ponies rubbed against it in the dark. All we have to do to be happy is love what we have. And know when to throw the stone away.

We visited Margaret and Roddy a couple of times. He'd got an oil job on the Flotta terminal, she had a three-month-old wee boy, an ugly blighter but good natured. They seemed very happy. Domestic bliss, maybe there was something to be said for it. It would be good to have something to devote oneself to. I remember standing in their warm kitchen holding the baby and felt very tender towards my friends, my lover, the baby, life in general.

And when we made love that night in our room without curtains, for the first time I felt maybe we were missing the meaning of the act.

I noted it, kept it to myself. After all, she already had something she was devoted to.

That last day together on Orkney, the one we didn't know would be our last, I see it as a dance. As we moved in a loose grouping about Mainland Orkney that day, we were bound by forces invisible and powerful as those inside Maeshowe.

We moved in pairs, or each alone, or in a loose four, across the treeless land. The sky as ever was enormous, the waters mirrored back its light, the wind tumbled peewits and curlews over the standing stones. I could live here, I thought, and feel in place. And Kim yearned for that too. But she was young and needed change as well; she needed to be near her peers, in kicking distance of Edinburgh or Glasgow.

'Or London?' I'd asked her.

She shivered.

'No, I corrupt too easily.'

Dunbar seemed a reasonable compromise, a neat East Coast fishing town like Eyemouth but a lot nearer to Edinburgh. Safe harbour, I thought, I'm ready for that. Soon as the Old Man's climbed.

We drove North from South Ronaldsay, across the Churchill Barriers, built to block off Scapa Flow after the *Royal Oak* was torpedoed. Something poignant about defences put up too late.

We stopped to let Kim get religion at the Italian Chapel. It always moved me too, extemporised from two Nissen huts by homesick Italian prisoners of war. In front of the altar she didn't cross herself but her father's religion was still there. Only the figure at the head of it had gone. Absented Himself, or himself. She was quiet and I let her be.

We came out blinking into yellow light. Graeme and Lesley were sitting near the shore, heads bent together.

'I envy the believers,' she said. 'Though God's surely not the right name of God.'

'If it's anywhere it'll be everywhere.'

She squeezed my arm. 'We'll work it out,' she said.

We spoke in shorthand then, and seldom lost each other. A glance, an image, a brief muttered phrase, and it was understood.

(I sit tonight at my table and watch the two of us walk away from the Italian Chapel, me in old tweed jacket and her in baggy breeks and my white shirt and Orkney shawl about her shoulders. There are kinder loves, like Ruth's, but ever since I've had to *explain*.)

We drove out to Deerness, to Skaill, just because we liked the name. Skaill turned out to be a farm, a house, a church. We wandered idly through the churchyard, reading minimalist novels on the headstones.

'Look at this.'

Les crouched beside a stone. It was to a man who'd died in 1960 aged eighty-four, and beneath that was his wife, died 1964, aged thirty-two. I see us grouped round Lesley – me stooping hands on knees, Kim upright, Graeme straight-legged and hands thrust in pockets – see the lettering and smile to watch us struggle with the arithmetic.

'Hm, there's hope for you two yet,' Lesley said and as Kim made to cuff her she swayed, grabbed her arm and pulled her over and the two of them giggled and wrestled like weans in the coarse grass.

'I really wouldn't mind being dead here,' I said to Graeme as we watched. On that little headland, sea and sky, sand and wind blowing always through the long grass by the fence, death seemed part of the natural order.

'Makes no odds where y'are. When yer deid, yer deid.'

He sounded awfully like my dad. There were some things we couldn't share.

Lesley running in green dungarees to the car, bagged the driver's seat.

'Skara Brae next,' she said as she drove. 'We did it in school. I had a mad crush on our History teacher. I thought she was lonely for a friend. I used to wander out along the East Sands at St Andrews, imagining a hundred different ways we'd meet and she'd say she needed me to come here with her on holiday. I didn't know what we'd do but I knew it would be lovely.'

She laughed and shook her head.

'Terrible shortage of men at St Leonards,' she added. 'Tried to make up for it since.'

I roll my second cigarette of the night and watch us as we wandered separately along the long curving beach by Skara. The shingle stones were flat and round, made for skimming, the water green-blue over the sand. I watched the waves mount, break easily, withdraw. The wind was strong and cool in my face and the day was very bright. I picked up a perfect skimmy stone and knew my old man would have to die soon.

'It's bonnie,' Graeme said, 'I'll grant you that. A long way from Thatcher-land.'

He whirled and skimmed one of the discus stones out to sea. Its forward motion defied gravity a while then slipped out of sight.

'She's irrelevant,' I said. 'She'll never know this.'

'Wish tae God she wis,' he grunted. 'Anither four years of yon, it makes you want to scream. They're out to break the miners this time.'

'Think they will?'

He squatted down and selected another stone, flipped it in his hand.

'Yup,' he said.

'*No!*' he screamed, raw in the throat, then whirled the stone away into the waves.

The birds flew away from us, we stood in silence watching the water. Then he smiled and seemed much younger.

'Och, that feels better,' he said. 'Maybe someday I'll live here,' he said. 'Politics isnae the only game in town.'

I had to smile. Maybe Kim was getting through to him.

'Absolutely,' I said.

He looked along the beach where Les and Kim waited at the Skara Brae site.

'You twa and yer Absolute,' he said. 'I don't know.'

'Me neither,' I said, 'but it helps.'

I slipped the skimmy stone into my pocket and started running towards the others and felt the day all around me.

If that day was a slow evolving dance, it came to its final set at the Broch of Gurness.

We parked the car and walked across the white sands of Evie towards the headland. The wind dropped, the sunset clouds were piled up like scrambled eggs, the water was green and the low hills toast-brown. We came round the corner in a loose four and the broch was silhouetted like a pepper-pot on the low headland. All in all it was one of the more edible evenings in history.

The curator had gone home for his tea, so we climbed the fence and had the place to ourselves. We crossed the grassed ditches and wandered through the Iron-Age village clustered round the broch. In comparison with the exclusive appartments of Skara Brae, this was a sprawling Council estate and a few thousand years later. But the same features persisted: door, hearth, box beds, storage tanks, built in the same way from the same stone. Not hard to see how these people like us had been born, played games, made meals, ornaments and rituals, fancied each other, had sex and children, lived a short while then sank back into the bare land.

It was so quiet I could hear a sheep tearing grass outside the enclosure. Kim was hunkered down at a hearth, ran her fingers lightly over the reddened earth. Graeme and Lesley were standing on the bank looking down at her.

Into the broch, the place of refuge, the stronghold. We filed through the entrance. The others disappeared into the narrow passageway between the walls, but I made for the well at the heart of the broch.

The steps were steep and narrow, I cautiously edged down into the half-light, peering for water or a sudden drop. I crouched and groped my way – and finally my hand struck water so still, dark and clear it was invisible over the stone.

I scooped it up and drank it. It was cool and stony, slightly metallic tasting. There was no sound down in the well and very little light. I drank again and a resonance went through me as if a bell had been very softly struck a great way off. The water was cold on my fingers as I crouched thinking of my failing old man, of loving Kim, my fears, children, and a voice like one she followed said *You'll never run dry.*

How many nights since then has that promise got me through.

I light up now and follow me down to the shore where I found the others. The sun plopped out again under the lowest cloud, red and raw. Twenty yards out seals were looking our way. Lesley whistled and they craned their necks, jooking from side to side.

We were standing apart now, at the corners of an invisible square. We could hear each individual wave crumple. I felt the sand under my feet, air on the back of my hands, smelt the water and felt its cool draft in my eyes and the last fire of the sun. My friends turned into black, wavering silhouettes and light ate round their edges as though they were not people but glowing coals.

Kim glanced at me as though for confirmation, Graeme was looking her way, at the seals, Lesley gazed across the water. We were in our final position. Then a sound like wobble-boards whopping in the air and we looked up as a flight of swans came in low overhead and turned pinky-red like tongues in the air. They passed over the long black skyline and we were alone in the gathering dusk.

We were quiet on the way back, almost embarrassed to look at each other, nothing left to be said. Crossing the Churchill Barriers the flat calm waters were perpetuated in the Western sky, and it felt like the car was skimming not driving, and we too were mirrors for each other.

Kim and I were up sharp and packed up our gear for Hoy. The morning was windy, the odd smirr of rain across Scapa. Not too promising but all we needed was one clear day. The main thing was to get to Hoy, camp round the corner from the Old Man and wait.

We finished and cleared breakfast. Still no sign or sound of movement from the other room.

I stood at the window, rehearsing the first pitch in my mind.

Come on, kids. Then the awkward traverse, up into the crucial hand-jamming overhung crack . . . We had to catch today's ferry. I chapped on their door.

A long pause, low voices, then Graeme shouted 'Just a tick!'

He emerged in jeans, pulling on his shirt. He looked dishevelled and weary.

'Youth, we got to get cracking. Morning ferry, mind.'

'Um. Jim . . .'

He looked vaguely round the kitchen, nodded to Kim. He took a deep breath.

'I canni go.'

'Whit?'

'Been thinkin aboot it. I'd better get back tae Glasgow.' He wouldn't look at me. 'I wis gonnae skive a couple of extra days, but it's no right. Anyway, the weather isni smairt.'

'You serious?'

I was greatly pissed off. Felt Kim's stillness behind me. He glanced up, nodded.

'Sorry, Jim.'

'For Christ's sake, man!'

Lesley appeared behind him, fumbling with the straps of her dungarees.

'We've been talking about it, Jimmy. I know it's kind of eleventh hour, but really we ought to. It's . . . better.'

If her look was a message I missed it.

'So that's it on the Old Man?'

'Ach, anither time, eh?' He didn't sound very convinced. 'You twa stay on and enjoy yersels.'

We stood like stookies while Radio Orkney played Country and Western. Yesterday's four was suddenly two twos. I couldn't buy this sudden attack of work ethic conscience.

'Will you gie us a lift to the ferry back south?'

I nodded. Les gave me another look like I should understand and if I didn't, don't ask. They went back into their room and shut the door. I turned to Kim.

'Search me,' she said. 'I love them both dearly but I wish they'd get their act together or call it a day.'

'Me too,' I said. 'Me too.'

I lifted my rucksack off the chair, dumped it on the floor and sat down. No hurry now.

'I'm really sorry,' she said. 'It's not my ploy but I know how much you've wanted this.'

'Ach, it's awright. No it isn't. When you first walked into the pub in Aberdeen, I was already dreaming of this climb.'

'That's a while back,' she said lightly. 'You've got me, maybe you can't have the Old Man too.'

'I can give it a damn good try! Och, I feel like a bairn whose trip to the circus has been cancelled at the last minute cos the adults find they've something else on. Some adults. If there was a cat here I'd kick it.'

She grinned and put her hand on mine.

'That's better,' she said. 'We can still have a fine time.' She hesitated. 'I know I've been distant this last while. I lose the thread when I can't work then I withdraw and resent it when you try to get me to open up and then everything's a right fankle. I try to undo it, but I can't.'

'Maybe we shouldn't live together.'

Her hand squeezed painfully on mine.

'I do want it to work,' she whispered. 'I need the base, something settled in my life. If you just give me room to wander away from it once in a while.'

I thought we both understood what she was saying.

'Sure,' I said, 'haven't I always?'

She leaned across the table and kissed me, light and lingering. Les came in noisily from the bedroom.   .

'You two at it again? You'll do fine without us.'

But her voice was too loud. Then Graeme emerged and they clunked around getting their last things together. No one said much. They loaded the car and we left.

'Pity,' I said when I got back. 'Yesterday was one of the best.'

'I know,' she said. 'There was a very strong feeling about. But now do you fancy a walk, or whatever?'

She'd built up the sittingroom fire, had big cushions on the floor.

'Can we skip the walk,' I said, 'and go straight to the whatever?'

Her passion opened like flowers in time-lapse, stirring petal by petal then rushing into bloom, then holding it there, quivering, for ages.

That's the skimmy stone finished with. Tomorrow before we

set off I'll let the child return it to the sea. Long overdue, like my understanding of that Orkney episode.

I pick up the last piece for the night, swing it gently, objectively, between finger and thumb.

Never run dry. I owe you that much, it's a promise.

THIRTEEN

Key

BABY, LET'S PLAY house.

Come autumn they flitted to Dunbar, to a tall narrow house by the old harbour. Crow-stepped gables and red pantile roof, low ceilings, deep windows, a pulley-beam outside the attic for hauling up large items. A house that leaked, boards that creaked when she walked about at night. A house within sound of the sea and wind in the fir trees. Nice house, this house.

It was hard not to giggle a little, playing that game, as if at any moment the grown-ups might return. None did, so they bought two bonnie breakfast bowls, two mugs, two plates, a milk jug that matched the teapot she'd brought back from Morocco. They decided if they got breakfast right, the rest would follow.

Together they floored, insulated and wired the attic studio where she would work. He built the bookcases, the work surfaces, the big table; she fitted the tool racks, the lighting, the sound system, and the locks on the kitchen drawers. In case she sleep-walked, she said, and giggled, or maybe burglars. He came back from the platform to find she'd added a bolt on the inside of the attic door and a Yale to the outside. She let him in and up the narrow stairs.

'I hope you're not affronted,' she said. 'I need one private space.'

He nodded. A corner of the kitchen to read and play guitar in was enough for him. His folks had always liked company; her father hadn't. She took two glasses, produced a foil-capped bottle of Sparkling British Wine bought with the last of her giro.

'Welcome to the Play Room,' she said. 'Adults by invitation only.' She nodded at a key on the table. 'That's your copy,' she said. 'For Emergencies Only. Promise?'

The bottle went phutt.

'This is everything I've always wanted,' she said. 'No excuses now, I'll just have to get on with it. Here's tae us.'

'Wha's like us. Promise.'

Her mum came through from Plean, said they must be mad

and in her young day etcetera, gave them her mother's cuckoo clock and six Robbie Burns tea-towels.

His mum and dad bought them the divan, the standard lamp, and the painting of the Bass Rock under a divided sky. His father was stooping now, his nose and ears drooped longer each year, his eyes paler. Hard to imagine Jimmy had been fearful of this man and had struggled so hard to deny him satisfaction.

'He's no so bad,' Kim laughed after they'd gone. 'In fact he's a bit of a sweetie. You do exaggerate.'

'He's mellowed, Kim, believe me. I've no memory of him ever hugging or holding me from the time I could walk.'

'But he must have cared for you.'

'I guess, but there were so few ways he could show it – mostly by teaching me facts and how to do things with my hands. What d'you think Scotland was like in the Fifties? The old man and me didn't exactly go around hugging and crying and saying how much we loved each other. Later we began to shake hands. Manly restraint! Have you ever given a thought to what it was like to be a boy then? It's a wonder we can show anything at all – except anger, of course. There's aye anger.'

She put her hand on his arm, mercifully didn't say anything.

'In my Mod phase – dinna laugh! – I had a Vespa 90. I hit black ice on the back road, wrote it off, hurt my knee, ripped my new breeks. The polis gave me a lift back home and when I came in my mum was real concerned. But the old man – he just said "Go back and git it. Noo." He wouldn't even give me a lift. I had to hitch back out there and push what was left of the scooter all the way back to Eyemouth, still in ma torn breeks, bleeding knee and all. I was greitin wi anger. I hated him. And I swore I'd never be like him. I'll nivver be hard like that.'

'My dad would never have done that,' she said softly. 'He had problems but he was kind.'

'When I was a laddie my dad was a hard man with a hard hand. He had high standards and a temper and he wouldn't bend.' Jimmy shrugged, his father's gesture. 'Not his fault. It's in the culture. Something we catch, like a cold. If I had children – '

'Where there's a cold there's a cure,' she quipped. 'Things are changing despite the politics and we're part of it. Now can we get this picture hung?'

She folded her arms and looked at it.

'This Huston is no a bad painter,' she admitted. Long pause. 'My trouble is, I suffer from delusions of adequacy . . .'

Dry dock, Kim called it, living together. The old, close-knit order of her student days was unravelling. Many of her friends had left Edinburgh and those still around lacked transport to get out to Dunbar. Joan had suddenly dropped out and moved without explanation to Shetland, with a man, Kim thought. Alison had been in hospital, fallen in love with the male nurse, and they were preoccupied with each other. Graeme was running for a seat on the Council, and with that and the coming Miners' Strike, said he'd no time for climbing or socialising, only for socialism. Lesley came by a couple of times, smiled at it all, took Kim to Greenham Common and stayed on herself.

Winter was hard and spring was late, tough on the North Sea, getting rough outside the pits. The only thing it was good for was winter climbing, and made a lot of hard routes piss-easy. In an exceptional week, Jimmy dossed in the S.I.C. hut below the main crags on Ben Nevis and each day wound himself up and soloed another classic route – Hadrian's Wall, Orion Face Direct, Glover's Chimney, No. 5 Gully, Zero Gully. Each day he climbed better than the one before, all his placements, all his judgements seemed right. The ice was made for him. He was so confident, it was almost worrying.

On the seventh day he went to take it easy doing Comb Gully, and suddenly was running on empty and struggled to complete that straightforward route. Enough. He packed up his gear and went home gladly to Kim and found the break had done them good.

'You should go away more often,' she said as she got dressed again. 'Does me no harm to worry about you and appreciate what I've got.'

'If I can expect this kind of welcome,' he said, 'there'll be no stopping me. How did the work go?'

'Good, at last. When it's like this I know it's the right thing and it's wonderful.'

'How about the headaches?'

'Dinnae fuss, Jimmy. Please.'

His fortnight on, fortnight off, was difficult for them both. At home for days on end, he could feel himself crowding her. She confessed that when he went off-shore she was at first relieved, then missed him, then resented his absence, and by the time he came back again had adjusted to living happily on her own. So the first few days of his leave were spent struggling to get in tune again, and the last few were spoiled by his imminent departure. Still, one more year and he could afford to jack it in and do something adult with his life.

It wasn't a fairy-tale, but good times or bad times, he always felt it was right. Like a man abseiling off a single peg, he had finally committed himself, the way the women told us.

Kim had some new ideas, and a first solo exhibition to work towards. She'd met an architect's model-maker and become fascinated by the surreal blandness of his miniature shopping malls, conference centres, coastal developments, airbases. To this she added her childhood joy in kaleidoscopes and toy theatres, in peeping into miniature worlds.

She got him to teach her what she needed to know. The tools, the materials, the techniques. She claimed she only kissed him a couple of times, in the way of appreciation.

'It doesn't matter,' she said. 'You shouldn't wonder.'

She was right, of course. Jealousy, insecurity, possessiveness, these were hateful and low-grade emotions. At that time magazines were still urging us, men in particular, to show our feelings – so long as they were the right feelings. Jimmy agreed, but still wanted to pull off Joe Sutherland's head whenever they met.

When he was at home – and that's how it felt now – he left her mostly to herself in the attic studio and got on with reading, cooking, the concertina and carpentry and practising slash-and-burn agriculture in the wilderness-garden, trying to make room for spring. For the first time in his life he felt no particular urge to be elsewhere.

Sometimes when she tired of solitude and Radio 4, she would call down for coffee and a reader and he'd sit on the bar-stool by the window looking across the North Sea and read out loud to her while she hunched over her bench and teased away at her latest world-in-a-box.

Now she fiddled with a scalpel and stared out the window at the rain driven over the slate roofs by a February wind sharp as mussel shells.

'I just want to be a decent artist, a good human being – and a loving bidie-in. Is that asking too much? Surely you don't have to be a manic-depressive adulterer to be a serious artist. Or is that impossible?' She stabbed the scalpel into the bench-top and watched it vibrate to a standstill. 'Don't answer that,' she said.

He put his arms round her thin shoulders but she was elsewhere. She'd been going through one of her lethargic white-faced spells when she spent most of the time in bed. Resting, she said, just resting. Don't fuss.

'One thing's for sure,' she said eventually, 'the Art is no excuse for behaving badly. I'll get some pain-killers if it helps.'

Tonight I turn the key over in my hand and walk in there again. It is afternoon. Out the window the gurly grey North Sea is in place. Rain whips raggedly across the dormer windows, gurgles down the rone pipes, whirls along the gutters outside. Smell of coffee and cigarettes blended with wood, glue, paint. The mutter of the radio, the rain, the quiet scratching as she sands. Bowed over her work, head inclined as she listens to him reading, she is in place. And he feels himself in place for the first time in his life and he has to pause for a moment in his reading before he can go on.

The involuntary shutter clicks again, the curse of solitude.

She let him into the attic. She'd been hard at it in his absence, working flat-out for the exhibition. He inspected her pieces while she pretended to be absorbed sorting her enamel paints. He was looking into little theatres, lit boxes, models. Viewing was restricted to a peep hole. sometimes distorted by a curved lens. Inside were half-demolished tenements attacked by angels in hard hats, airbases encircled by segments of oranges and defended by tiny bunches of bananas. There were missile launchers outside blue twilight shopping arcades, the Bruntsfield flat's sittingroom, a sea-shore drawn apart like curtains, the council house in Plean with her mum watching TV, a child kneeling by her side.

'It's like playing dolls' houses,' she said. 'If it's not fun you might as well not bother. Don't you think?'

In a minutely rendered room there'd be one or two things not quite right. The mirror on the wall might reflect not walls but moorland, or the ceramic figure hesitating at the door was oddly blurry and unfinished. Little flourishes of surrealism without the smarty-pants. The pussy-cat emerging through the wall was the size of the settee and its eyes were reed-fringed lochans with what looked very like a fish jumping in each of them.

And her finish was getting better. What she made looked less like an interesting idea, more something complete in itself, enigmatic, self-contained. Beautiful. 'Ach, if it's not beautiful,' she'd say – and she didn't mean pretty – 'why bother?' And she held onto that word, bearing it defiantly through an ugly time, carrying it in the face of Graeme's ridicule and her peers' incredulity.

She had fun with dimensions. Sometimes her human figures were flat cut-outs standing in a 3-D room. In the Plean room everything was flat, the bed, chair, desk, the kneeling child – everything except the matchbox sized plastic TV with cherry blossom painted on the screen and if you looked closely you saw the floor round the set and the child was covered in petals.

He glanced at Kim, and she looked rather chuffed with herself. The doubts would come later.

'Look at the ceiling,' she said.

Jimmy set his eye to the peep-hole. The ceiling too was flecked with blossom as if it had floated up from the telly and shaped in it was the face of the rapt kneeling child.

'You're a dreamer,' he said and kissed her. 'It's beautiful. It makes me prickle.'

'The blossom's real,' she said, 'I nicked it from the garden down the road.'

She led him over to a large model by the side window.

'This is the last one,' she said. 'I'm empty now. Maybe I'll become a housewife or a nun.'

She stood fidgeting beside him as he bent to look through the peep-hole.

'It's just a notion,' she said. 'I'm not sure. Probably utterly naff.'

'Oh stop gibbering, woman.'

He was looking into a version of their bedroom. It was lit for night, an orange streetlamp at the window. An oversize cat was sprawled on the bed where a couple lay. One was turned away sleeping. The other, a woman, was looking up at the ceiling. The cat had a tiny crucifix hanging from its collar. The smoke from the cigarette in the woman's hand went up to the ceiling and in its fine gauze was the suggestion of a face like the imprint in the Turin Shroud. An incomplete white moon hung outside the window and glinted on the walls. Then as his eyes adjusted he could see the moon was glinting on blades that projected from the walls. He looked again and the whole room was full of emerging knives. The woman lay in the bed with her eyes wide open.

'Jesus,' he said softly.

'Ach, I'm no sure' she said. 'Do you think it fits with the others?'

'No,' he said. It didn't fit with anything. It was not remotely like a toy. 'It's stunning.'

She shrugged. 'Well, you're always on at me to do something more personal. You know, all that looking-into-yourself stuff. So I gave it a try. Maybe I should burn it. I don't like giving people the bad news.'

He looked again through the peep-hole into the roomful of knives. Living with talent can be unsettling.

'Keep it,' he said. 'We need the bad news too.'

She hesitated then switched off the light in the box and turned away.

'Just a wee visual haiver,' she said. 'I wouldn't pay it any mind. Isn't it terrible about Graeme's mum? How could anyone be so cruel and desperate? Poor Graeme. I think about it all the time.'

That first solo exhibition made her. Not in a big way, not fame and fortune, but she was getting there. The exhibition toured later, pieces went to France then Germany and started that connection. She thought it a lot of fuss about very little.

'If I was a man,' she said, 'there wouldn't be half this attention. Still the Arts Council award should keep the landlord happy a while. Fancy a wee holiday with the bidie-in?'

It was spring, of sorts. He'd been out strolling and shopping in the chilly sunlight, saw a convoy of Police vans heading North for the Fife pits. Another day of picketing, scuffles, cameras and arrests. Graeme's talk was all fight this and smash that but to Jimmy it was depressingly obvious who'd win the struggle. All they could do was keep some kind of light burning for a better day.

When he came back in and saw her face, he thought at first she'd had another bad session in the studio. She put her arm round him.

'Your mum's been on the phone,' she said. 'Your dad's dead.'

Tears came, painful and scarce. He sat at the kichen table and noticed the shopping bags looked sadly abandoned, open-mouthed on the floor.

'He had another stroke,' she said. 'He was on the pier at Eyemouth and he was probably dead by the time he hit the water.'

So the spey-wife got it right, Jimmy thought. He died in the water. Huh.

He phoned his mum, then went and sat in the garden. The ground was cleared and dug over, not much new had come through yet. It seemed odd that the day hadn't changed at all. He had a cigarette and wondered when his father had smoked his last pipe. It would be lying in a bowl somewhere, meticulously reamed out. Tears again, just a few, enough to make the garden swell and wobble.

Her hand was lightly on his arm and she kept quiet. The cold sun shone, birds were busy at mating and territory, the cigarette burned, the struggle went on. Only his father had ceased to take part in it. They'd never gone on that last fishing trip together. The last words his father had said – waving from the door – 'Glad ye came by.'

If we knew our last times were our last times at the time, he thought, it would be unbearable.

Funeral day was thick damp haar off the sea, and the foghorn going. A lot of folk at the crematorium.

'As big a turn-oot as many a long day,' his uncle Bob said with satisfaction, like Bill MacLaren reporting the attendance at a Borders rugby match. 'John wis a ken-speckled man in this toun.'

Jimmy nodded. He felt sorry for Bobby, sorry for all the old ones who weren't dead yet. Even the children hurt to look at, they had it coming to them. People filed in slowly, a shuffling procession towards death, some nearer the head of the queue than others. Why these struggles, these arrests, this violence? he wondered. What can we be but terribly gentle with each other?

And he had seen for the last time his father's hands, the shrunken, liver-spotted hands that had cuffed him, corrected his grip on rifles, spanners, torches, rugby balls, and overlaid on his, had guided his first casts with a rod. The hands white on the rail in front of him were his father's, long, broad-palmed and knuckly, no doubt about it.

His mum on his right, Kim on his left. Alec, his Maggie, their bairns. Graeme and Lesley for the first time in ages, both looking tired and worn. He was touched they'd come from their causes. People were very kind.

Then the coffin, then the flames. He stood in a line with his eyes pouring and shook the hands that came towards him, nodded at whatever they were saying.

When he could see again he was sitting at a long table with food in front of him and he found he was very hungry. He ate, and it tasted good. He glanced round. Everyone was eating. His mum smiled at something Graeme said. One of the bairns gurned, somebody laughed. Outside the world turned, muffled in an East Coast haar. Further inland it would be fine, just a local condition. The sun would be shining on Rest and Be Thankful at the end of his father's old single track road.

He reached out for his glass. He wasn't the man his father was, but what man feels he is? He pictured the stand of trees by his house, and the space left when the biggest one had come down.

The wine tasted, oh it really tasted fine.

He was with his dad in Soho in the late Fifties. Dad looked younger, almost spivvish as they turned into the jazz club. Jimmy bought the drinks, offered his dad a Passing Cloud and lit up for them both. His dad nodded thanks. Unusual and pleasant to be so at ease together.

His dad wandered over to the piano on the low stage and idly ran his fingers over the keys, grinned to himself. To Jimmy's astonishment he then sat down and began to play. Some kind of improvised boogie. Lots of heavy left hand. His father liked music but Jimmy had never heard him play a note in his life. He stood beside the piano and stared. The big left hand swung lazily across two octaves.

'Why didn't you tell me you had the gift?' he muttered.

His dad shrugged.

'Ach, used tae play. Then you lot cam by and there wisna time.'

His father swung into waltz-time, slid into a minor key. Jimmy was very impressed and very pissed off.

'You shoulda tellt me.'

His father nodded at a guitar leaning up against a bar-stool.

'Why don't you join wi me?' he said. 'It's in R minor' he added.

R minor, Jimmy thought. What the fuck's that?

But an audience had gathered so he picked up the guitar and quickly found R minor and so long as he kept it simple it wouldn't sound too bad. He felt just fine, kinda proud and astonished and still a bit cheesed off as they flicked the improvisation back and forward between them. The audience nodded, they approved. He glimpsed Kim working behind the bar, head down, very busy and too far away to hear properly.

His father returned to 4/4 time and began to wind the piece down. He tailed off gradually, put down the lid of the piano and walked quietly off-stage, leaving Jimmy to finish the piece. Which he did, that was how it was meant to be, an improvisation begun on piano and ending on four spaced chords.

He put down the guitar, there was some applause, the audience drifted away. The manager wore black, seemed pleased.

'Is your father alright?' he asked.

'Aye, he's fine,' Jimmy answered. 'It's meant tae end thataway.'

He went outside to find his dad. It was dark and mild out. The old man was leaning back against the wall, hands in pockets, in good trim.

'Christ, you might hae tellt me!' Jimmy said. 'I thought I'd got all the good stuff from mum. You had the gift and you didna let on.'

His father looked down at a poppy-strewn pavement.

'Sorry,' he said. 'I should hae. Jist tae busy, ken.'

He had never ever apologised before.

'Ach, disna matter noo,' Jimmy said and they walked off down the street, looking for another show . . .

He hit the alarm and lay on for a couple of minutes. Still negotiating wi the dead, eh? R minor is a bit bleedin obvious but.

He wanted to tell Kim about it, get her opinion on this gift his father had concealed from him. More than an ability to punch the ivories, that's for sure. Pity she had been too busy working to hear.

He reached up and thumped the bunk above him.

'Come away, Tumshie. Daylight's burning!'

'Away fuck,' the gloomy Swede muttered and swung his long white legs over the side.

'Anither three days and that's what I'll be at.'

He tried phoning Kim from the rig to tell her about the dream but got no answer. She'd said she might be going away, maybe to see Lesley at Greenham. Now the exhibition work was done, she didn't like being in on her own for long.

When his stint was up he choppered out and took the train down to Edinburgh, then on to Dunbar.

Been away. Now at 'The Diggers' with Joe and Rita etc. See you there? Kim.

He dumped his gear, had a wash, took the next train back into Edinburgh, walked into the Diggers and found her in the Jug Bar hunched round a table with friends her age. When she wasn't working she needed to chatter and drink and socialise. She looked up, nodded diffidently. Returns were always difficult. He wanted to hug her but she was at the far side of the table. Well, he'd be finished with the rigs soon. He was ready to fill the space.

He bought a round, squeezed in opposite Kim and raised the finest pint in the country to his lips.

In bed at last, he put his arm round her. She accepted it but nothing more. They lay together in the dark.

'So,' he said, 'what's doing?'

'Nothing much,' she said. 'I went with Graeme and his friends to that cottage in Arran. He needed a few days off the Miners' Strike.'

'Good,' he said. 'Did he climb much?'

'No. Mostly it rained. We stayed in.'

'You're looking better for the break.'

There was a long pause.

'Yes,' she said slowly. 'You see, I've been sleeping with him and I feel like a million dollars.'

'I feel terrible,' she added.

He pictured hitting her, saw it clearly, his hand swinging across to clout her like his dad had him, but already it was too late and too ridiculous.

'Oh boy,' he said.

'You must have guessed it would happen sooner or later,' Kim muttered.

'No.'

It had been a joke between them. Now they looked at each other in the dim light of the Teasmade, helpless it seemed.

'I didn't go there intending,' she said. 'I was just headachy and fed up. But as soon as I walked into the cottage, we both knew it was going to happen. I'm . . .'

'You're?'

Sorry? Happy? Feeling like a million dollars? And why dollars, he wondered.

She spread her hand over her face.

'Maybe it was just sex,' she said.

Just sex for a whole week in Arran. Lucky Graeme.

But he didn't own her. He had no exclusive claim on her. These things happened. She wasn't his. He said all the right things to himself.

'And now?' he asked.

She gazed at him across the miles of inches between them. The night was very still. He was hanging at the end of an abseil, waiting to see if he could touch rock.

'I want to do it again,' she said.

He hit her then, a scuffed slap on her face.

'Yes,' she said quietly, and began to cry. Automatically, he moved to comfort her. She flinched and part of him began to say goodbye.

'My head aches,' she said quickly, 'but I feel alive for the first time in ages. You've done nothing wrong – I wish you had – but I'm too young to settle. I've known it ever since we moved in here but didn't want to admit it. Those headaches . . . It's been too much too soon. Graeme feels really bad about it too,' she added.

'Nice of him.'

'Don't be bitter.'

'Bitter? I want to kill him. He kens what you mean to me.'

'Jimmy,' she said, 'he didn't exactly seduce me.'

He didn't want to think about that, didn't want to see the two of them in the cottage, moving towards each other and what came next, didn't want to see that movie at all though he would, over and over and over.

'If you're going to hurt anyone, it should be me. Or just fuck me. Hurt me. Maybe that's what I need. Why don't you?'

'I – '

He got stuck.

'Love you,' he said.

'I know,' she said gently, and in her sympathy he knew something was gone.

'Maybe I love him. He's been so down, I couldn't bear it. It wasn't just sex, you know.'

Which is the better reason for sleeping with someone else?

he wondered. Love or just sex? And what has just got to do with it?

'So what happens now?' he said at last.

'I don't know. We said we'd just see.' That 'we' clung and burned like napalm. 'I'll move out if you want . . . Maybe it's just a fling. Oh shit,' she said and rolled on her back, 'this is so banal.'

Yes, commonplace and agonising to a degree he didn't know possible, and it had only begun.

'What about Lesley?'

'She was already back in the States. I think she's got someone there though Graeme won't talk about it, you know what he's like.'

'I thought I did.'

'He doesn't know when she's coming back. Don't give me guilt, I'm sure she'd understand.'

'Really.'

They lay on their backs in silence, rigid and inches apart, as though turned to stone, like effigies of Lord and Lady in a corner of an abandoned church of a religion in terminal decline.

I lean forward, carefully turn down the flame and blow hard across the top of the glass funnel.

I say goodnight to the sleeping child I sometimes call mine, and feel my way downstairs in the dark without hesitation. It's easy once you're familiar.

PART II

Scissors, Paper, Stone

FOURTEEN

The Golden Triangle

THE TIDE SURGED past the harbourhead. The moored boats jittered, streetlamps shattered and reformed prettily but it meant nothing to me. Graeme looked up at the dark outline of the ruined castle wall above the harbour. It curved away at the top, leaning into an arch that was no longer there.

'You've climbed that?'

'Never crossed my mind.'

'Ever seen anyone dae it?'

'Not to the top. It's falling apart.'

I felt his restlessness fix on it like a grappling iron.

'Let's knock it off.'

'Go break your neck.'

He shrugged.

'Suit yersel.'

He bounded up the wee hill and stood at the foot of the wall where it hangs over the big drop on the other side. He stroked the greasy, rounded stones and looked up, then down at the sea flickering like a knife in the dark.

'Race you,' he said.

I stood behind him, hands in pockets. I couldn't fathom him. Maybe that was the attraction for her. A boot in the back and he'd be over the cliff.

'You've the advantage of local knowledge,' he said.

'Five or six years worth.'

I waited till he figured it out. He looked down and sighed.

'If it's gonna fall, it's gonna. So, are ye on?'

'No way.'

He bent down and started unlacing his shoes. A moment later I was too. Worse than daft.

We went at it in stocking feet, hurrying up the loose slippery holds like deranged spiders, feeling our seperate ways through the mirk. We made the top in a dead heat and sat facing each other, panting, astride across the beginning of the curve out over the rocks below. For a moment it felt good, daft in the right way, like in the old days.

And then we sat in silence, nothing left to say to each other.

That quick, taut chapping on my door earlier that evening, I'd known it was him but not what I was going to do. He used to just walk in but not this time. I let him wait then opened up.

He hadn't changed much, a bit smaller maybe.

'You're no gonna clobber me, then?' he'd said at last.

'Dunno,' I said. 'Not yet.'

'Wouldni blame you.'

'Uh huh.'

He stood getting wet, dark hair plastered to his forehead. Celt in the steady summer rain and not a happy man. I was in no hurry to let him in, anyhow the house was empty of anything that mattered. A few days before, I'd finally said 'You'd better go' and she had, white-faced, silent, toting a rucksack. Kissed my cheek, waved vaguely at the end of the lane, went.

'It jist happened,' he said, not looking at me.

'Really. You knew what she meant tae me.'

He straightened his neck like it was an iron bar and finally looked me in the eye.

'It's nae excuse, Jim, but I only betray ma freens when it's important.'

'Some politics you got there.'

'Meaning?'

Good, he wasn't going to be humble. With luck I'd be able to hit him. I wanted to hit someone and it couldn't be her.

'So it's important?'

'Yes,' he'd said and kept his black eyes on me. 'I'm afraid she is. You must hate ma guts but I had tae come and tell ye.'

I took a step forward and closed the front door behind me. He didn't step back, just watched intently. He was taking in my right hand and I reckoned if I hit him once maybe he'd let me, but if I hit him again we'd be at each other till one of us was done.

We'd thought ourselves exceptions, the good guys, keepers of the faith.

'We'd best go for a drink, then,' I said. 'You're buying.'

We walked silently through the rain past the harbour and up the wynd to the pub. No, we didn't get drunk and matey and laugh about women and make it up. Nor did we settle it with fists, not yet anyhow. We couldn't believe in that dumb joss. We were stranded, had no idea how to act.

So he bought a round then I did and we drank them slowly. After the first pint it was clear I wasn't going to hit him and he wasn't going to blether about being sorry. Which meant he was still in the game. It wasn't his way to apologise for something he intended to keep doing.

'Lesley?'

'If she comes back, I don't know. She's something going over in the States but that's between us. Maybe I'm no that bothered. But I hae tae tell you, I do want Kim. Badly.' His eyes flicked up at me, I wished he wouldn't do that. 'Verra badly. She's in ma blood, man.'

'So you take what you want and tae hell wi the morality. I used to admire you and your politics. Solidarity!' He winced. 'Aye, when it suits you.'

'Man, it wis you who tellt me tae.'

'Fuck Kim? Oh surely.'

'On the Orkney ferry last summer. You said in the end we should take what we want.'

'This wasna quite what I had in mind. Anyhow, since when did you listen to anything I said?'

He grinned and for a moment it was there again, like the dead returned, that warmth between us.

'I aye have. You know that.'

'Nuh.'

I looked down at my hands, flexed them, sat back and took a long breath. Christ, the things we say.

'Jim,' he said quietly, 'it's been on the cards for a while. Whit dae you think aa that on Orkney wis about? Mibbe she didni know, but I did. And Les.' He hesitated, seemed to change his mind. 'That's why we bailed out early, before it went further. Till then she'd jist been a pal, swear tae God. Mind yon sunset at the broch?'

'I mind it.'

'That wis when I clocked her. Jist saw her different and couldni forget it.'

That sunset at Gurness. Of course he'd seen into her and loved her, for a moment we'd seemed more than flesh and blood. Me awa wi the fairies, him clocking Kim and Lesley knowing it and then the swans whapping over the horizon and the silence after. He'd looked and seen her differently and that was that.

'It wisni all me,' he was saying. 'No excuses, but when she came to Arran she was really wanting. Otherwise I'd nivver hae touched her. Honest.'

Sitting opposite me, biting his nails, scarcely meeting my eye, he didn't look like Glasgow's hottest radical Councillor. She had got to him. Desire had got to him, like a torpedo through the dark. No safe harbour and no safe ship, not even in Orkney.

'I'd best be making tracks,' he said. 'Back hame.'

'You do that.'

I appreciated him letting me know he wasn't going on to Kim's new bedsit in Edinburgh. We'd finished our drinks quickly then wandered down towards the harbour and my place. Then he'd seen the ruined wall and he'd just had to go for it.

Now I shivered in the small rain. The wall could cowp us any minute and I couldn't stop feeling sick. He fumbled with his right hand and levered out a rock, lobbed it into the darkness.

'You're right,' he said quietly. 'This wisni wan of ma better moves. Mibbe – '

But I was already on my way down.

We parted at his car.

'I thought you'd lay wan on me.'

'Me too. No point, but.'

'We let her decide, then?'

'She usually does.'

'No competing.'

'I said that once.'

'I know,' he said. 'The Etive Slabs, I mind fine. I thought: what have we here?'

And for a moment there was the old warmth again.

'I loved you once,' I said and caught him off balance more surely than any punch. 'I appreciate you coming over but it'll be a long while till the next time.'

He wiped his hand across his mouth and slid into the car. Then he rolled down the window.

'There'll be better times,' he said.

'I doubt it.'

I thumped on the roof and he sped off through the rain. With luck or justice he'd end up under an artic.

I watched his lights disappear then wandered numbly out along the pier. I came to the edge and stopped. The water below was dark, unfathomable. To lose a lover is also to lose a daily game, and a house-mate, and a closest friend. I'd lost two in one throw, and Les was out of contact in the States.

I turned away from the edge, looked up into the night and finally felt something, damp and real on my face.

'Again,' the child says. 'Again.'

She's getting bored already and we've a long ride ahead of us. She'd been desparate to come along. I'd tried suggesting she could as well wait and see her next morning, but she's stubborn as hell. She had to see her tonight. She'd promised to be good while I did my business first, and she was trying.

I take my right hand off the wheel and hide it by my side. She does the same with her left. We look each other in the eye for a moment, trying to second-guess. She starts to giggle.

'Go,' I say, and produce my hand clenched. As her wee hand comes round she adjusts her fingers, shows a flat palm and laughs triumphantly.

'Paper wraps stone!'

I nod and laugh too. This time together is precious and anyway we all cheat once in a while.

'Are we nearly there?' she asks.

'Soon come, darlin,' I say as we take the old back road into town, heading for Leith on our first leg of the drive.

She heaves a sigh but goes back to sculpting her playdough as she sits strapped in beside me and I run the scenes you'll need to see.

Kim sat in the studio and was alone with her notebook and her inner voice. Jimmy off-shore again, Graeme teaching, everything broken and nothing resolved.

Do we have to resolve everything? she wondered.

The house was empty and silent, no life down below. Even her kitten Charlie had taken himself off in disgust.

If this is so wrong, Kim thought, why do I feel so alive? That's got to be worth something. Moving across the kitchen towards him, knowing yet not knowing, about to find out, my wee heart banging.

I'd forgotten what it is to have a man in your mind like a mirage in the desert. He's essential and unreachable as water.

He's someone I can't quite arrive at. Maybe that's what Jimmy was always getting on at me about, and now it's my turn.

We're not fixed at all, it just depends who we're with.

Maybe I know Jimmy too well, he's an open door to me.

People say that's good, but it's the door that's open just a chink keeps you coming back for more –

She stared hard at the harbour, concentrated on counting the creels stacked below the wall, and hummed loudly till the vision of that room, that door, faded. You must be careful, her voice whispered, not to pull the little triggers –

And then she had to start all over again. Humming, breathing deeply, pacing the attic floor. Over the years she'd worked out many ways. By the time she was fourteen she could make herself feel nothing, just by willing it hard enough. But it was so tiring and once in a while she would let it slip.

'You've two brains and two hearts,' Jimmy had shouted the other night, 'and neither knows what the other's up to.' He couldn't have known that was the most frightening thing he could say, nor why she'd gone ice-cold till the poor man apologised.

She sat down at the bench and fiddled with her father's compasses and made herself think about something else. Thought about sex. Tried not to think about sex. Sex is not that important. Work's important. So are friends. So – but not to admit to Graeme – is political activity. All the News these days makes me want to weep. It's not as if they don't know what they're doing.

But the only thing that's really important is something I can't even name but I know is there.

So does Jimmy and that's always connected us.

When I finally get everything I wanted – security, a studio, a good man to share it all with – I go and blow it up. Just for that heart-hammering feeling.

You're a greedy bisom and can't let green cheese pass yer een. Mum aye said so and she was right.

Kim Russell/Ruslawska stabbed the compasses into the table. Spread her hands on the wood and looked at them.

I need the security too. I need my faithful, reliable companion and I want my mirage in front of me so I need never look back.

Security and excitement – why shouldn't we have both? Why ever not?

She leant forward and began to scribble notes, notes with little drawings in the margins, the notes I checked this morning, waiting to see what it would become.

'Jimmy, I need a pee,' the wean says.

'Can you wait till we get to Leith? Twenty minutes.'

She considers her need. The urgency of her body, the control she can have over it, the length of time. It's good to sit beside her and talk to her like an adult only more slowly. She hates baby voices and already we can talk over lots of things. Rina is given to considering things, you can see them stir in her round dark eyes.

She nods.

'Yes,' she says.

I hope she knows her mind and her limits better than we did. I put my foot down and hurry it along a bit.

'Can't we have more imagination?' she was saying. 'I don't want to lose you but I can't give him up.'

'Let me guess,' I said. 'You can't help it.'

'No! That's not my excuse. Lack of will has never been my problem.' She looked out over the water as though looking for her true problem. 'Truth is,' she said quietly, 'I can't stop it because I don't want to. Maybe I'm not really a couple person.'

She paused and flipped her roll-up into the Water of Leith. That was Kim's way of cutting down, smoking less of as many.

'We should try adapting our ships to suit us, not the other way round.'

'What's this leading to?'

She took my tobacco and began rolling another. 'I'm saying I want to see you both. Regularly. A triangle.'

I stared at her.

'You serious?'

'Why not? Couples, I'm sick of couples. Who said it had to be that way or nothing? It's not working for us, so let's try something different.'

With the sun pouring down on us as we bobbed slightly on the floating pontoon of the Waterfront Wine Bar, and my third glass of white wine in my hand, and her sitting beside me in a yellow summer dress, it all seemed reasonable.

Why should I grudge her? If I claimed to love this woman, surely . . .

'I know it's a scunner,' she said and put her hand on my arm and kept it there, idly brushing the hairs. 'But it needn't be a problem even if other people think it's weird. I don't want you less because of this. More, if anything.' She smiled to herself. 'I'm sure there's enough of me to go round.'

'Darlin, you sound like a leg of lamb.'

She hesitated then laughed with me. With the sunshine and the wind and the wine, it seemed a game, a comedy of hearts, and we briefly saw that it was.

'I love you,' I said, because it was true.

And because it wasn't a plea or a reproach, she wrapped her fingers round my forearm and spoke gently.

'I know – but why not spread it around a bit? It might even bring me to my senses.'

'What if the truth is I can't stand it?'

She lit her skinny roll-up.

'I'd have to leave.'

'You've left anyway.'

'You ken what I mean.'

I leaned back in my chair and looked out over the clarty water, and marvelled again at the whiteness of the swans drifting on it. Perhaps it was possible.

'You've put this to him?'

'Aye. The wee Protestant soul is shocked. Like most male radicals, he's awfy conventional. But he'll consider it if you will.'

'What's the deal? Two weeks on and two weeks off?'

She laughed.

'Something like that. Whatever suits. Shall we give it a try?'

At least it would be different from the sorry old best friend yarn. We might learn something by it. I watched the swans preen and settle by the pontoon. Wine bars, restorations, repro Scottish vernacular – the familar dirty run-down docks area was beginning to change. Good or bad, there were new developments and I might as well accept that.

Half of her or none.

'Aye, sure,' I said. 'Why not.'

She re-filled the glasses.

'To new ways of shipping,' she said. 'I really think we can do it.' She put her hand cautiously on my arm. 'I don't like to ask, but can I keep on using the studio sometimes when you're away?'

140

Only if you'll love me, the child in me screamed.

'Yes. Only you mustn't – '

'Of course I wouldn't,' she said. 'Not in your house. I promise.'

She drew deep on the cigarette then threw it away. We sat in the sunshine not saying much till the wine was finished and then we went home and pulled off her yellow dress and made love or had passionate sex or something that felt more scary and real than in ages.

'Okay, honey bee?'

Rina makes a face that reminds me of her mother, and hands me her latest playdough masterpiece. It looks like a human ear or maybe a cabbage leaf, but I've learned not to ask. I thank her and stick it on the dashboard.

She ought to sit in the back but as I say, she's stubborn and anyway I like having her beside me. She sits well strapped in by the harness I adapted. The diamante brooch glitters on her wee green jacket, special dispensation for a special day.

Kim was sitting in my kitchen as if she'd never left, her feet up by the window. I hadn't expected her but didn't ask and just carried on doing the dishes, noticing how everything felt in place and all fuss a waste of breath.

She said she'd come by to thank me for the use of the attic studio while I'd been off-shore, and to pick up her sleeping bag. I didn't ask for where. It was summer morning, behind her laburnum hung like yellow grapes over the garden wall. The sunlight picked on a glittering pendant in the hollow of her throat. A present from my old pal?

'I call it the Golden Triangle,' she said. 'It's giving me lots of ideas, mostly with distorted perspex and mirrorglass. What d'you reckon?'

'I can see the possibilities,' I said. 'Sometimes.'

She nibbled her index finger and carefully laid a ragged crescent of nail on the window sill.

'When I don't feel a right wee hoor, it makes me feel so . . . fecund.' She looked directly at me. 'Being wanted by you both. Loving you both. Giving myself.' She started on the next finger. 'Sometimes I feel so selfish, and then I think – why not?'

'Know how you mean.'

'So it's okay?'

I looked down into the basin, the little foam bubbles hissing and breaking. I rinsed a plate and looked down to the bottom.

'I've been looking too much at how things used to be,' I said slowly. 'Or how I hoped they would be. I hadn't faced how it actually is, this Golden Triangle of yours. But now I have . . .'

We'd become an adventure again, not an institution. Even the way she made love had broadened and changed, which was hunky-dory if I didn't think too much about why. Sometimes I'd caress her and wonder where I'd learned that caress, with Bridget probably, and that gesture would be passed by Kim on to Graeme, who'd acquire it and some day maybe please Lesley with the same touch, who would in turn pass it on to whatever lover. Maybe one day it would come right round the world and back to me.

And when Kim wasn't here, well, that wasn't so easy but I'd considered the alternative.

'Now I have, it's okay. When it's not, I'll quit.'

Aye, that'll be right.

She looked relieved.

'I'm proud of you both. You don't run each other down. I know he wishes he could see you, he thinks the world of you.'

'Oh jolly jolly good.'

We let an angel pass while I wiped down the surfaces. Gotta keep up standards. I shook my head.

'What is it?'

'*Golden Triangle*. For fuck's sake.'

'Maybe that's what all this is about,' she said. 'Fuck's sake. And I used to think I was above all that. A right wee prude.'

'Aye, I suppose now your biggest problem is adjusting to the different pillow heights.'

'How on earth did you know that?' she said.

We looked at each other and there was nothing else for it. We started laughing and my heart was abruptly full of lightness. I thought of those dark green trees that when the wind blows through turn silver.

'I'm so lucky,' she said. 'It could be wonderful if our hearts are big enough.'

She was shaking some grit from her shoe. A leaf of light shook in her throat. It just came out, a bit hoarse.

'You're so fuckin precious tae me.'

She raised her eyebrows.

'What brought that on?'

I shrugged.

'Felt it, said it.' I sat on the corner of the table. 'Were you thinking of staying?'

'I hear you've met someone in Perth.'

'Met is all.'

'Nice?'

'Nicer than you.'

As if that was the point.

'She knows about me?'

'Of course. It's the least I can do.'

'What does she think?'

'That you're a chancer and pain in the arse.'

She grinned and got out of the chair. Put her arms round my neck, kissed my cheek, brushed my lips. There was no one else like her. Which was a pity, because there were many better.

She swayed against me.

'Jealousy,' she said, 'is a great aphrodisiac.'

Stone breaks scissors cuts paper wraps stone – the Golden Triangle hung and spun that summer into autumn, sometimes buckled, sometimes radiant. In the Borders the leaves hung on late and gorgeous, though my school biology told me they were just shedding poisonous waste. At times I thought waiting was the worst, waiting to see how it would fall.

'Look at me,' Kim whispered. 'Why won't you touch me? Am I any different just because I sleep with someone else?'

'Yes,' I said. 'For me you are.'

She impatiently pulled away the duvet and crouched in front of me with her precious tormenting mongrel body.

'Look at this body, seeing you place so much importance in it. Has my hair changed? My eyes? Do you think my hands are different now I've held someone else?' She cupped herself in the curiously tender way of women. 'These breasts? Do you think I'm different inside, that he's left a mark? Take a good look, Jimmy. I'm the same, damnit!'

Whatever I felt, it wasn't simple desire.

'Doesn't it bother you at all?'

'Yes, but I'm working on it. We've all got conditioning to deal with. I'm still the same,' she said softly. 'I still want and need you – can't you just relax and enjoy me?'

'I can't do this any more,' I said. 'It's time you chose.'

She leaned towards me, eyes wide open.

'How can I chose between two people? How can anyone?' I felt the warmth of her body, her breath, was almost persuaded. Then she giggled. 'You're different planets, not sticky buns!'

'And I suppose you think you're the sun. You act, we react. Sod off and stop messing up my life, and Graeme's, like you had the right. I don't know how you got off wi it so long. I've had enough.'

She was silent, turned her head away like I'd hit her.

'Fair enough,' she said eventually. 'But I'm *not* a bad person.'

She dressed and left. From the window I watched her walk down the road, a hand up to her face as she passed people. Shading her eyes from the sun, I thought, then realised it was a grey day.

Alison leant towards me in the pub.

'Bet you'll be seeing her again,' she said.

'You think so?'

'She was round talking to me and Gerry half of last the night, pouring out her troubles. You two are bound with cables. This one will run and run.'

I shook my head.

'Christ, Alison. I hate this.'

She put her hand on mine.

'I know,' she said. 'So do we all.'

'I suppose I maun thole it.'

'Ye maun thole it, hen. But we'll be here.' She squeezed lightly and my chest felt like a lemon pulped on my mum's glass lemon-squeezer. Juice swelling in the corners of my eyes.

Gerry plonked down the drinks.

'So let's hear the latest from Heartbreak Hotel,' he said.

I managed a wee smile. Liked the man, so large and patient, took to his Geordie manner, the rough tenderness so like ours. 'Naw, I've burdened you two enough this past while.'

'Don't be Scottish, man.'

'But I am!'

'Then – change it!'

'Brilliant,' I said. 'Change it. Want to change the height of Ben Nevis while we're at it?'

'Don't see why not,' Alison grinned. 'Not if we each bring our ain wee chuckie stane.'

'This won't take long,' I tell her. 'You take your playdough and I'll take my papers and we'll be out of here in no time. Okay?'

She nods, she understands a deal. We toddle together through the old dock gates, me with my files and her with her box. Maybe I've been too quiet and brooding, but she silently slips her hand into mine and I think again of those dark leaves flipping to silver, so commonplace and indescribeable.

And just when I see Graeme about to make a face and mouth *sentimental git*, she lets go and puts her hand behind her back.

'No cheating,' I say.

She nods and stares at me hard, as though concentration was enough to read another's mind. I get down to her level and we face up like gunfighters. The wind blows across the empty cobbles. Me in the new leather jacket, her in a wee green coat and the brooch glittering like a deputy's badge.

'*Only fun when it's serious,*' Kim whispers.

I narrow my eyes. She mimics me.

'*Only serious when it's fun,*' Lesley says, laughing.

'Go!'

Her hand comes round, stone as expected. Her pattern is not to repeat herself. I'm a fraction behind her, enough to change my mind and roll my flat palm into a fist too. We chap them off each other.

'Draw!' she crows, still young enough to enjoy the game for itself, whatever the result.

We hurry into the office of 'Marshall-Renilson Domes' to fulfill our needs, mine to earn money and hers to have a pee. She's doing well as we ever did.

FIFTEEN

Scissors cut paper

BUSINESS DONE, FED and watered, we're ready to hit the road
again. But first Rina has to sit on my lap and we pretend she's
in control. There's no hurry, waiting for the afternoon rush-hour
to disperse and forby there's no point in getting to the airport
ages early.

She grasps the wheel in both hands, I help it round with one
hand at the bottom. She feels like she's steering as we go round
and round the empty car park, and I think well we all have that
delusion. But I still hold on, just to be on the safe side.

The way he looked when she came unannounced up the garden
path cut her like the East wind. He quickly replaced it with his
neutral, cautious expression, but it was too late.

You poor man, she thought, wanting me. As well someone
still does.

She glanced up at the dormer attic windows. The bright red
frames she'd painted the week they'd moved in, willing it to
work and already that dragging feeling in her arms with every
stroke. Those curtains with zig-zag stripes, well they'd been a
mistake too. None of them hung straight and it showed.

There's only one thing I'm any good at and that only sometimes.

She adjusted herself to his kiss and hoped to God she'd
remembered to take off Graeme's ear-rings.

Soon as possible she went up into the attic studio. Her playroom
where she'd sketched and dreamed and made things at the table.
Now her tools and toys were dispersed in three households and
she herself was scattered and divided.

She took out the compasses from the drawer and thinking of
nothing in particular scored a circle on the old workbench.

In it she drew a triangle, its points just breaking the circle.

She dragged a line across the circle like an arrow through
a heart.

She hesitated then scratched a little fish outside the circle and triangle, down to the right, with a wee open mouth and a suprised expression. Swimming away.

And from the end of the arrow which now looked like a fishing rod, came a curly line, with a hook. And on that hook she impaled a worm, stuck the hook through the body of the worm and gave it a bit of a writhe and felt sick.

She sat back. What am I supposed to do with this information?

I'm just a wee chancer. Pretending to be some kind of artist. Kidding myself I could have Jimmy and Graeme. Faking that I'm grown up. That there's nothing wrong with me. There is is is nothing wrong with me.

At least we gave it a whirl.

She lit the gas ring in the corner and stuck the kettle on. Padded round the room, loosening her shoulders and neck, wondering if that drawing would work as a mobile. There's things more important than love and sex. Like making bits of the beautiful world. We are what we're devoted to.

Graeme isn't devoted to me. He's got his politics and his conscience, and Lesley. I'm not top of his list. That's obvious now. I'm important but not the most important, maybe that's part of the appeal for me. The fish just out of reach.

And Jimmy? How do you value what you know you have?

Do I? This new woman. He may decide – who'd blame him. I ken fine what Jim wants. Been tempted, just once or twice, in the heat of the moment. But it runs in families.

She turned away from the window, hummed 'All things bright and beautiful' till the moment passed.

She rattled her nails on the fish-tank glass. His moving-in present to me. If I really loved him I'd let him go. Or maybe I do, so I don't.

Feelings are over-rated. Blind man bumps into a blind woman in a fabulous bazaar. 'I'm looking for treasure,' she says. 'Search me,' he replies.

Men who can't love? More like women, some women, this woman, who can't receive love when it's offered.

Because it's too scary.

Because we can't live up to it.

Because to be loved unreservedly is terribly corrupting.

She breathed over the glass at her favourite, Greedy bastard's eaten all his kind. But is it fair on him? she asked. *Gloop, gloop,* her favourite mouthed back. What's it all about? *Gobble gobble.* Is it worth it? *Blub.* Am I in my right mind? *Bloop?*

Between them they gave me everything I wanted and yes at times I made them happy and felt like a good person. It's not so weird. It could have lasted.

She returned to the table, glanced at the doodle. Could work on that. Imagine a sculptural equivalent of kids' drawings. We're kids anyway. Joan Eardley. I'll never be that good. I want to be normal and happy but the great ones seldom are. The beautiful world isn't pretty, just enduring. So . . .

She pared her nails carefully on the grindstone, then sat down to her notes. Where does love go? Why?

Up in steam, whispered the kettle in the corner, *because of the fire down below.*

'So what are you doing here?' He grinned, more or less. 'According to the calendar, it's not my week for you.'

'Lesley's back,' she said. 'He says he's realised she's more important. I think he's given me the push.'

She stood at the kitchen sink and began to cry. Given the push, he thought, sometimes she's still in the playground.

'This is ridiculous,' he said into her ear. 'Why should I be comforting you?'

She rubbed her eyes and looked at him. His heart was hammering like fury.

'Because we're friends and you love me,' she said, and sometimes she told the simple truth. 'I won't stay, though,' she added. 'It isn't fair. Just give me a little more time.'

He said nothing but held her cautiously. She leant back against him, hard yet full of tinkling bits inside, like a vacuum flask someone has dropped.

I take control again, strap the bairn in, and work my way out of town towards the Glasgow motorway. She's not too pleased with this development and soon throws her playdough to the floor.

'Mouldy old dough,' she mutters.

'She'll be half-way over the sea by now,' I remind her. 'We're driving towards her and she's flying towards us at hundreds of miles an hour.'

She brightens up at this and we put on B.B. King, and soon

she's singing like a linty as we scoot down the darkening road towards Prestwick and the airport.

Next time I came back from the platform, Lesley was standing at my door with a grip on the ground beside her. She put one arm round my waist and squeezed, held on like I was holding her up. Her face was swollen, two livid scratches across her forehead. Her right hand was heavily bandaged.

I unlocked the door, put on the heating, looked around. Everything was exactly as I'd left it but colder, down to the last drooping plant and stray cassette box. She hadn't been here.

'What the hell, Les?'

She looked out the window at the garden.

'I got hit,' she said, 'by something smaller than a truck.'

'Bastard. You've not done anything to him.'

Silence.

'Graeme wouldn't hit me,' she said at last. 'Though God knows he's had cause. Anyway, he knows I'd hit him back and harder. The Karate Kid.'

'Then?'

She turned and looked at me. I'm so slow.

'Kim,' she said.

'What's going on here?'

'You haven't sussed yet, Jim?'

The American tinge was deeper ingrained now, like her tan. She had no loyalty to being English, said she didn't know what that meant any more.

'I gave up understanding anything months back.'

She sat down slowly like all her bones ached. She didn't look that young, and certainly not indomitable. None of us were beauties any more.

'After Graeme and I had talked it through – you ever seen a man trying to rip himself down the middle? – I went over to see her in Edinburgh. I thought it was time we straightened things out.'

'Damn tooting right.'

She almost smiled.

'I told her I wasn't really angry at her – '

'True?'

'I guess not. But these things happen, you know?'

'I used to think we could do better than that.'

She brushed back her hair with her good hand. The old jaunty crew-cut had grown and keeled over.

'You'll have a dram, for God's sake,' I said.

She nodded vaguely.

'It's not so surprising it happens among friends,' she said. 'People don't often fall in love with strangers. I was away, Graeme and me have been very untogether. I'm more . . . disappointed.'

'Christ, I felt more than that. Violated. Invaded. Like Grenada or something. Couldn't show it, of course, or I might lose her.'

'Know how you mean,' she murmured but wouldn't look at me.

I poured whisky, wondering what the hell was going on. I hoped she was going to stay with Graeme. Kim had been wobbling on the edge of coming back. I hoped it would be for the right reasons but suspected it wasn't but I'd want her just the same. Love can be fairly humiliating. For the first time I wondered if love was still the word for it.

She held the glass in both hands and stared at the carpet.

'She's not entirely callous, Jimmy. She does feel bad about it. Only she can't say that. There's a right case of knives in that young woman, and she's terrified to look inside. One can't help loving her.'

'I'm working on it.'

'Jimmy.'

She drained the glass, took my hand and held on to it. We sat side by side on the settee like a parody of a courting couple.

'I told her Graeme said he did – does – love her but when I came back here he had to make a choice. Your triangle – well, nice idea but really out to lunch. It's not on. He's much too old-fashioned, you're hanging in because you think you've no choice, she's all over the place with her little ass on fire and her mind on higher things. I told her Graeme had made his choice and it's me.'

'You don't look overjoyed.'

In fact she was mangling my hand.

'It's more complicated than you think.'

She took a deep breath. I put my other arm round her, she was trembling like the platform on a bad day. Whatever was under those bandages must be hurting. I waited, trying to concentrate on her and not myself for a change.

'Jim, we've always been friends, haven't we?'

'Surely.'

'Like brothers?'

'Brother and sister, anyway. Yeah.'

'This is difficult.'

I hadn't the foggiest what she was on about.

'When I told her Graeme wasn't going to see her any more, she went . . . peculiar. Like she was shaking and staring at me, but she wasn't seeing me at all.'

I knew what was coming.

'I felt she could do anything. She was saying things . . . Even her voice was different, some odd accent. I panicked, I told her the truth. I've known it since Orkney – well, before that – but I never meant to say it. Because I love her.'

'Sure, lots of us do that – '

I stopped.

'You heard. The same way you do. I love her and want her like crazy. I have for years.'

I opened my mouth, shut it. We looked at each other.

'Trust me,' she said. 'Believe me.'

And slowly, slowly it began to fit.

'And you told her that?'

'Yes.'

Her shoulders quivered but there were no tears. She was no better at crying than me. We held on to each other. I looked into the weave of her green sweater and tried to make sense.

'Don't even know if she heard me. Or understood. Can you imagine what that's like, Jim? To say you love someone when it's utterly, impossibly, totally not on for them to love you back? Oh, she likes me, and given half a chance I could probably give her a hell of a good time for a night, but love – '

She was shaking under my hands. Not Lesley. Not indomitable, care-less Les.

'So I'd blown it and thought I'd best leave.'

'Oh boy.'

'Right.'

She sat back and stared at me. The room, Dunbar, the rest of the world and the night all round us, had all vanished. Everything narrowed to her naked eyes and the long face radiating grief. No politics, no government, no climbing, just the heart blazing away like a ship going down.

'She went for me. She was holding one of her little wood-carving scalpels and it went through the back of my hand. Otherwise she'd have had my eyes. She's severed a tendon, Jimmy, maybe two.'

I glanced at the bandaged hand. I had a notion cut tendons don't heal. No tendon, no finger movement. I'd seen it once on the platform.

'I mean, she was possessed. She wasn't responsible.'

'What did you do?'

'Hit her. Solar plexus. It's a reflex. I thought I'd killed her, I mean she's so small and light and all. She banged off the wall and fell on the floor. She couldn't breathe. For a moment I thought of mouth-to-mouth . . .'

She laughed, kindof. I winced.

'You see,' Lesley said quietly, 'I do love her. That's why it all hurt so much. Because it was Graeme, not me.'

She leaned forward and spelled it out.

'I wasn't jealous of her – though I guess it was a bit sneaky – I was jealous of *him*. That she wanted him, that he got to sleep with her and hold her and have her love and it's just not fair – '

For a moment, the voice of the English nursery. She closed her eyes.

'Aw shit,' she said, 'I wish I'd stayed in Texas. Gals are tough there.'

Then mercifully she began to sob. Raw at first then more easily if you can call it easy. Of course she wanted Kim, that much made total sense to me. After all, I had for years. I held her and waited for the easing.

'But those flings you had? That guy in the States?'

'I never said those pashes were with men. You all just assumed it and we let you. Maybe that was wrong of us. Sure, of course Graeme knew. It upset him but didn't threaten him.'

'I'd always wondered.'

'He could live with it because it was understood I'd never sleep with another man, and I haven't. He has his own problems – goes back to his mother's death, I guess.'

I poured us another shot of her duty-free Jack Daniels. We sat on the floor leaning back on the settee, gradually leaning against each other as the night went on and the bottle went down, filling in the gaps, the secrets, the distances. Mostly I poured and listened while she drank and talked in snatches, took painkillers and nursed her hand. We were closer than we'd ever been, all pretences stripped away down to the raw original, as though alcohol was some kind of paint-stripper.

Some of the things she said that night float still in my memory, like rafts and bits of timber from a vanished ship.

'. . . I've nothing against penises. Hey, some of my best friends have one! Whatever you think, he's been my closest and most loyal friend. A mate with a prick – well, why not? Sex isn't the problem. Being bi isn't a problem and it's not really about sex. Well that's bull because of course it is, *but* . . .

Thanks. I warn you, when I get drunk I get soft on Country and Western. I start to drawl and cry and sing 'Crazy'.

If I start on 'Stand By Your Man', you must throw me out . . .'

'. . . Sexual ambiguity I can handle, it's not such a big deal to me now. It's passion that tears me apart, right along the dotted line. And I feel that way only about women. A certain kind of woman. Usually tense, skinny, fucked-up, talented. Vulnerable and defensive. Heartless if you like. Recognise her? The only difference is Kim's not Jewish.

And usually straight. So there's this certain kind of woman and only good Lesley can hold her and save her, understand her, stroke her fevered brow at the end of the hard day's grind. Lesley will also show the little darlin where her true sexual interests lie. Good ol' Les . . .

You can guess what they called me at school! That never bothered me. Up your ass, sister. Most of them were dick-heads anyhow. But there was this girl and, yup, she surely broke my heart. Don't believe anyone who tells you love's easier and kinder between women. That's bull. It's the same old heaven and hell, maybe worse because you know each other inside out.

The ones that jump mean it, don't they, Jimmy?

Sure you haven't got any Hank Williams records?'

'. . . I love Graeme. You do too. Don't make faces at me, pal. He loves you too. Sometimes I wished you two would just go to bed together and get it done with. Imagine it in one of those angry male novels he's so keen on. The hard man hero says Well, bugger this and goes to bed with his best mate, who's the only person he really loves anyway. Now that *would* be radical! I look forward to that, but it'll be a while . . .

But the way I love him is *safe*. He's been my refuge. Port in a storm, yeah? Because I don't have a passion for him. I liked him, cared for him, slept with him, respected him, above all he's my friend.

But being in love is terrible. About as sweet as getting ploughed under by a real big one when you only meant to go surfing . . .'

'. . . I could seduce her, like as not. I've thought about it often enough, when it's been late and we've had a few. Oh I've burned for her and never ever made a move. Under the right conditions, like if she was high or lonely or frustrated – sure, she'd probably go through with it. Hell of a lot of straight women would. Do. Her ol' pal Les could give her a damn good time. But there'd be no point, you see? It would just be more hell, because she's straight and I can't change that.

I mean she's got a hetero heart, babe.

Like you and Graeme, but not me. Now I've blown it, even as her friend.

Big dykes don't cry. Aw, shit . . .'

'Get the guitar out, Jimmy. You gotta know 'Lonesome Blues'. Play 'I'm Down to my Last Cigarette'. Sing 'Crying'. I'll do the Orbison, hell my voice is shaking anyhow. Christ my hand *hurts*. 'Love Hurts', let's start with that . . .'

We stumbled upstairs in the wee hours, drunk and played out. Together we made up the bed in the spare room. Nearly everything that could be said, had been. We straightened the duvet and looked across it at each other.

'Hell of a day, huh?'

'No wan of the best.'

Put it down to spending the whole evening talking about love and sex, thinking about her sexuality, trying to draw off some of her pain. I'd known her for years, admired her from the beginning, watching the flash of her red hair and blur of her movements as she went on the attack in the gym. Now I looked at her differently. Maybe this was what had happened with Graeme and Kim.

She looked back at me steadily. Hazel eyes in a pale, tired face. Vulnerability always gets me.

She knew. We could soothe our loneliness and have our revenge. Stick the knife in Graeme. Perfect. We owed nobody.

The slight smile on her lips was oddly apologetic.

I cleared my throat.

'Too obvious,' I said.

'Afraid so. Keep the dick-heads guessing,' She almost smiled. 'G'night, Jimmy. Thanks, ya know.'

'Night, Les.'

I went to bed and felt virtuous.

It was her crying woke me. Even through walls, grief is not a sound you can mistake.

Don't just lie there thinking about it. Do something useful.

I tapped on her door and went in, switched on the light. She lay curled up in a sweatshirt. I sat on the side of the bed, stroked her forearm above the bandages as if my fingers could draw out pain like a skelf.

'Everything hurts so much,' she said simply. She looked about fourteen and finished. I thought, if love can do this to Lesley, God help the rest of us.

'Pillow friends?' I said.

'Please,' she said. 'That would be best.'

She straightened her long legs and I got in.

She stayed. She slept a lot, went to the hospital a couple of times, took too many pain-killers and jumped when the phone rang. It was never for her. I cleared the garden, read and pottered round the house. Neither Graeme nor Kim phoned and somehow we couldn't phone either of them. We were all stranded, waiting for a ship to come by.

The rain came and stayed. I sat at the window for hours, drew the unresolvable equations on the misty pane. *Jimmy loves Kim wants Graeme needs Lesley craves Kim depends on* . . . 'The queer quadrilateral', Leslie called it. It would have been funny but for the stang within.

Sometimes we went out to the pub which gave them something to talk about. We went down to my mum's for a Sunday lunch. She raised an eyebrow when she saw Les' hand, so I filled her in so far as I understood it, which was no distance at all, while Les was out playing with Alec's mob. She shook her head, sighed, didn't offer judgement or advice. She was at an age when little shocked her. Later she took Les into the kitchen, they were in there for ages.

'What was that about?' I asked as we drove back.

'Girls' talk,' she said, and nearly smiled for the first time since Reagan's re-election a week before. 'Your mother's a star. Now I know where you get your nice bits from.'

'What about you?'

She was only beginning to talk about her family. It didn't sound happy.

'Most of me comes from my father, and he's a sports-loving USAF imperialist. You knew he was involved in Greenham? I even saw him once, through the wire. I'm the boy he didn't have. My mother? It would take a fork-lift truck to raise her consciousness.'

Mostly we stayed in. We had long bouts of talking and long exhausted silences. (There are times like this evening, driving through the half-dark with the dozing child, that I want to see her so bad.)

'Has he phoned?' I asked when I came back from shopping to go off-shore again.

'He? Uh, no. No.'

And then I realised it was Kim she was waiting for, and when she didn't phone I think she knew it was down to her. She finally took herself off to Graeme's for a summit conference and I went off-shore feeling hopeful.

Her telegram came from London.

Dear heart it won't work. Have your triangle back. Else black coffee and cigarettes. Going back to Texas. See you loving Hank.

If it hadn't been for Tumshie's reflexes, I'd have had my hands crushed on the pipe deck that night.

'Did you and Lesley – ?' Kim asked later, but for once I didn't answer.

'Pit stop, sprog?'

She stirs then looks at me for a moment as though she's just been born and wonders what it's all about.

Truth is I need a break from this. Sure, I like the half-light when the colours fail and darkness rises along the roadsides like silt and the sky is pale behind the flat trees. I like it when distance is uncertain and depth has nearly disappeared. But like many things I love, it's kinda tiring to navigate.

'Beans and chips,' I offer. 'Don't know about you, but I need a coffee and a pee.'

Her hands wave vaguely as she struggles to sit up.

'Are we there yet?' she says. 'Where is she?'

I turn off the main road south of East Kilbride, onto the wee road that follows the stone walls of these moors, looking for the unexpected inn dad and I once found on a fishing trip. I tell her about it, exaggerating a bit. She likes to hear stories about the past.

When we get to the inn, she turns and looks at me and I know there's a challenge coming. She hides her hand.

'No cheating,' she says. 'You must try to win.'

I promise. Not much gets past her.

We bring our hands round: me scissors, her stone. She knocks her fist against my fingers and laughs delightedly. And as we head for the lit door I think: she's learning. She's learned to repeat herself.

Or maybe she just forgot what happened last time.

The Golden Triangle resumed. Kim oscillated between us but it was not the same as before. It wasn't an experiment in living, just something we were trapped in. When I mentioned Lesley she said they'd talked a bit and there'd been an accident but they'd sorted things out, the way women do. Maybe it was as well she'd gone back to the States and her boyfriend there. Really there wasn't much to say. I was stunned into silence and missed the moment to push her any further. And in truth I was wondering if it was a safe thing to do.

Several times when she was away I went up the stairs to the attic door. I was fairly sure some of her notebooks were still in there. Each time I finally turned away and went back down. I'd promised her privacy. And even if I'd used my key and gone in there, it might well have made no difference.

Inside the inn Rina and I hit the beans and chips and chatter away, but it's too late to stop now, too late to stop thinking about the nights Kim spent in that room alone when I was away.

Kim put the last viewing-box aside. It wasn't rubbish but it was repetition, craft but nothing more.

She switched off the spotlight and laid her head on the table. Maybe for me it's just safety in numbers. I want two men not because my heart's so big but because it's small and shrivelled and scared. My heart's the size of a peanut.

It felt true and the first tendrils began creeping towards her.

She wanted to phone Jimmy but he was off-shore working the

night-shift. Graeme was away for the weekend, climbing with a couple of mates. They'd had a set-to about that but he wouldn't put aside his climbing for her any more than she would her own work for him. She could rage all she wanted but he wouldn't give way. Graeme, well he could turn round and in some fit of conscience drop her any minute and maybe that's what made her heart beat faster. It was very dangerous.

Yet he was capable of love. You just had to dig for it. But she . . .

The fear fastened round her wrists, she felt its cool furry touch on her knees. And the voice in her head, the one that seemed to tell the truth, began to stir.

And Lesley was back in the States. That was a relief in some ways but she missed her. Had Lesley really loved her? She supposed it was possible and other people knew how to love, to give themselves over. She alone was heartless and incapable even of Art. For weeks now she'd made nothing worthwhile at the table and that was the worst. Nothing else could justify her sordid existence.

She swivelled restlessly, trying to break away from what was filling the room, but there was nowhere else to go. Downstairs, outside, it would all be the same. She selected a carving tool, checked the edge with her thumb. What she had done to Lesley was unforgiveable. Of course she'd known for ages Lesley lit up when she was around, hadn't admitted it, had encouraged it, flirted with her even. It was nice to be fancied, she'd played up to it.

She flicked the knife into the air, caught it by the handle on the way down.

Again.

Too easy. She broke people's hearts, cut their hands, they must think she was crazy. There was no excuse, none.

She flipped the knife high, banged her hand palm down on the table, shut her eyes and waited.

She opened her eyes. The tool was embedded, still quivering, in the little bay between her thumb and index finger. Missed by a mile.

Her fear was wrapped around her now, its furry, familiar tendrils spreading from her sick head. She closed her eyes and saw only red. Lesley's hand, the blood so bright, erotic, awesome really, running down over her wrist as she'd bent over her. She should have, could have surrendered then.

She clung to the knife. Hail Mary, mother of God please please help me. She pressed her forehead to the table and fought as her fear bloomed scarlet. She threw at it memories of green places, of beaches, skies, sculptures, Chagall, Jimmy in Orkney, Graeme in Arran. It absorbed them all and then swelled again, and she groaned at the sound of her father's voice shouting from the bedroom, worse than usual, and *Housewives Choice* on the radio in the kitchen as she hesitated across the hall and he called again and she hesitated one unforgiveable moment more and then the crash –

She made it to the loo just in time. When she had thrown up everything that was in her, down to the bilious green, she leaned her forehead on the cool white porcelain. Her fear dwindled back to the seeds that she believed were planted in her brain. They could lie dormant for years but they'd always be there. She could never have children.

She got to her feet, cleaned the basin and stumbled through to the sittingroom. She looked at the whisky Jimmy had left – much too scary. She thought of the phone, no point. She thought of the pub down the road, human company, people who knew her but didn't really. There were at least two men there who would jump at the chance to fuck her the moment Jimmy's back was turned. They'd be crude and brief as that word, and there'd still be the night after and the one after that. Anyway, she'd promised Jimmy: not in his house. Fair's fair.

I could be anybody's and it wouldn't help because I'm nobody's, not really.

She lay on the settee holding the travelling rug and slowly brought her knees up to her chin. Wish I was a wee hedgehog so I could curl around myself and sleep through this and not wake up till it's spring again. She giggled at the silliness of it. She'd be back on top tomorrow. In two days Graeme will be back and next weekend we can go to Arran, just the two of us.

But no one will ever find me, because I won't let them.

My house should have been built on higher ground on better foundations, further up the slope from the harbour. I'd always been vaguely aware of that but chose not to think about it, till one night the wind moved round to the East and backed up the equinoctal tide, and by then it was too late to move or sell up.

I went down to the basement, where water was already oozing in. I bolted the big iron door to the passage that ran into the old harbour wall, knowing that if the water level outside got much higher, it would blow the door off its hinges. But a flooded cellar I could live with, if it would stop at that.

I sat in the kitchen, hoping Kim was secure somewhere, listening to the wind howl, and bracing myself against the battering-ram impact of the biggest waves on my outer wall. The tide had still an hour to run. The house was old but solid, I might get off with a soggy cellar and weakened foundations. Then I saw water sweating up through the floorboards, silently filling the room up to a few inches. Then the swell outside must have receded and the water drained away again, leaving sand and weed on the bare boards.

I hurredly packed books, the kitchen table, the coal bucket, up against the front wall, jammed cloths under the doors, knowing fine if the water level was higher outside than inside, there was no keeping it back. No house was that watertight.

I thought of phoning but there was no point. There must be enough people in trouble all the way down the East Coast on a night like this. Too late for a builder to do anything about it. I sat on, watching the wall and making temporary repairs. If I could hang on till the tide turned, as it must, I'd be in the clear.

The room shook and all round the walls plaster split and fell. Seawater sprayed in through the cracks. A wave swirled round my knees, then retreated, sucking open all the doors. I slammed the doors shut and wedged them and it was then the roar began from way in the distance and I could picture the wave outside coming clear over the harbour with nothing to break it this time, and there was no time to leave by the back because I'd jammed all the doors, and as I was getting to my feet the wall in front of me disintegrated and the sea thundered in –

I woke screaming, hurling the duvet from the bed, and sobbed like a terrified bairn because I was alone in my house and it was all true. My house should have been built on higher ground on better foundations, further away from the sea but it was too late.

'Well, it all sounds terribly civilised again, this triangle of yours,' Alison said and shifted number two bairn to number one breast. 'Very state of the heart.'

'Civilised!' I thumped my forehead off her livingroom wall experimentally. I was being hysterical but it made me feel better. If I exaggerated enough I'd end up laughing.

'My heart's in shreds. My digestion's completely scunnered –

I can't even drink whisky any more. I listen to Country music. I've become an embarrassment. This is serious!'

Through in the kitchen her man Gerry switched channels on the radio and got Lou Reed singing 'Pale Blue Eyes'. He didn't have to do that, nor turn it up so clear and loud.

'Just as well we've got some beer in, then' she said. 'And careful you don't knock the pictures off the wall, doing that.'

'You ask how I feel?' I groped for an adequate word. 'Broken-hearted. Ludicrous, isn't it? There's nae dignity in it. The truth is, I'm fuckin broken-hearted.'

'If that's how you feel, there's dignity in it,' she said. 'And nae need to use language.'

I turned to her with my arms out wide.

'Christ, Alison, what am I going to do?'

Gerry walked in with a tea-towel over his shoulder. He seemed to be dragging one leg slightly, probably injured himself again playing football.

'Suffer,' she said. 'And keep talking with your friends,' she added.

'Good to see you,' Gerry said. 'Pain's what we call experience whose value we ain't understood.'

'For Christ's sake, Gerry,' Alison said as she wrapped the twins away, 'the man's in a right stushie and all you can offer is positive thinking. He loves her.'

He lowered his large, hairy, comfortable bulk into the chair opposite.

'Man, you're not in love, you're in a state of dependence,' he said. 'Like your country. It may once have been healthy but it ain't now.'

I shaded my eyes. Wisdom I did not need.

'Put her aside, Jimmy. Break away. These ties diminish you.'

Alison put her hand on his shoulder.

'But he can't,' she said gently. 'It's not possible, not yet.'

The old lemon squeezer pressed in my chest again. Gerry sighed and got to his feet.

'You'd better stay here then,' he said. 'I suppose this means you're going to keep us up half the night again and flirt with my wife and drink all our Grouse.'

I put my hands wearily over my eyes.

'Everything but the Grouse,' I said. 'Thanks.'

SIXTEEN

Disappearing Gully

I PUSH THE REST of my beans away, feeling none too good, and glance at my watch. She'll land in an hour and a half.

'Let's hit the road, kid.'

She sooks the last of her Coke.

'Soon come,' she says.

It's right dark outside. A whiff of snow off the high moors sets me aching for a moment to be back in the winter hills again. Then in behind that, like a punch in the guts after the smile to the face, comes the way it felt then.

The salted road was a black tawse banged down on Rannoch Moor. Whack! That'll learn you for dreaming, boy. I lit a cigarette and shook my head. A violent culture, sure, and I was part of it.

Early January '85 and at last the snow. Cold and hard outside the pits, and a rough fortnight on the platform, my soberest Hogmanay on record. Cokes and cigars and watching the folk at the Tron Kirk on telly. Still, it had kept me from doing damage once Kim had tossed a coin and gone to spend her New Year with Graeme in Wales.

A hoodie craw tilted across the road, veered into the wilderness in the heart of Scotland. I thought of Lesley in Vermont, skiing with two fingers of her right hand stuck out in a powerless V sign, instructing the young and wealthy . . .

The white palm dipped under the blow and I wound down into Glencoe, towards ancient grudges and betrayals, hands tight and careful on the wheel.

I pushed into the Clachaig with my climbing gear and there were MacBeth, Gypsy, old bauldy-heid Andy Clackmannan, the poet with her rinky-tink mandola. A wave from Cathy and Shonagh, and Nick Fairer up from London with his side-kick Slide. My old, abusive, trusted winter climbing mates. Shake hands all round, our first meeting since the end of last winter.

'So how's it going, youth?' from Andy.

'Like *A Bat Out Of Hell*,' I said, 'way over the top.'

Ach, patter, patter. Still, he chuckled and made room for me.

'Well,' Gypsy drawled, 'didn't expect to see you *this* weekend.' He winked, nodded towards the bar.

He was standing there, back turned, neat in denim. My favourite Glaswegian, my old pal.

I should have walked out and driven to my brand new friend in Perth. But they were watching and they all knew, of course, no secrets in the climbing world. I stood like a stookie, trying not to show.

'McGlashan!' Gypsy shouted. 'Reckon you owe this man a pint.'

Graeme's lips moved like he was trying to whisper to me across the distance.

They were all watching. Show a moment's weakness and they're on you like wolves and as merciless. Except when it got really bad, then you could trust them with your life if not your lover, way beyond other folk.

'The usual,' I said and sat down among my friends, kept my hands out of sight a while.

He passed over the pint, sat down opposite. I raised my glass, nodded acknowledgement. Why the hell wasn't he still in Wales with her?

Then she walked in the door, brushing snow from her fleece jacket. Her eyes went to me, back to him, flicked over the expectant faces round the long table. MacBeth drew on his fag and looked down at the floor, squeamish at heart.

'Happy New Year, glad you made it,' Kim said and put her arm briefly round my shoulder, kissed my ear, then sat at the far end of the table, away from us both. She had her moments.

'So, you fixed with anyone for tomorrow, a ghràidh?' Shonagh asked. 'The Ben's in good nick.'

'I'm not fixed, m'eudail,' I managed.

I'd come up on impulse, to climb with whoever was around, or solo if necessary. My house was a wilderness till she next returned.

'Graeme's on his tod,' Cathy said. 'Why don't you two team up?'

I glanced at Graeme. He didn't want to, nor did I.

'Sure, why not?' I said.

'Suits me,' he said quietly. 'Where?'

Gypsy leaned back in his chair. 'Ice axes drawn at dawn!'

He laughed and Graeme looked down at his hands. Small and strong, a bit hacked about, the hands that pleased and shared my lover. I watched myself smash the glass and put it to his face. A violent culture, sure, and I was part of it.

'Disappearing Gully,' I said and sat back while the poet fine-tuned her mandola and sang 'I Loved a Lass'. Just once her eyelid flickered my way. I took out my guitar and in Lesley's memory bopped through 'Walking After Midnight', and for the first time accepted it was down to me.

Kim's hand on my sleeve at the bar.

'For God's sake be careful!' she hissed. 'The two people I love most in the world.'

'Me too,' I said, 'but my heart's not big enough. I think I resign.'

She stared at me. Hail and farewell.

'Dinna fash yersel,' I said. 'I'll take care of him.'

We trudged apart up through the dark towards the foot of the Ben. Flurries of fresh snow swirled through my head-torch beam, mesmeric and bonnie but not a good sign. Six in the morning and a wild world. Way back Graeme's light bobbed and weaved, coming on slowly. He was a rock jock, not a mountaineer. Let him suffer.

I slugged up through deepening snow, wide-awake and calculating the next moves.

Dawn at the C.I.C. hut below the great crags, mist, a smirr of snow driven in the gale. A grey, bleak, unpromising day but climbing's no dafter than roping your happiness to someone else. Not her fault, she hadn't asked me too. It just grew that way.

I hunched in the lee and weighed the odds. This was no place for playing hard men. They just get killed, and that's dumb not tough. If I pictured Disappearing Gully rightly, it would chuck down spindrift but nothing bigger. Getting off the top could be the hardest, a pure compass job in a full gale. Mountaineering, not climbing. For someone who hadn't been out much in bad conditions, someone like Graeme, it would be fairly desperate.

Ho hum.

On the other hand, we could just say sod this for a game of crazies and go back down to spend the day in the chalet with friends swopping yarns. Aye, and him and her, all day. If she touched him when I was there, I'd be shredded. Why even pretend to be tough?

Then again, I'd long wanted to do Disappearing Gully, and who better to do it with? Why, we might climb into it and just vanish altogether.

He staggered up, dropped his sack and a few curses. He looked pretty shagged, maybe she'd kept him up late.

'Does this make ony sense, pal?'

We talked it over but we were always going to do it. We strapped on crampons, took out an axe each and groped up into the Coire na Ciste. It was not an uplifting day but still better than being in Fort William in the rain. I led on past the Douglas Boulder, waiting for short breaks in the mist. Found the big gully then paced carefully.

Yup, this must be it. Disappearing Gully, a modern hard Grade V. A messy icefall soared into a dim chute then nothing. Spindrift slid down and blew in our faces with depressing regularity. Cathy and Shonagh had described it as 'interesting', meaning at the top end of my abilities. If it wasn't in good nick, we wouldn't get far.

We prepared in silence. I sorted out my rack of ironmongery along the waist loops of my harness. I took my time about it, getting into precision mode. Took out slings and karabiners, a screw-gate, the descendeur, still clumsy in my mitts but slowly remembering how this went. Finally I roped up.

'She's a bit twitchy about this,' he said.

He stood with his end of the rope in his mitt.

'Really,' I said.

'She says you've resigned.'

'Yup.'

The longest look at the foot of Disappearing while snow settled on our helmets like daft crowns.

'Yup, I've decided to untie. You two are on your own.'

'Jim, we never meant it tae be like this.'

I could kill him for that 'we'. I clipped a couple of ice-screws and drive-ins to my rack.

'But I'm crazy about her.' His voice was hoarse. 'Canni let her go.'

'Fuck solidarity, eh?' I said. 'No wonder you're losing the Miners' Strike.'

'Whit you haiverin aboot?'

'Need a couple of spare friends,' I said. 'Size 3 and 4.'

He handed over the spring-loaded cams and I clipped them in.

He hesitated then tied himself in, put me on belay. We were connected till the end of the day. I put my mitts through the wrist loops of both axes, looked up and took a few long breaths. Christ, it's a steep one. We loved each other once and we blew it.

'Climbing,' I said, and began.

Gradually I remembered how to do this. My axes investigated, stabbed, found good ice. Tested it, moved on up, breathing a bit fast. Nothing wrong with adrenalin when appropriate, like for fleeing, or fighting.

I hacked out some loose rubbish and it slithered down onto Graeme's bowed helmeted head. Left foot, right front points in, right axe lodged high, test, lean out, left axe in, pull up. Method and faith and some improvisation – climbing's like life, Cathy used to say, only easier. Her life was as much of a shambles as mine, but she sure was a better climber.

Forty feet up I found the crack I was looking for. After a bit of jiggling the nut held good. I clipped the rope through and relaxed a little. Down below, Graeme's red helmet glimmered through the mist and spindrift. He would stay there, patiently, until I signalled him.

I eased away from my temporary security.

It was slow going, the route not being in very good nick, just loose choss. I scraped, huffed and puffed, struck a few sparks as I groped from one iffy position to the next.

Time passed – the hardest, the best. Serious play. My world narrowed to textures of snow, opacities of ice, spikes of black rock inches from my face, the axes dirling in my mitts, the red and green ropes swooping down between my feet.

'Of course it's escapism,' Shonagh would say cheerfully. 'But at least the mountain isn't impressed by our bullshit.'

A tough Skye lassie, an ambitious hard climber with a streak of the necessary craziness, yet I'd seen her leave the Clachaig bunkhouse in tears over a man.

I pushed up on a nice mantelshelf move, whacked in the axes, leaned back and looked up. I'd seen few uglier scenes. But I could exit out of this, I could live without Kim. It had been less than six years together. A rough calculation suggested we must have made love some five hundred times. Very nice but no big deal.

I got a gobfull of spindrift and heard Shonagh laugh. Bullshit, Jimmy! Yeah yeah. Couple of times I'd seconded her the winter before, an education that. She'd climbed a blinder but confessed her blues all the way back. We'd sat in the car outside the Clachaig till she'd stopped greitin and was ready to put her best face on and walk through the door . . .

My calves were starting to shake from too much teetering on front-points, and upper arms were burning and weak above my head. I'd surely run out most of the rope. Five hundred times seemed unlikely. I could remember perhaps a dozen occasions, but those would never leave me be.

Break-time.

A flared crack took a poor friend. Found some okay ice and got a drive-in half way in, tied it off. That seemed about it for belays so I clipped myself in and kicked out a ledge of sorts. Down looked fairly grim but it usually does.

He wouldn't hear me through the wind, so I sent down the sequence of tugs we'd established over the years. Took in the ropes and put him on belay, stuck a frozen Mars Bar in my gob, and waited.

He came up damn slowly. This was more awkward than anything he'd done in winter before, a big adjustment from hard rock. Sweat began congealing inside my thermals. A long pause. Finally he signalled for tight rope, slightly panicky, I thought.

I grinned and nearly dragged him up the awkward step. Suffer a bit, you bastard.

That wasn't very nice. Then again, I wasn't very nice. Certainly not the easy-going, reliable – heh, be honest, passive – Good Guy I'd tried to be for her for years. I was a howling spindrift of hateful thoughts and low-grade feelings. Not a good guy at all.

His fall was sudden. It jerked me forward and the friend flew out. The drive-in wobbled, held. The ledge started to crumple. Christ's sake, man!

The strain stopped. He'd re-attached himself to the face. I quickly jammed the friend back in, stomped out a marginally better ledge and, sweating now, faced out into the grey and took the rope in as he moved.

He appeared at last out of the gloom, grunting, swearing to himself.

'Steep?'

He rubbed a frozen mitt across his face, brushed ice off his eyebrows.

'Nae real. Bleedin nightmare.'

I nodded, shifted over and let him clip in to the belay.

'Thanks, pal. You caught me quick, but.'

'Ye near cowped me.'

He grimaced. We were now well into the throat of the gully. It soared up into the grey, looked overhung but probably wasn't. Little spindrift avalanches gathered on our shoulders.

'What now?'

Good mountaineering is knowing when to say No. The triangle had had its moments. It could have worked.

'Push on,' I said. 'If it gets much worse, we abseil off. We can still crack this.'

He hesitated. With balaclava and helmet, each of us showed only a few square inches round mouth and eyes, and I watched his carefully.

'Ach hell,' he muttered, 'why not?'

'Consider the alternative,' I replied. It was one of our old routines.

'Sweet Fanny Adams!' he supplied the line and it suddenly seemed unfortunate. Kim, her body, her sex, passed between us and the moment was gone.

'Aye, well,' he said. 'Right then.'

He didn't like it but he was thrawn, right through.

He started on up, awkward and unsure. He wasted a lot of time looking for belays – the long run-outs of winter climbing made him uneasy. Tension twanged down the ropes to me.

One little twitch, I thought, and he'd be off. And so would I, most like. So what? In time you can live without anyone, of course you can, but there's no joy in it.

Time passed. Occasional scraping sounds came down with showers of ice. I thought I heard a muffled shout, tightened instinctively, saw something grey fall past me, maybe just a clod of snow.

Waiting's the hardest. Admit you wake wishing you hadn't, drag yourself out onto the scaffolding deck, work on automatic day or night, and all the while your anger grinds like glass in the gullet, cuts deeper every time you swallow it. And you cannot shout or skelp her, not even be angry, because you hope to keep her. And these images of her delight in him . . .

I hunched my shoulders and waited. A culture of stoic suffering is limiting but has its uses.

Hours later, tugs came down the rope. I disengaged myself from the stance and stiffly put my axes to the test.

The climbing wasn't too bad but he took the slack in poorly. I kept having to stop and wait for the rope to come tight again. What was he playing at? The crux was awkward, with poor ice. A corner pushed me out into space, I felt like a bone stuck in the throat of the gully as it tried to swallow me down. Christ's sake, take in the slack!

Finally I pulled up into the ice cave, none too chuffed. Then I saw his right hand was bare, a white stiff claw.

'Dropped me glove,' he said hoarsely.

'Jesus.' So that's what had whirled down past me. No wonder he'd had trouble taking in the ropes. He could lose his fingers.

'Give me that,' I said.

He held out his hand. It felt like wood. I unzipped my jacket and carefully slid his white fingers under my oxter.

After a few minutes I gave him his hand back and he stuck it inside his pile jacket and stood there grunting, almost sobbing. Hot aches can make hard men cry. No shame in that.

Finally he looked across at me. His lashes were clogged with tears and snow, the dark eyes stared out from a long way back. He was being stripped to the bone and it hurt.

We were halfway up a serious route, the light was already dimming. He'd lost a glove and could lose a few fingertips and then he wouldn't climb too well again, nor paint, nor touch Kim the same.

I turned my back to him.

'Bottom of my sack,' I said. 'There should be a spare.'

He rummaged awkwardly, found it. Between us we jammed the Dachstein mitt over his half-thawed hand.

'One of hers,' I said. 'Good thing you've small paws.'

He almost smiled, I kinda shrugged.

'Keep working the hand,' I said. 'The belays here aren't good enough for abseiling down. We'll have to top out tonight.'

Coming out of that cave was hard, the ice steeper than I'd ever known but quality stuff. I climbed as fast as possible before the short day ended.

Then at the crux the ice went wrong. I tapped gently and it sheared off in plates. The snow on either side was just choss, and I sent it tumbling down the chute.

I made a couple more edgy moves and then ground to a stop.

I was thirty feet above my last runner which was iffy anyway, no secure points of contact and nowhere left to go. I couldn't reverse the last two moves nor go on. All I could do was bide in this impossible position till both of us froze to death, or let myself fall and pray the runner held.

I let my face fall against the ice.

Okay. I looked up and at full stretch scraped loose snow off a nick in the rock, just got the tip of my pick on it. All I need is just one good placement, one secure point of contact. Please.

It took five minutes to prove there was no such thing.

I settled for wedging my other pick into a crack off to the left, and twisted hard. It might hold. I'd have to torque hard on it while pulling absolutely straight on the right or it would skite off that nick and I'd be away, probably kill us both, for all the belays below were lousy.

Some of my friends could do it, but me, I was out of my league.

I closed my eyes.

'You're the two men I love most in the world,' she said.

I enquired within whether I was a man or a spineless invertebrate and received the usual answer.

Nevertheless I was going for it and pulling with all the power and control left in me. I rose up over the bulge, careful, careful, put my right boot out, lodged one front point. The axe wobbled, I was twisting desperately, pulling up. Left foot round and up, up, scraping on the lip, another inch, yeah! onto the ledge and stood right up on it and sank one axe high into pure ice, then the second, and stood there a moment, heaving. And as I powered on up towards the exit that had to exist, I was weeping.

I hauled him up that last pitch, mostly on tight rope. Didn't think he'd be too concerned about dignity at this stage. As he struggled with the crux I wasn't entirely in my right mind and idly considered untieing from him.

No point. I'd seen this movie somewhere before – two men, struggling on a mountain for a woman. But that was all old choss from the black and white days. Climbing wasn't like that. Kim wasn't like that. Men like that were dated as Mastodons in ice even if they didn't know it yet. No point at all.

He floundered through the cornice break and stood in front of me on the summit plateau, swaying slightly, caked in snow. At other times we might have hugged, the way we used to do after something specially gnarly and good.

'The Old Man of Hoy will be a piece of duff after this,' he mumbled. His jaw was frozen.

'Let's see the hand,' I said.

He pulled off Kim's mitt, I turned on my head-torch to see better. His hand was blotchy and red, but only the fingertips were white. He'd lose some skin, maybe the odd dead nerve, but he'd be okay. Better than Lesley, for sure.

'You played a blinder, pal,' he said and held out his hand. 'I'll leave her be.'

'Go to hell,' I said. 'She's no yours to give.'

He turned away and slowly walked out right to the edge of the cornice. He was a crazy man. It could break off any minute. Then I remembered we were of course still tied together and with me securely belayed he was risking nothing, just making gestures.

Then he stopped, turned to face me in the dimness, and slowly began to untie.

So I had to get off the belay, and stomped towards him through the wind and horizontal snow. I stopped a few feet short of the edge.

'Christ, you live dangerously, pal.'

He said nothing, just waited.

'You mad bastard,' I said. 'It's too late for that.'

'What am I tae dae?' He sounded bewildered.

'Win the next sodding Election, for all I care.'

'But can ye understaun it?'

'I understand it,' I said. Forgive is something else. 'Now can we get out of here?'

I turned and started plodding away. A pause, and then he followed me.

Working fast, we stuffed the gear away and tied in close to each other. It was now proper dark and we were alone in a winter storm on top of the Ben. I tried to hold the compass steady in my head-torch beam while the wind thrashed us. One hundred paces at 240 degrees then switch to 290 degrees and plough on towards the Red Burn descent. Miss the turn and you're over the edge; drift too far left and you're into Five Finger Gully, which is avalanche-prone and desperately dangerous.

'Now we do everything right,' I said.

Then we set off on the bearing. He broke trail in front, I followed with the compass, using him as a sight-line to hold our course when the wind blew us sideways. We were aiming for a hundred yard gap over a distance of three-quarters of a mile in a world without definition or horizon, and we had to walk that line without error.

It was hard, but nothing compared to what we do to each other.

Four hours later we dropped like sacks of tatties into my car and sat unable to speak or move. A full winter storm on Ben Nevis can be survived but scarcely comprehended. Me, I was wabbit, scunnered, dumfounert, forjeskit, then just weary beyond words.

He slumped back in the passenger seat with his eyes closed, arms hanging down at his sides. Melting ice dripped from his mitts. Even crossing the golf course we'd ricocheted around like pin-balls, slammed up against the fence and clung to it for the rest of the way.

I straightened up and fumbled the key into the ignition.

'Didni know it could be so hellish.' He tugged her mitt off with his teeth and cautiously waggled his fingers. A touch of frost-nip on two tips. 'Reckon I owe you wan.'

I giggled, began coughing, nearly threw up. He sat there nodding away like he had Parkinson's. Neither of us was entirely in his right mind.

'By God you do! But I'll settle for a pint and a shepherd's pie at the Clachaig.'

I manoevred cautiously out of the Siberian car park. After all, we're alive and these things happen. That's why they happen. Now let the bullshitting commence.

We walked more or less upright into the Clachaig around closing time. The place was packed and storm-bound, serious jollification squeezed within four walls. Drink, music, laughter, abuse and flirtation, all the human things. Outside for miles on end was the wilderness we'd struggled through. For a moment it blew in the door with us.

'Here come the long and the short of it!' the poet shouted. I wished she'd save her wise-cracks for her poetry.

'Shut that bleedin door!' Gypsy yelled.

Relief on the faces of our friends round the long table. I'd have been worried too. She looked like she was going to be sick. We were just too far apart for her to touch us both at the same time. She hugged him first and then me. It just fell that way.

'Don't you ever do that again,' she hissed. 'I'll no be a climber's widow.'

Graeme and I looked at each other.

'But you're no married,' I said.

'That's what you think,' she said and stomped off to the bar.

We dumped our sacks and sat down at the table to general abuse. Seeing the weather coming, they'd all had the good sense to do short routes or pack it in early.

'Dè a thachair?' Shonagh asked, but I buried my face in a pint to give myself time to decode that one.

'Diabhlaidh,' I managed at last. Hellish was about it.

'Thought you two had had it,' Andy Clackmannan murmured. 'I was hoping for your record collection.'

'But did you do the route?' Shonagh insisted.

I looked over at Graeme.

'Aa the way,' he replied. 'But I'd rather hae been in Fort William.'

We related our wee epic in the climbing manner – playing down the difficulties, exaggerating our fear and incompetence. She sat massaging his hand while I concentrated on the other end of the table. The poet pushed her granny glasses up onto her fringe, glanced at me.

'Maybe an old codger like you will ken The Incredible String Band's "October Song",' she said and began. Only Clackmannan and I were old enough to know those words, and remember a time of soaring hopes however misplaced, of a joy now buried under winter. We sang as best we could, through choked throats, fortunate or otherwise.

Then Shonagh sang unaccompanied the old Gaelic heartbreaker 'Cumha na Cloinne', the Lament for the Children, and that about wrapped it up for me. After the shepherd's pie I went behind the bar and made a phone call, had a more or less satisfactory response. I came back and announced I was offski, was informed I was a crazy man. Eleven o'clock on a Saturday night, up since five in the morning and a howling blizzard outside – what's the hurry?

I kept my eyes averted from my own little corner of hell where Kim sat stroking his hand.

'Got a hot date in Perth,' I said, 'and the snowplough's just gone through.'

173

Shonagh shook her head and whispered in my ear.

'Come see me soon, a ghràidh. We'll do some easy routes together. Feuch gu fon thu mi. Promise you will.'

'Carson nach fon thusa mise?' I hacked my way through that lovely language.

'Keep the day job, doll. But thanks for trying.'

'Yeah, think I'd better listen to that cassette again.'

'Stick at it. Give Perth a good time, but remember where your friends are. Beannachd leat.'

'Aidh, beannachd leat.'

A good mate. As well I wasn't her kind of trouble, nor she mine. So I said my goodbyes, thanked MacBeth for the chalet doss. I was running on empty and desperate to get out of there.

Kim followed me out the door. We stood in the porch watching the snow blitz past. The melt dripped from her chopped dark hair.

'Like the ear-rings,' I said.

'He gave me them. Months back. I hope you're not affronted.'

'Haven't seen them before.'

The snow whirled past like some unwritten contract ripped into millions of pieces.

'I always took them off when I came to see you. Put on your ones instead. I forgot to change yours once and he went moody on me all weekend.'

I laughed quietly, then she did too.

'Do you have to, Jimmy?'

'We're not big enough. At least, I'm not.'

'Maybe it's just a fling,' she said into my shoulder. 'I'm oscillating like crazy.'

'I'd better away. My friend's expecting me.'

I brushed her lips. A dream, however braw and persuasive, is still only a fine example of a dream.

'Can I still come and see you?'

I stopped half-way to the car. She looked so small and weary my heart went to her. I wished she wouldn't do that.

'If you want to.'

I slung my gear in the back and set off before the road ahead vanished completely.

I played cassettes loud for energy and company. So wabbit I was, hallucinating with it, only the hands on the wheel felt mine.

When the snow plough turned off at the end of Rannoch Moor, I'd had it but pressed on anyway. Visibility was down to a few yards and sure enough I finally missed the road and buried the car in a ditch.

I mentally apologised to Perth and reached in the back for my sleeping bag.

Double yellow lights crept up from behind. I wound down the window and looked back. A Land Rover with snow chains. It stopped, the window came down and the inside light went on and a bull-like head peered out. Our old pal Mick DeTerre. I wasn't even surprised.

'Hi, man.'

'Kim fucked off then?'

We were winding slowly but steadily along Loch Earn. I grunted. He laughed quietly, put his paw on my arm.

'So it goes, man.'

So it seems.

'One crazy woman,' he said, 'but alright.'

I thought that was rich coming from him and said so. He laughed again.

'The Struggle continues.'

He asked after Joan. I said far as I knew she was living quietly in Shetland, running a salmon farm, sailing, being celibate. She was involved with Amnesty and the Church in Salvador, wrote a lot of letters and co-ordinated campaigns. I'd scarcely heard from her. He nodded several times.

'Yeah yeah,' he said quietly.

'Still got the guns?'

'Under my feet, as always.'

He tapped the floorboards with his Doc Martens, clicked his teeth.

He woke me. Lights in the distance. Perth. I checked my watch. Two in the morning.

'Is it a woman?'

I nodded, no energy to speak. My thermals were stinking. He stopped the Land Rover in a lay-by, switched on the light.

'Can't disappoint the lady.'

He laid out two generous lines of cocaine on a map case, looked at me and grinned.

'The guerilla's friend,' he said. 'And the lover's. We all have our roles to play.'

Liz opened the door. I was swaying but my head was now clear as ice, the untrustworthy kind. My new friend was in a towelling dressing gown, holding a book and looking warm, sleepy and rumpled. She smelled of bed and coffee and I longed to sink into her.

'A boring weekend so far,' she said. 'Went to a party and nearly got laid but thought of this new AIDS thingy and went to bed with Raymond Chandler instead. Yourself?'

'Eventful,' I said.

She hesitated.

'You'd better come in then.' She sniffed. 'Boy, do you need a bath.'

I opened my eyes. I was wearing Liz' dressing gown, in the hall, sitting propped against a radiator. She was slumped and snoring gently across my knees, auburn hair over her face. She looked vulnerable as we all do sleeping, though she said she could look after herself. I'd been known to say daft things like that too.

I smoothed her hair back, lifted the brandy glass I appeared to have in my hand, and toasted the wall in front of me. We'd been good to each other, it wasn't passion but there are other ways. There'd be Sunday breakfast on Sunday afternoon, then a walk, the papers, then more bed.

I stared at the white wall. Disappearing Gully. Soon I'd wake her and we'd get back to bed. Just sharing what there was to be shared, both of us hoping for more but guessing it wouldn't be with each other.

I sat on a while longer, curiously and briefly at peace, considering the movie so far, considering the lives we'd lost.

Here she comes, not so very late, through 'Arrivals'. The child breaks from me, runs under the barrier and into her arms. Assorted wifies smile and nod, a grave young man leaning on the rail looks like he's going to burst into tears. I go to meet her as all my prepared spontaneous quips go out of my head. It's been a fair while, an eternity by child's time.

We hug, her ear warm on mine, her breath on my neck. We hold each other long and close enough to be sure that the other's real, lightly enough to reiterate our limits. Irina clings to us both, babbling away her green coat and my Grand Slam T-shirt, and I imagine we make a pretty family picture.

'Welcome back,' I say.

'Good to be back,' she says. She's tired but her eyes hold mine and mean it.

Rina sits on the luggage trolley as we wheel it to the door. Lesley looks to me over her head.

'Thanks for holding the fort, Jimmy.'

'Ach, the Apache's settling down now. But I'm glad of the reinforcement.'

She nods.

'The Apache's had a hard time,' she says carefully. 'I'm here to do the right thing.'

SEVENTEEN

Stone breaks scissors

THERE'S A PAUSE as we load her cases into the car. This will take some getting used to.

She's let her hair grow, long and red and loose.

'What happened to the butch crop, then?' I murmur.

She laughs, more soberly than she used to.

'I've given up protecting people – except you, Scottie,' she adds to the child who's clinging to her long legs. 'Like the leather jacket, Jimmy. You given up old fogeydom?'

'Ach, tweed jacket, leather jacket – same difference. Still soft and squishy underneath.'

I take it off and hand it to her. She tries it on and crouches to check herself in the wing mirror, then flips the collar up and looks again. Tries a sneer.

'It suits you.'

'Yeah, the Wild One.' Her American accent has nearly driven out the old boarding school. She caresses the sleeve. 'Feels great.'

'Thought you'd quit that scene.'

'Oh, I can handle it once in a while.' She shrugs her shoulders deeper into the jacket and my stomach turns over, for it's Graeme's gesture. 'This fits great across the shoulders.'

'Have it. No, really. As a welcome back present.'

'Are you going away?' Rina asks anxiously.

Les crouches down and looks her in the eye, strokes her hair.

'One of us will always be here, darlin. You can depend on it.'

'What's depend?' she demands.

Lesley hesitates, glances at me.

'It means you can trust. I promise. Always.'

She considers this, looking from one of us to the other, then silently gets into the back seat. Lesley raises her eyebrows. Talk about it later. As I turn to open the driver's door, I feel her fingers brush the back of my neck.

'Thanks for the jacket,' she says. 'I'll think of it as a loan. You can have it back anytime.'

'Ach well, we're all on loan.'

'Even her?'

'Especially her.'

'I know that.'

'But till then . . .'

'Yeah.'

Now we're on our way home, the child's mood changes. She's high as an untethered balloon, bouncing up and down in the back seat next to Les. Tears before nightfall, my mum would say. The past bears down behind us with its muckle blinding headlights while I keep one eye on the road and another on the rear-view mirror.

They're playing Scissors, Paper, Stone. The child's a fanatic. It helps take her mind off things. Lesley wins.

'Best of three,' Rina says.

Lesley, who's been made to promise to try her hardest, wins again. The child thinks about it.

'Best of five,' she announces.

And I couldn't resist trying one more time, not once Kim suggested it.

When I got her note asking me to come and see her, important, soon as I was on-shore, I couldn't wait another week. If I'd worked that day I would have broken my hands or legs or worse, for my concentration was shot. The last months had pulled me tight as the reeds round Lesley's fist back on Orkney; one more flex and I'd break.

So I arranged a twist-off. It wasn't so hard to do, though as an engineer it hurt. Small hours of the morning, under the lights of the drill floor, part in shadow and nearly alone as the next section of pipe was being taken up on the derrick, instead of giving the final lock I slackened back a couple of bolts on the drill string. Sure enough, just as we were ending our shift the drill pipes separated and left the shaft plugged a few hundred feet down. A classic twist-off. It would take a few days and a lot of money to extract this cock-up, and they'd send us home meanwhile.

As we were about to go under the shower, Marshall the drilling supervisor gripped me at the elbow, the way my father used to.

'I don't know what you're about, Jimmy, but you take a break. A very long break, right?'

I nodded, couldn't look him in the eye. He'd get it from the Company Man, and I regretted that. Still I was grinning as I stood under the shower washing off the grease and dirt for the last time.

I was choppered out that evening with the rest of the crew. I looked back at that glittering hulk that screwed the planet and powered my car and extracted Scotland's oil. As it dwindled below I thought: Yup – boom-time's over and we all got shafted.

The headlights from the juggernaut behind are blinding. I wish it would overtake or back off. In the rear seat they're now on the best of twenty. At least this game has done a lot for her early counting. Rina wins the last one and now it's ten each.

'A draw,' Lesley says. 'That's a good result.'

'Again,' the child insists.

'Are you sure?'

'Yes.'

'Last time, then.'

A long pause in the back.

'Stone breaks scissors,' Rina shouts then slumps knackered and content against Lesley, who puts her arms round her, folds her in. In the mirror they look so right it hurts.

'What is jealousy?' she pipes up. Then, like she'd been saving this one for ages, 'What are angels?'

I shake my head, listen as Leslie does her best to find a straight and simple answer, though she seems to be describing envy not jealousy, and good people not angels. Kim would have known those differences.

I say nothing, for the worst is coming up behind and I accelerate, trying to keep it all at a bearable distance.

'What's the worst thing I could say now, the very worst thing?'.

She lay half beneath him. His cock and then his soul began to dwindle.

'I wasn't thinking of you.'

She said it to the wall, with just enough emphasis on 'you'.

They lay across her single bed-sit bed. Through the wall Marley was singing 'Don't you worry about a thing', and that song was ruined forever. She sat up and pulled her T-shirt down over small breasts at least three had yearned to receive.

'I'm sorry,' she said, which was rare. She looked miserable or maybe just embarrassed. 'I shouldn't have dragged you up here. I just hoped that we . . .'

She rolled off the bed, pulled up her knickers and jeans. She'd been hoping for what – a flash of lightning? Revelation?

'This is sordid,' she said to the floor. 'I'd hoped if we could . . .'

She re-tied her laces, shrugged on the old cord jacket. She glanced in the mirror, bent her head to one side then the other in that tender, efficient female gesture, then laid the two small Golden Triangle ear-rings on the shelf.

'I've lost my best friend too, you know,' she told the mirror.

By the time he'd finished turning that one over, she was at the door and looking back at him.

'I've got to meet some friends from the gallery,' she said. 'We shouldn't see each other for a fair while. Now the strike's over, I'll be spending more time at Graeme's, see how it goes. We argue all the time, but there's a spark there. My work needs . . .' She shrugs. 'Nae excuse. If you've blown it on the rigs, think of it as an opportunity to do something new.'

Her hand on the door handle, him trying to signal across the distance between them.

'Not again,' she said carefully. 'I'm afraid you must take that as meaning forever.'

Later he got up, went through to the bathroom and marvelled at the absence of tears. That *forever* echoed on a bit, though.

He studied her little jars and bottles on the shelf. He opened and sniffed a perfume and for a moment possessed her.

He looked up and saw himself in the cabinet mirror. Ravaged, he thought, you look well and truly fucked over. Mr Good Guy, Mr Understanding. Look at you. A right desperate, pathetic bastard. Jump every time –

He picked up her toilet bag, dug in his nails and ripped it apart. More tubes and bottles showered into the sink, hairgrips, her pills. He slashed a few tubes with her nail file, looked up, didn't like what he saw, swatted everything off the glass shelf. Jars, ear-rings, glass animals smacked off the wall. Smashed the perfume bottle under his heel, put an elbow through the mirror. Glass showered into the bath, the cabinet slumped, he grabbed with both hands and heaved it off the wall, broke it over the cistern then smashed, squashed, bent and broke anything in sight till he was on his knees heaving against the bath. He saw her diaphragm container. Opened it. It looked up at him like a yellow rubber eye or a whale's rolled-up condom. Anyway, she'd said she was back on the Pill again though she didn't like chemicals. Babies were the last thing she wanted.

Saw Lesley's diamante brooch winking on the floor. Picked it up, jabbed once, closed the container, drop-kicked it into touch.

Then he emptied his wallet for damages, slammed the door and ran down the stairs. He crossed the Meadows, blind, bumped into a bench, cursed it and sat down and wept for the third time in his so-called adult life. He couldn't stop greiting and he could go no further.

I have to pull in, get out of the car and let something whoosh by me.

'Are you alright?' Lesley asks. The child's dropped off, cuddled into the lining of the jacket.

'Yeah. Just need some air for a minute.'

In the distance is the glow from the city I'll always think of as Graeme's town. I take a deep breath of night wind, feeling the wet driven into my face, and go blank for a while.

Back inside I roll the third cigarette of the day, one for each leg of the drive, a fourth allocated for bed-time. Lesley wrinkles her nose but says nothing. Over the years we've accepted each other's strange habits.

'Has she been affected at school?' she says quietly.

'Not that her teachers notice. Maybe a little subdued.'

'She's bright.'

'And beautiful. Can't imagine where she gets it from, can you?'

We're talking half in whispers, as though Rina might be eavesdropping. Perhaps she is. Lesley runs her powerful hand up my neck, kneads the tension there.

'Can't you? Look, I'm sorry I couldn't get back sooner, what with the contract.'

'I've enjoyed the time. I got into work most days, except when she was sick, dropped her off at school. Mum and Alec's wife helped out. Weekends are knackering but basically she's a joy. You don't have to stay longer than you want.'

We're still awkward. Politeness doesn't suit us. This will take a while but we have to start somewhere. Her hand gives a final squeeze and drops away.

'But it's not a solution. Not best for her.'

'Nope.'

'Well, then.'

'Thanks.'

'Shucks.'

I let my shoulders drop. That feels better.

'And romance?' Casual-like.

'Sorted now. I've made my decision, though it's hard leaving the States.' She leans back, sighs. 'Dependence, independence, I don't know.' A long silence. She's looking shattered now, jet lag, and I'm only half here.

'Did she ask for the pussycat brooch or was it your idea?'

'Hers.'

She shakes her head.

'Mary Mother of God. She'll need it explained some day.'

'I already am.'

'Huh?'

I leave it, settle my shoulders back and drive on. Soon she sleeps. I watch the headlights swing and illuminate, like a film projector's beam, the darkest scene.

EIGHTEEN

Shetland

HE SAILED TO Shetland near the edge, looking for shelter or a place to fall off.

'Why Shetland?' Alison had asked on the phone. 'It's the Falklands without penguins. She's had us up till three in the morning, worried about you. Shetland! You might as well stick your head in the gas oven and get it over wi.'

More like a fridge than an oven, he thinks as the ferry rolls north. The bar is open but that seems like a bad idea. The Bon Accord lounge proclaims HAPPY TO MEET, SORRY TO PART.

That and the whiff of curry and chips drives him back on deck. He looks down over the stern, sees himself falling, sucked into the screws and chopped like salami. These flashes are almost daily now.

How long, O Lord, how long?

'Fourteen hours, mate,' says the man in the donkey-jacket beside him. 'Hell of a trip, eh? Best get legless, I say.'

Jimmy grips the rail and stares grimly forward, though there's nothing much out there.

The ferry rolls into Lerwick after fourteen stomach-turning hours from Aberdeen. Shivering and sober, he looks out at the trawlers, the oil storage tanks, trucks, containers, gas compounds, then the brown moorland wilderness beyond. His father's people came from here. It rings true, so stripped bare, extreme, nothing hidden. This is no Edenic Orkney, nothing green and kind about it. This looks terminal.

The ship is secured, the sea sickness that had made death seem preferable is already fading, but the rest remains. All he wants now is bog and cliff and a celibate friend, a safe house and somewhere to lie up, and few questions asked.

Joan stirs and wakes sweating. She reaches for Ian, but that was two years ago. She whistles and two of her cats leap onto the bed and fight for the right to sit on her head.

Half-light through the thin curtains. He's coming today. The windows rattle and she can dimly hear the pier-head breakers. He'll have had a rough crossing. She must get down to the cages, check their moorings.

Scufflings in the corridor – the peerie stray is sorting out its place in the pecking order. One of the ponies whinnies. The garden gate is banging, she must fix it soon before the sheep get in and eat up the garden she's trying to create against the climate.

The dream. She grimaces in the grey light but is forced to remember. Her half dozen ewes were grazing by the burn. She looked down and saw four of them had a gulf, a slot eaten out of their backs. Yet they grazed, feebly, unaware of their condition. Wolves, she thought. But there are no wolves in Scotland. She was looking down right to the intenstines of one, saw the flabby heart jerk. They're being eaten away – by what?

Then she looked at the two that still grazed, fat and unmarked. One glanced at her with indifferent eyes. She felt sick and weak.

The sheep are eating the sheep, she thought. *I can do nothing about this.*

The black cat on her neck is slung to the floor. She says sorry, but it slinks away reproachfully. She lies calming her breath, fixing her eyes on the patient Christ on the wall.

The nausea subsides. Six cats need fed, the ponies put out, the Raeburn refuelled, the gate fixed. Then off to the salmon cages, hand-feeding, then over to the experimental fresh water tanks, read up the latest environmental reports on Nuvan . . .

It's fully light now and the tame thrush sings on the window ledge. She mouthes 'Thanks' to Christ, then swings her bed-socked feet to the floor. There's much to do, a lot to care for. After all, she thinks, I've the right to choose peace of mind over happiness.

But there is happiness sometimes, careless and unasked for, like when the sun breaks through and the thrush opens its throat and gives it laldy.

Steep-sided voes flash in and out of sight as the bus twists north on the new oil-money road. The light changes by the minute in the sky, on the sea which seems everywhere, over the dark peat cuttings and the empty land. Clouds swirl and disappear over the bogs, sunlight hits on a tiny patch of pasture. In every dawn he has staggered into, on the platform, on the hill, at home or abroad, there has always been this momentary surge of energy. It is not optimism, he can't imagine that. It's just being still in the game.

The driver greets each passenger as they get on at a cross-roads, a telephone box, a ruined croft and its breeze-block offspring. Much cheaper to build new than restore the old, something to do with crofting grants, he gathers from the large woman who's subsided beside him. She glances curiously at Jimmy, as if surprised to meet someone she doesn't know. They chat while he enjoys her long, slanting vowels, a throaty accent and rapid dialect quite different from Orkney's easy cadences. Who is he, where is he going, why is he here?

Good questions all. She establishes he's going up to near Hillswick.

'Quat's du dain der?'

'Excuse me?'

She pauses and shifts to their common language.

'What are you doing there? You'll be visiting friends?'

'Aye, she works on a salmon farm on the West side.'

'Ah, the Wast,' she says. 'That'll be da Sooth-moother wha writes in the papers about da pesticides.'

He says, no she's not English. The woman laughs and says she knows that fine, but the ferries from Aberdeen come into Lerwick by the South Mouth channel. All incomers are Sooth-moothers. And what does he like about Shetland?

He hesitates. The light, he replies. The bareness.

Her laughter wheezes comfortably, she takes out her cigarettes and offers him one. He accepts, and they talk on, and he's comforted beyond measure by these little transactions, the murmur of conversation on the bus, a baby's round blue eyes and a collie dog's sharp brown ones.

'Du luik like a Norse man,' she says. He's chuffed, admits the Renilsons were Lerwick fishermen two generations back. 'Du shood be at hame.'

'Ta,' he says. 'But I'm just up for a wee holiday', though last resort might be the truth of it.

The light shifts from platinum to silver-blue, the long grasses bend round Joan's garden. Behind him, miles of empty moorland are spattered with peat-workings, the odd rickle of stones, a few mottled sheep. Down below is the harbour, the village, then cliffs. Were he in the mood, there's some finger-twitching rock-stacks out in the bay. One looks like a huge black ship in full sail, petrified. The Drongs. Joan had warned him to stay away from it.

He turns away and carefully opens the rickety gate to Joan's old two-storey house. Stunted roses, blasted crocuses, some scraggy plants, the makings of a garden pond. Cats at the window, a peat shed, smoke whisked from the chimney. Journey's end.

He drops his case and rucksack full of climbing gear. Somehow it was right to come like this, by boat, by bus, by foot, like a pilgrim. He no longer has a job, his car's sold. He wants only the bare minimum, jettisoning the rest like a sinking balloon. He feels inside the letter box for the key as promised, finds it but can't extract his hand without letting it go.

Oh aye. He shakes his head as the rain blows into his eyes. These squalls out of nowhere . . . He pushes the door. It's unlocked.

He stands in a dim hall. A flurry of disappearing cats. Smell of damp, peat smoke, cats and just a whiff of fish. He finds a light switch. Wellie boots, a spade, the Virgin, a saddle over the bannister, thick socks and a mug of tea halfway up the stair. A couple of large-scale maps, drawn on and annotated – El Salvador, Afghanistan.

He spots the note by the mirror and leans across to pick it up, carefully avoiding seeing himself in the mirror, which seems to be a new phobia, along with a reluctance to enter rooms in the dark.

Hi! Sorry about the bruck (mess) – I'll have a good redd up later. Please: more peat in the Raeburn (in shed), feed the cats lunchtime, and can you do shopping for tea tonight (Pierhead Stores). Glad you're here! See Chernenko's dead – how did they tell? The new one's a lot younger. Back after work. God bless, Joan.

P.S. Anything but haggis.

What's wrong with haggis? he wonders.

They hug akwardly in the small kitchen, then glance when they think the other isn't looking. He'd forgotten her physical awkwardness – the large hands and feet, her abrupt speech, the broad forehead, her striding walk. And her heavy honey-coloured hair, now up in a tight bun.

He's filled out a bit, she thinks. And he's lost some of his bounce. His eyes are almost green and he still doesn't know where to put his hands. He looks worn out, the wee soul.

'I'm so glad to see you,' she says. 'It's been too long.'

'Yes,' he says. 'Me too.'

*

On the moor as it grows dark, the pony's mane is coarse and pungent in his fingers. He smells peat and the sea. Yellow lights snap on in the dusk. Somewhere Joan is whistling for the other pony. He stands transfixed. Perhaps here he can finally let it go.

The pony snorts.

Jimmy checks the casserole in the oven then opens his cask of red wine. He finds two glasses and carefully fills them, puts hers by where she sits in the rocking chair, feet up on the mantelpiece, going through Amnesty material, Church reports, letters and photos from correspondents.

'Ta,' she says. 'Ten more minutes.'

He sinks into the old wing-chair at the other side of the fire. Maybe it's the wind, but already he feels sleepy. Soon she'll put her work aside with a sigh at human misery and endurance, and then it will be unwinding-time.

(It will become their nightly ritual, the times they'll remember best. Evenings by the fire, smell of red wine, food, his roll-ups, singed socks. A time of dangling conversations, tentative confessions, of silences tactful, distant, or simply companionable. The kind of time that lingers long after it's gone, like the sweet whiff of peat smoke the morning after, making you smile and shiver both as you kneel at the ashes.)

'So much for Afghanistan,' she says and puts her work aside. 'I'm sure our letters will have the Politburo shaking like a jelly. So where's Kim?'

He gives her the short version, the single rather than the twelve-inch disco mix. The long one bores even him and he's feeling oddly shy, and anyway she's more important things to consider.

'Do you still miss her?'

She is shocked by his eyes. He looks down at his lap to roll another cigarette. He lights up and looks at the fire, the piano, the curtains.

'From one second to the next.'

'That's only natural,' she says encouragingly. 'It'll pass in time, if you want it to. You do want it to?'

He sips the wine. They'll seldom drink much on these evenings. Joan's made it clear she doesn't like intoxication, and he dare not get drunk. It's so predictable, and he is hanging on, very hard, to nothing at all.

He clears his throat.

'The day I stop loving her, I'll throw a party. And invite her.'

And later, after the meal, she gave him the outlines of her life in Shetland. She had, she said, got out of the way of talking about herself. She knew lots of people but she was not, well, intimate with anyone. Except maybe the tortured – literally – individuals who sometimes came for sanctuary and rest, and they mostly wanted to be left alone.

'Smolts and salmon, sailing, village life and Liberation Theology,' she summed up and tugged at her hair. Like she was trying to ring a bell inside her head, he thought. 'It's not everything but it's enough. Maybe we all once wanted more, but I can't handle it.'

There are no curtains in this room, so you wake too early. The air is chill and damp, with a hint of cat. Then you remember where you are.

You sit up with blankets wrapped round you and see a pale slash of light across a dawn sky. It has the dull glint of your father's old open razor. Below it, a pink watery stain starts to spread onto the sea.

It is dawn in Shetland, you can see it is beautiful but you cannot feel it. A thrush is singing, you strain to hear it better, but there is only territorial grating. You must take that as meaning *forever*.

You lie back, close your eyes. Words like *Please* and *Help me* drift about the room like bits of wreckage.

You fall asleep again as full day floods in your window, and upstairs the woman of the house swings her feet down to the floor.

In the silent house next morning Jimmy spread out the map. Nearby: Grind o' da Navir, The Holes of Scraada, Hamnaure, The Villians of Hamna Voe. Give them a wide berth for sure. Where else? Zoar, Tonga, Swarta, Giltarump. Whit? Quoy, Quarff, Quendale, all these Setters and Bisters and Tings. It was like listening to Shonagh's Gaelic, a foreign tongue and yet the deep sense one once knew what this meant, and on some level still do . . .

(I can still recite them, the Shetland litanies, as we drive through the night. Rina has begun to memorise those names, and this too is part of what she inherits. She and Lesley are far gone in sleep, the cats' eyes stitch up the middle of the road, and I no longer mind how close to home we are. Concentrate. For a little while longer be responsible.)

Too many choices, and anyway maps and reason and all other forms of canny navigation had led him to this. Instead he stepped out the door each morning without anywhere particular in mind, and started walking along the single-track road. If a car came, he'd stick out his thumb, whichever way it was heading. If no car came in five minutes, he'd cut off across the headland above the voe, or head East across the bogs on the peat-extraction track. When he came to another road, he'd walk along it for a while and see what happened.

In this way he could end up peering over the Hermaness cliffs at the northernmost end of Unst, or riding past Sullom Voe on a delivery van, trudging through the rain towards Jarlshof, sitting drying out in a Lerwick café. People were very kind. He liked to hear them talk, it stopped him thinking for a while. For the first time in his life, he had no purpose, no game-plan, no ploy. He just went out the door and waited for whatever came along.

So for the first days he hitched and walked himself into exhaustion. He sheltered behind peat-stacks and pens, listened to anyone he met, shared vans with dogs, sheep, creels and drunk fiddlers and oilies, wandered through the cleared crofts of Kergord, sat alone behind harbour walls watching wind on water till thought and feeling and memory finally ceased, till he was stripped down to zero.

'Would you like to see my stars?'

He rouses himself from the armchair, hoping Joan's not going to turn astrological on him.

He follows her upstairs and into her bedroom. In three weeks he has never been in it. She has her sanctuary and he has his. She draws the curtains then switches on the light.

'Now we wait for a minute.'

Curious and uneasy, he looks round her room. Hot-water bottle on the floor, bedsocks over the footboard, many books, the Bible, a cheerful Mary with Child on the wall, posters. There are photos of family, families in El Salvador, nuns he guesses must have stayed here, but none of herself. And by the bed, a large framed photo of a man.

He picks it up. Not Mick DeTerre. Eyes in shadow, bearded, not a happy face.

'It is a kind of madness, isn't it?' she says by his shoulder. 'Very little to do with love, really.'

She takes the photo from his hand, hesitates, then puts it on the dresser by the window.

'That was Ian. I went with him as far as I could. He O.D.'d in the end.' She looks out the window. 'It's a weakness of mine. You can become very dependent on supporting someone.' She glances at him. He blinks, lets it pass. 'Then I cleaned myself up and moved here. It's been hard but . . . better. No more addictions, thank you.'

He stands in her bedroom and tries to digest what she's handed him.

'Except maybe to a quiet life?' he says.

'You don't see them?'

'See what?'

'The stars, of course.'

She leans against the door, hands in her back pockets, Betty Davis style. How can he see the stars with the curtains closed?

'Sit on the bed and look up.'

She turns off the light and he sees the stars.

There are hundreds of them, at an unknowable depth above him. He sees Orion, the Pleiades, Casopeia, the fuzz of the Andromeda glaxy, the haze of the Milky Way. It's a miracle. He is standing beside his father on Eyemouth pier on a hard winter's night. His father's hand encloses his as he explains about the world, the sun, stars and galaxies. He tells him our sun is like one wee fishie swimming with a shoal of a million others, and out beyond that is the huge sea with other shoals spaced out in it, and that sea is part of a larger ocean, which is a corner of all the oceans of the universe, which is Everything, which has no end, no shore at all.

'So you see, we dinna come tae muckle,' he'd said. Then he squeezed his son's hand and added, 'But if we bide on here a while, we might see a shootin star.'

In that moment Jimmy had looked up and learned there was something too big for him ever to have or to hold. He feels something streak through him, brief and flaming.

Joan's face glimmers across the room. His mouth is open but nothing comes out. He had forgotten his father had taken the time to take the child out on a hard winter's night, hold his hand and show him where he stood. He had forgotten his father cared for him.

'Look at the moon,' she says softly and points. He twists to look behind him. A full white moon hangs glowing over his shoulder. He is in a woman's bedroom and the universe is all around him.

'Light-hoarding paper,' she says. 'Took me a whole winter to cut and stick them, but it got me through . . .'

She slips out and leaves him there on the bed, head upturned, staring into the illumination that has opened above, inside, all around him.

Joan wakes in the night with a once-familiar ache. Bloody hell, she thinks, apologises to the invisible, non-fluorescent Christ on the wall. It's been ages since her last period, they'd stopped after Ian, after all that. She'd got used to being post-menopausal in her late twenties. Saves a lot of bother.

She switches on the bedside light and pads to the bathroom, sighing theatrically. Now where did I put them?

Back in bed, she switches off the light and watches the stars come out. The moon glows on the peerie cat. She sinks back to sleep, irritated, gratified, mildly disturbed. Here we go again.

He knew then those first weeks had been an anaesthetic, not a cure. He got out his gear and took to soloing on the rotten cliffs round Weinnia Ness, routes that don't appear in any climber's guide. He came back in the evenings with little to say as they ate together by the fire and drank wine, sparingly. She wrote her letters, compiled reports while he stared into the fire for hours. They tried not to interfere with each other. They let each other be.

But tonight he finds himself studying her as she bends over the word processor. She is wearing her working glasses, old-fashioned and effective as herself. Her hair's up, exposing large ears and the nape of her long neck. Necks are vulnerable. He's vulnerable to necks.

He watches her work. Her hands are large but deft, organised. He likes competence. He can see a red spot by the end of her chin. Then he's embarrassed, it's almost indecent to look at a woman, a friend, so objectively.

She frowns and mutters to herself. He could as well not be there, she is so used to being on her own. And now he's sweating, because he sees she is not ungraceful or unwomanly at all. It is not that she is plain, it is that he is seeing her plain.

The sun doesn't shine out of her mouth. She is more like the moon, reflected light, where he can look directly and see every little spot and crater. And that means . . .

A few months back, he'd seen Kim at a bus-stop in Edinburgh. At first he'd recognised the coat, not her, because what he was looking at was a very ordinary young woman fidgeting at a bus-stop.

Relieved, slightly let-down, he'd hesitated then crossed the street towards her. After five minutes of course she was the sun again, his world revolved round her. And when she blurted she was on her way to see Graeme, it had begun all over again.

But for a few minutes he'd seen her true. Without projection, without illusion.

He leans forward in his chair, trying to work his way up what feels like a lifeline. His world has narrowed to Joan's profile and one red plouk. His heart is hammering. This is the reality of Joan, of anyone. Nobody is the sun, not even Kim. It's all reflected light. Nobody's sae special. Or everybody is. The rest is make-believe, exaggeration, like the Sea of Contentment, the Sea of Tranquillity, all the dry seas of the moon.

He's read the books. He must recognise projection when he sees it. Loss of projection means sitting on Joan's bed in clear daylight and seeing bits of paper instead of stars.

But that's terrible. No, it's bearable, desolate but bearable. *Face the facts, laddie*, his father says. He is sweating not because of desire but because of the death of desire. And it must take such courage for her, to be alone so long. He is on his feet, aching with tenderness for her ordinariness, stepping towards Joan –

'That's me done,' she announces and reaches back to untie her hair. She looks at him, raises her eyebrows. 'Seeing you're on your feet . . .'

He brings tea and digestive biscuits, they sit in silence for a while. She looks at him.

'Funny thing about salmon farming,' she says.

'Oh aye.'

'There comes a point,' she continues determinedly, 'when the smolts, which have spent all their life in fresh water, have to go to the salt water cages. In a wee while we'll be taking delivery of the next crop.'

'You mentioned.'

'The problem is the timing. You see, Jimmy, there's only a very small window that opens up when they're ready for the change. Really small, maybe a couple of weeks. If they go into the sea too early, they're not adapted and they just die.'

He leans forward and gently pushes the peats with his foot.

'What if they take too long – I mean, go out to sea owre late?'

'They don't thrive, usually they die too.'

He sits back, nodding.

'Figures. Must take some careful monitoring.'

'It does. The secret is hand-feeding, keep a close eye on them by the day. Of course, the fish sense when they're ready for the change, but someone close to them has to see it too.'

He manages a wee smile at this. She sits, waiting. She's learned how to wait. Finally he drains his glass, puts it down carefully so she can only just see the slight tremble that disturbs her.

'If it stays dry, I'm ready for the big cliffs round Swarthoull tomorrow.'

'Is that wise? I mean, soloing.'

'Well . . .' He shrugs, then blurts it out.

'You've been very kind but I seem to have tramped all over this island and got nowhere.'

She glances automatically at the Mother and Child on the wall.

'Well, I hope you mean to be careful.'

'Careful enough.'

When she went by to go to bed, he held out his hand and squeezed hers as she passed.

'A very small window,' she said. 'Goodnight.'

'G'night, Joan.'

At the door, softly.

'God bless.'

'Och, you ken I can't believe that.'

'Sure, but you're a jammy lad, you'll be saved anyway.'

He sat on alone, thinking about the stars in her room. To him they are like needles, thousands of tiny memories that prick and torment till sleep finally comes. She must be lying and looking at them. How does it feel to be her? What does it cost to get off an addiction, and what's left afterwards? Why is everyone stronger than him?

Just the same, it was good of his dad to have taken the trouble, to have held his hand while showing him the big picture.

He filled up the Raeburn and shut it down for the night. Can't push these thoughts no further.

*

Solo climbing on uncharted routes on big rock is a mug's game. As he carefully descends the steep grassy slope into the bay, Jimmy knows that fine.

He stops at a ledge over the sea, traverses along till it peters out. He leans back and looks up. Three hundred feet of unknown rock, a schist seamed and scored with cracks. In fact, looking more closely, a right tottering heap of shit. It's just good sense to test everything and trust nothing. Avoid commitment to any single hold, though sometimes there's no alternative.

He laces up his rock boots. No helmet today, no point. No harness, no rope, no abseiling tat. Free climbing.

He rubs chalk into his hands then fits his fingers to the rock and begins.

Day-long conversations with rock over the sea, aiming for the sky at the top. Something is taking shape at the back of his brain, he doesn't know what yet. The front of his brain is taken up with black rock, red rock, lichen, the faults and crannies of Weinnia, Turls Head, Zoar.

He climbs steadily, indifferently. Climbed damn well, he would have said. But that's haivers. Good climbing isn't Russian Roulette, and soloing poor rock on sight without abseil gear is plain daft. So when his hand feels blindly over a roof and closes on a nub of rock and he pulls on it in a blaze of rage and indifference – that is not true climbing, that is stupidity.

He comes home silent, unsmiling, pale as death. Has a bath, eats his tea, drinks a glass with her, is brittily cheerful trying not to be a drag, then goes off to bed. She has been in his room, seen the sleeping pills, the pile of Kim's letters. She must not interfere. No more madmen and strays. It's a form of arrogance, thinking she can help, more about her needs than his. At times she feels lonelier than before. She sits down and writes a letter to Gorbachev.

It comes as it had to, in the heart of a chimney, well up the route. He reaches and pulls on an obvious jug-hold, but it breaks away. Way off-balance he grabs for another, totally reliant this time. It holds. He twists his head and sees the offending piece bounce once then ricochet into the sea way below. He sees himself peel off and fall not in a tumbling scream but curled up like a rubbery seal, a ball that miraculously absorbs each blow, hits the water then uncurls and swims away, laughing. That's how it would be for him – a dream, a release . . .

His knee is trembling. He clutches into the chimney's heart and heaves and carries on. Very carefully.

He taped his knuckles as she poured the wine.

'So how did it go today?' she asked.

'Well, I failed to fall.'

He laughed to let her know it was just a meaningless crack.

'It's a mortal sin, Jimmy,' she said. 'I tried it.'

They sat and looked into the flames for a while. Forever, he thought, is much too long to wait.

'And if you don't like my theology, call it an offence against life,' she added. 'It's not on.'

The chicken was fine though dead, and the wine was cheap but good. That surprised him, for the whole world had been reduced to ash weeks, months, before, though not many people in Shetland seemed to have noticed this. He'd been wading in a spaceman's leaden boots through the airless dried-up seas of the moon – and still the wine was as red and good as at his dad's funeral.

She paused on the landing before bed, looked back down the stair at him.

'Jimmy.'

'Uh?'

'There's nothing weak about grief. But trying to sneak out the back way, that's despicable. Goodnight.'

She padded off to her room in her bedsocks, the badge and luxury of the woman who sleeps alone.

He listens to her footsteps moving about upstairs, then silence.

He wasn't Catholic but it had stuck. There's no way out.

It feels as though a hammer has been tapped on an empty bowl, and laid it to fragments.

He stumbles out into the garden, leans dry-heaving over the wall. He looks up into an overcast night. Nothing up there. But inside, on the pedestal where the bowl had been enthroned, there's a stunned vacancy.

He gasps for air. Luckily, Shetland is full of it.

Later that night the rain set in from the West. He lay awake, pictured it coming down in stair-rods through the night, shaking on the coarse heads of heather, sputtering into ancient bogs, leaping over cliffs back into the sea. In the chimney the wind muttered all the things she'd said. In the cracked ceiling he saw needs and terrors long-forgotten, the terror of the child alone, the source of dependency. And they used to say he supported her. He saw her the last time, pulling down her T-shirt and turning away forever.

It goes on and on. He could take a pill but he's sick of evasions. The rain gusts on the window, he tosses and turns, pulled one way then the other. Finally he lies still, on his back, arms out on either side. It is three in the morning, too long till dawn. Joan will be sleeping, in any case he's not her problem. It's not fair to wake her.

He has finally come to the end of the abseil, and he's hanging out in space. He cannot save himself. And no one else will. He cannot think nor feel nor will a way out of this. He can do no more.

He lets go.

Something will catch him or it won't.

He falls and falls and falls

He opens his eyes. He's still spread-eagled on his back. He seems to have landed in another day.

He'd hoped for something more definite than that, like revelation, death or a religious experience.

Nope.

He dressed and feeling a bit white about the gills went out into the rain. Just to confirm something, he climbed the little sodden cliffs below her house, sliding and cursing in a sweat till there was panic and water everywhere, on his face, in his eyes, under his arms, falling from his open mouth. He gripped and skidded, made the top and walked droukit to the Pierhead Stores.

'Wet,' he said to the woman there.

'That it is,' she said. 'Yes, this is what it is.'

He took the supplies, wondering if she was simple or an enlightened being.

Back at Joan's he put the roast in the oven and had a bath. He stuck his feet on the taps and sighted along the body that had once known Kim. His cigarette smoke uncurls question marks, the rain still rattles on the roof. He knows nothing, bugger all, sweet Fanny Adams. A mystery. He squeezes the soap and draws a face on it. This is what it is. That, if anything, is what it is.

He looks tired, Joan thinks, but differently.

He hugs her briefly with one arm, that's unusual, his other hand holding the kettle. The table's set, he's even put a cloth down.

'What's this?' she says, looking at the dried blood across the knuckles. 'Can't you keep out of trouble for one day?'

'I'll try,' he says. 'Good day? Tea?'

'I'm tired of fish and sick of this pesticides row,' she says. 'You'd think I was trying to poison the planet. I mean, am I likely to pollute my own voe? Please.'

He nods and fills the kettle, his back to her.

'Nuvan,' he says. 'I've been reading the papers, and your test results. I'm no biologist but some of these claims seem wild.'

His shoulders seem to fill the window. She likes the way he concentrates on little things, the pot, the tea, pouring milk into the mugs. This is so comfortable, she thinks.

'I think we both need a break. There's a sailing club dance up on Unst this Saturday,' she says. 'Fancy a wee jive?'

He turns, the lighter clicking in his hand, a tiny blue spark across the kitchen.

'You askin?'

'Ah'm askin, hen.' For a moment the seventeen-year-old from Plean peeks out.

'Okay,' he says. 'Ace,' he adds cautiously, then prods and lights the gas.

'Why do we keep wanting more, Jimmy?' she said.

'Because we're restless greedy sods,' he said, carefully rinsing out the glasses. 'Oh, and we live too long. Next question?'

She paused, crouching at the Raeburn as she stoked it for the night.

'Peace of mind,' she said quietly. 'For a long time I've thought it the most important thing, but that wis just me being lazy.'

She slammed the fire-door shut, whirled the vent closed then re-opened it, half a turn.

There are seven of them in the car coming back from the dance, none of them small and none sober. Joan is on Jimmy's knee, he is slumped against the window and appears to be asleep. She feels the rise and fall of his chest against her back, as if she were reclining on a rhythmic sea.

A good dance, even by Shetland standards. In the usual breeze-block community hall were all ages from grannies to bairns – locals, returnees and Sooth-moothers. The long tables laid with sandwiches and tea at the interval, whisky, canned beer, plastic cups.

After the slow start while the young lads got tanked up, the dances blurred together. Shetland's truncated version of the

Eightsome Reel, Dashing White Sergeant, Two-Steps. Jimmy had been astonished to see the Shetland speciality, Quadrilles, was happily coached through them, well away and beyond worrying about making a fool of himself. He'd even been coaxed on stage for a song – did he have to pick 'I Loved a Lass'? – and added another guitar to the endless Country and Western waltzes. By the end, a stagefull of fiddles (surely those children should have been in bed, but good to see the girls getting their hands on the fiddles), accordions, two mandolins, banjo, electric bass, several guitarists, some already playing in their sleep, drums. A Shetland band. One or two of the fiddlers staggered down from the stage and swayed through the dancers, still playing . . .

In Shetland they don't have to call it a community, it just is one. And a voice in Joan adds: you don't have to call it love for it to be.

The car swerves South through the night. A distant glow from the oil terminal lights the underside of the clouds. She sees Jimmy's mouth twitch as the fat girl and her partner in the front seat harmonise 'Careless Love'.

They stood on the pier waiting for the first ferry back to the Mainland. The clouds slid back like well greased hatches and it was dawn.

'Look!' he said softly and pointed down.

The otter was way down in the transparent water, turning slowly between the uprights of the pier. It rose to the surface, old flat-head, as they peered over, checked them out, jooked from side to side. It looked up at Jimmy, opened its mouth, then flicked and was gone.

'I see that one here quite often,' she said. 'Don't tell too many folk, but this place is Paradise if you like yours stripped.'

The ferry came, they drove on and sat in her car. The sky was laid out in washes of light, pale green through salmon pink. The brown lands of Yell mumbled and snored down to the shore. For a moment he almost felt it beautiful. The otter gestured in his mind, way down.

'It's very hard to kick a habit,' she said and put her work-hardened hand on his arm. 'Especially the ones that could destroy you. I do know.'

He cleared his throat.

'I enjoyed that. Dancing. It's great to let your body do the thinking for a change. Or maybe you wouldna approve of that.'

'It's you Proddies have a problem with pleasure, no me. God's no against pleasure.'

She grinned, seemed flushed or maybe it was the rosy light.

'Haven't seen you go to confession in a while.'

'Maybe I've had nothing to confess.' The ferry slid up to the south pier. 'Yet,' she added, and drove off.

'It wasn't all addiction, it wasn't all need,' Jimmy tells her that night. She sits back, he seems ready to yarn.

'Kim came back from Morocco once and I was waiting for her at Glasgow Central. I was dead nervous, you never know with reunions. She was last off the train and staggered up to me, all tanned and thin, with an immense rucksack. She dropped it and looked at me, that swift keek like a couple of taps from a blue metal-punch.

And she smiled, one of her rare, utterly delighted smiles. I'd known her for years, argued, fancied other women, but still for me the sun shone out of her mouth. She pressed herself against me and rubbed her cheek on my chest the way she did.

That's her art, hiding and suggestion. The woman spent six months learning to inscribe on mica for God's sake.

She was half-giggling, half-greiting – who knows what she'd been up to in Morocco and I didn't care. But as she'd walked towards me, for a moment I'd seen her from outside, as another person in the world, all tanned and skinny and laden. Separate and herself, not mine, incredibly precious.

It had happened once in France too. That's love, not need. It does exist and I'll no deny it.'

He pauses for a long time. She waits. Coming from a man, this is new to her.

'I'm thinking love is because of the distance between us. And it's the distance that aches, don't you think? Maybe she was right, we can't cross it.'

Long pause. Even his voice has changed, she thinks, comes from deeper.

'Except once or twice in a lifetime, briefly.

I opened my eyes in her room that night. The curtains were open and there was an orange streetlamp outside. We were lying exactly as we'd fallen asleep: me on my back, Kim lying on her front, half-across me.

It wasn't so much waking as rising to the surface. It was like floating on a brimming bowl.

Her face was turned to me in the streetlight. Mouth slightly open, sleeping. I saw her crown tooth, the one she thinks everyone notices, that scar-line across the bridge of her nose, the vaccination mark on her thin shoulder, those pale lines across her wrist.

I saw she wasn't a kid any more – she never had been. Her ribs made shadows as she breathed and I lay memorising that room. The Art Deco mirror, the black fringed shawl draped across it like a wing, the Rembrandt and Chagall prints. The painted Moroccan plates unwrapped on the floor by the bed, the empty wine bottle, her father's rosary she took everywhere, hung on the far wall.

I had to memorise it because a wee voice said in my head, like it was already over, *That was the best of times*.

Then she opened her eyes. She didn't say anything, didn't frown or blink or smile, just looked back at me. It was like for once she opened all the curtains and I went way deep into her – her soul, I guess you'd say – and there was no distance any more. None. No separation.

You see, it was the top of the tide and I don't think it'll be like that with anyone again, even if I do get over her.'

He clears his throat, hesitates. Joan is leaning forward in her chair, staring into the fire.

'I didn't know it was possible to love anyone so much,' he concludes flatly and puts his empty glass aside.

She sits back but says nothing. She pours herself a rare second glass and fills his while she's at it. She looks down at her hands and begins.

'You probably think I'm a repressed Catholic spinster occupying herself with good works.' He winces. 'Or a would-be saint without a sex drive. Or that I'm waiting for the perfect man to drop out of the sky? Maybe I was.' She looks across at him. 'You think I moved way up here to avoid things, don't you? Which you envy but think is a little weird.'

She coughs, clasps both hands round her glass and leans forward. He sips and waits. Misery is so self-centered, that's what makes it misery. Now she has his complete attention.

'Remember when we first met? I felt straightforward then, not complicated like Kim. I don't know what happened. Mick, then Ian . . . I'm not that person now. Maybe I wanted to save someone, now I'm hard pushed to save myself.'

She sips and puts the glass aside.

'I know it's just what you call reflected light,' she says carefully, 'but you can bide on here longer if you want.'

Then she tells him the things she's been thinking, the way it's been with her recently. They look into the remains of the fire and finally it's time for bed.

'We're much the same, you and me,' she said at breakfast. 'People can give themselves completely only once, twice at most. For me it was Mick, then Ian. After that there's nothing left but fear and the habit of giving. And affection. You'll think about it?'

'I'm honoured.'

'So you should be.' She yawns and winks at him. 'So you ruddy should.'

'There's something I want to do first,' he said. 'But I will. Think about it, that is.'

Two days later he stood at the base of the Old Man of Hoy, wondering if this was sensible.

He opened his sack and sorted out harness, boots, helmet, chalk bag, ropes, abseiling tat. It was a grey day, the wind was gusting, the sea loud around him. It wasn't so good to be back on Orkney. He'd clenched himself from Kirkwall airfield to Stromness and caught the little ferry over to Hoy as soon as possible.

Tightened and re-tied his laces. Surely was a lonely place. A partner would have helped, someone to jive and bullshit and seal the commitment.

Pulled the helmet strap tight under his chin, looked up. The middle section bulged out over his head. The sense of exposure up there would be colossal. Climbing paired, he'd have felt fairly sure he could lead the whole thing.

Buckled the harness, clipped on the chalk bag, eased open its neck and rubbed his fingertips. No one was watching except the mad bonxies screaming round his head. No one to impress or woo or win. Frankly, who gave a shit whether he did this thing. The satisfaction of sending Graeme a card to say he'd soloed it would last about five minutes, a very small slice of *forever*.

He studied the whorls of his fingerprints through chalk. It wasn't the right sort of day. Too much wind, bit chilly, threat of rain. The sandstone lips and ledges of the upper section were famously slippy and friable.

He didn't have to do this thing.

Then again, a crumbling, eroded, four hundred and fifty foot phallus, even a square sided one bulging in the middle and tapering to a split top, is not easily ignored. He'd rehearsed the finish so often, chimneying up between the two summit blocks, looking right through to Pentland Firth on the other side. Not so much being born as being re-conceived, emerging from the top. Surely that must make a difference.

He unkinked and re-coiled the two ropes. He hadn't touched them since Disappearing Gully. He worked slowly, thinking it over. Thought of Joan working on the loch, her bedroom stars and her calm ways.

'We live easily together,' she'd said, 'and you don't get on my nerves. You could consider it as a base.'

This really wasn't necessary.

He dropped the ropes in the sack, slung it on and tightened the straps carefully. He'd been rehearsing this showdown for years, like the punk gunfighter in the Western you know is going to get killed because he brags and sweats and basically isn't good enough.

He wasn't feart. Nervous, maybe. He walked across the sandstone slabs and touched the rock. This could be his last climb. He bowed his head and collected himself for a minute.

It's what you do when no one is looking that counts.

The first pitch was straightforward enough. He took it steadily, getting into the rhythm. The soloing of the past weeks had put him in good trim and being alone had almost begun to feel normal.

He pulled up eventually onto a good sized ledge, natural place for a breather. The next section was crucial – awkward traverse out round the corner onto the other side, down and across to the start of the overhanging crack. That crack was the crux of the route, a sustained series of hand jams out over the bulge. Grade E1 5b. Fine for leading, worrying to solo. One slip and the long cheerio. Fair enough.

Time to look ahead. He got in a good peg, then a solid friend, took out his first rope and clipped it in. Tied on to the other end. He'd free-climb the overhang of course, but when it came to abseiling down if he got to the top – when he got to the top – if he didn't have a back-rope set up he'd be left dangling off the overhang looking a right wally. Like the last six months.

He lifted and dropped his shoulders as his father used to before starting something big, then edged carefully off the big ledge.

The wind hit hard as he came round the corner of the stack, cold and gusting. He never liked traverses and this one on a series of little sloping sandy ledges, was worse than usual. He worked his way across, hold by hold. His hands were already losing feeling, the sack caught the wind and pulled him off-balance. He hesitated half-way across and looked back at the corner which already seemed miles away, cursed himself for a wee timorous beastie and kept going. The wind and sea way below were loud in his ears, the sandstone gritty on his fingertips.

Then he was at the bottom of the overhanging crack, looking at an old bolt left from a previous ascent. He clipped to it and relaxed a moment. Not pure soloing style, but why not take advantage of what's on offer?

Why not? No illusion, no anxiety. Friendship. Paper stars.

He unclipped, got his hands into the crack, clenched them and pulled, enjoying the abrasion. He was going to solo this fucker. Don't ask, *do*.

Savage fun. His arms were burning and blood greased his knuckles. Still he hand-jammed up, move by move, clinging under the bulge, working up through it. It seemed impossible, but really just improbable. The holds appeared when he needed them. He heaved up to an old wooden wedge from the first ascent, thought about a belay but kept going. The crack leaned out and out, the last few feet of the crux and it's all coming true, get past this and –

A fulmar shoots from the crack, spitting oil. He flinches instinctively, his right hand jerks, left foot slips, and he peels off.

He is falling and there is time. Time to curse that bird and accept it. Time to know he'd been maybe a hundred and twenty feet up with a hundred and forty foot of back rope, so he must deck out.

It's not so terrible.

He falls and falls

The jolt shoots through his hips, crushing his chest, straight through to his skull. His eyes open and the rock blurs towards him, he gets his shoulder round and crunches into it. Another cry, whack on the helmet, and he's clinging to sandstone.

He looks down. Twenty feet off the deck. Glances up, his back rope's vibrating, must have snagged, in the crack most like. These things happen. A mystery. Get moving before it starts to hurt.

He pictured prussiking back up the rope, completing the route, conquering the Old Man, all that stuff.

Nah. It was over. He tried to untie with one hand. The knot was jammed solid from the fall and his wrist felt wrong. Be like that. He was grinning and spitting blood and muttering as he unbuckled the harness and left it hanging there. Let them figure that one out.

He down-climbed what was left, remembering nothing about it. He skidded the last few feet and fell back on his arse. Things began to get normal. Everything hurt.

He got to his feet and stumbled away.

Busted knee, two cracked ribs, buggered wrist, missing tooth and one heavily bruised ego. Joan shook her head and helped him down the corridor and into the sunlight.

'And now?' she asked in the taxi to the airport.

Two days in hospital had been long enough to think it through.

'I don't deserve another miracle,' he said.

He forced himself to look at her.

'It's not right,' he said. 'It's too soon and I'd be bleeding all over you. I hurt someone in Perth that way. It's terribly tempting but . . .'

She closed her eyes for a moment. She opened them and nodded, confirming something.

It's a calm night for the sea crossing. He'll be on the Aberdeen ferry by now.

Joan lay back and stared at the cruxifix on the wall till her breathing settled. Nearly but not quite, she thought. Maybe it's as well. There's other things to live for.

She hesitated then pulled on her bedsocks, picked up her Spanish dictionary and settled back into the pillows. She could keep this up forever, if need be.

At least that's how she told it, dry-eyed in the days after the funeral.

NINETEEN

Stone breaks scissors

MY JACKET CREAKS as Lesley stirs in the back.

'Are we nearly there?' she asks sleepily.

'Very nearly.'

In the mirror I see her hesitation.

'How's she been keeping?'

'A lot better lately. I'll fill you in later.'

'It's been rough?'

'What do you think?'

'Yeah.'

Pause. I blink and flex my hands on the wheel, the way the old man did. Nearly there.

'Is she really okay?' Lesley persists.

'Who knows? She thinks so.'

No reply. She's starting to droop again. I glance round and see the child's flopped across her lap. I mind that, falling asleep in the back seat under gran's travelling rug on family journeys, dad driving and the cats' eyes swinging out of the dark and vanishing behind. The kind of security that doesn't come again.

'We owe her this much, don't we?'

'Aye,' I say, and then wonder who we're talking about.

I was cleaning up the house when she tottered up the lane behind a stack of cardboard boxes. They swayed when she saw me at the door.

'I'm sorry,' she said rapidly, 'I thought you'd be off-shore.'

'I'm finished wi the North Sea, remember?'

'Ah.'

I helped unstack her boxes.

'So what now?'

'I'm letting the house and going away.'

'Oh,' she said. 'When are you going?'

'How should I know, I haven't been there yet.'

She considers this, recognises it as one of her standard replies about her own work. Nods.

'So how was Shetland?'

'I saw an otter.'

'You sound different.'

'Well, I guess.'

'How was Joan?'

'Well, I thought.'

We were speaking too loud, as if to someone some distance away.

'Jimmy – '

Graeme was walking up the path.

'All going up in steam,' she muttered and escaped up to the attic.

I made three coffees on automatic.

'She looks terrible,' I said. 'Hectic.'

'She's been working like crazy.'

'That's good.'

He took his coffee and prowled round the kitchen. He never did like sitting down, in bars or his own flat. Kim always curled up in corners. I wondered if they were going to live together and how it would go. Not my business.

'Sorry about the strike.'

'We coulda won, but something's gone. Everyone for themselves these days, eh? It's no the Scottish way. Christ, I hate it.'

He rattled his fingers on the window, nodding away to himself.

'It's no going too well,' he said quickly. 'Her work, I mean. She gets headaches and sometimes she sleepwalks, at least that's what she calls it.' He glanced at me. 'Did she do that before?'

'Once in a while. The headaches aren't good.'

We stood in silence, hearing her footsteps on the floor above.

'She got me to fit a lock to the kitchen drawer. Said she was worried she'd sleepwalk and stab me.'

'Aye, you don't have much luck with the women, do you?' He put down his mug and went very still. 'One decides she'd rather be gay and the other wants to take the bread knife to you. Of course, it could be coincidence.'

His hands came up. I kept holding on to my mug, it might be useful.

'You live dangerously, pal,' he said hoarsely.

I shrugged and looked out the window, kept an eye on him but.

'I said that to you once. On the Ben. Mind?'

'Course I fuckin remember. I was quakin in ma boots. Really thought you were going to do it.'

'Me and all. We're a violent bunch when it comes down to it.'

'Speak for yersel. You ken ah'm a pacifist.'

'Wouldna hit a Tory, eh?'

'Heh, that's richt.'

He slowly picked up his mug again, I eased my shoulders down. He glanced my way.

'We heard from Joan through Alison, sounded like you were crackin up, like.'

I drank the coffee, made a face.

'Na, just a wee fracture.'

I felt I had to say something like that.

'We wis worried.'

'Jolly nice of you. By the way, I went for the Old Man.'

'Solo?'

'Yup.'

'And?' he said at last.

It was silent upstairs. I wondered what she was doing. Taking a last look, maybe. Packing up her kettle and her notepads. Her tools were long gone.

'Packed it in at the crux,' I said. 'It didna feel right.'

'Good decision,' he said and sounded relieved. 'No point topping yersel for something like that.'

'No point at all.'

'I was worried. You were on ma mind.'

'No need – '

She stood in the door, looking a bit peelie-wallie.

'I've packed up,' she said. 'Do what you want with anything else you find about the place. Can you give me a hand down wi the boxes?'

'In a minute, Kim,' Graeme said.

She went back upstairs in a bit of a huff. I wished I'd spoken to her like that more often. Sometimes he didn't seem to give a toss. She always liked a challenge.

'Jim – '

'It's only a hill of beans, man,' I said, and we shook on that, kindof.

We carried her gear out to his car. Kim dithered near me while he loaded up.

'So you finally let it out,' she said quietly. 'Good for you. You really wrecked the place.'

Something there I didn't care to think about.

'Sorry about that.'

'Deserved it. I'm not proud of all this, you know. It's not how things were,' she said to her hands. 'I'm not nostalgic like you. It's what might have been . . .'

'That's it,' Graeme announced and slammed down the boot.

He got into the car and waited, looking over at the ruined wall we'd raced each other up that baffled night. It was still standing. Things are much tougher than they seem. She turned to me.

'Please dinnae be a stranger,' she said.

Then she gave me a quick blast of the aquarium. There was nothing in there but blue. I looked away. I'd never kiss those lips again, though we might be inches apart. We might even hug cautiously, brush hands while passing each other things, but she'd never close her eyes again and raise her face to mine. Never hear that soft sigh like the opening of an automatic door.

People said in time that wouldn't matter. Really, people hadn't a fuckin clue.

'Yes,' I said. 'God go wi ye. Do something fantastic.'

She hugged me quickly, hard. I felt her thin bones.

They drove off, I waved and turned away but my heart ran after them, yelping like a pup.

I went inside and closed the door. I washed the mugs and left them to drain. Then picked up the Yale key she'd left on the table and went slowly up to the top of the house.

The door was wide open. Her kettle was still on the gas ring and stacked neatly on the workbench were her notebooks, the private ones she'd sketched and scribbled ever since I'd known her. I looked down at them. *Do what you want with anything you find.*

My choice. I wondered how much I wanted to know. Everything, maybe that had been the problem. I stood and flipped through the top one and very soon felt sick. I'd been braced to read some hard truths, but not this.

I took a deep breath, then sat down to read everything from the beginning. It took all day and when I'd finished there was nothing to do but shut up shop and go a long way away for a long time.

'We're back, Les' I say, shaking her gently.

I carry in her cases while she stumbles over the threshold with the child a breathing deadweight in her arms. She looks round the hall, nodding to herself like all is present and correct.

She looks down at what she's carrying and seems puzzled, as though any moment it should revert to something reasonable like an aqualung or a pair of skis.

'I'm beat,' she says and shakes her head. 'I feel I'm playing mother, only it's not a game now.'

I help Rina, who's in automatic, sleepwalking mode, wash and change and clean her teeth, assure her she can sleep with Lesley this night at least, and put her in the downstairs bed, find the indispensable teddy, light the night-light. She's asleep by the time the match burns my fingers.

Lesley is standing in the door.

'You're good with her. Relaxed.'

'Well, I've had some practice.'

She looks blank for a moment.

'Sorry, I'd forgotten about Ruth. I'd better crash. Ignore me if I prowl around at some funny hour.'

'If you do, you'll find a letter on the kitchen table. Kim's last. I thought it might help fill you in.'

'Jim, I'm scared. Look at me. Do I look like a parent?'

I put my arm round her shoulder, the way old pals do.

PART III

The Internal Combustion Engine

TWENTY

Reconditioning

IT'S LATE GLOAMIN at the table, Kim's studio table like one of Graeme's early paintings, all old scores and nicks and scorch marks from cigarettes, knives and soldering irons, the table I made for her, the one she left behind. The wind's a breeze tonight and its passing through the firs blends with the sea and the distant rip of engines on the new by-pass. The moon is low and full, a gowk's moon my father would cry it, spreading iodine stains through thin clouds.

And the baby, the child, wee Scottie? Though she's not here to see it, and me I'm old enough to know better, I've lit the sputtering oil lamp as a moon for her. Unless she wakes crying for her mother, she'll be asleep back in her old room in Portobello, surrounded by her court of teddys. Lesley phoned this evening to say they'd settled in alright, though she still felt between places, could be she needed her lover. She laughed, as I do now but quietly.

Now everything that can be settled, is settled, and in this quiet house there's time to finish this for you.

The American frigate in the Gulf that had been hit by the Exocet had lowered its defensive screens to communicate. Many men killed, more injured. Apologies all round.

He folded away *The Scotsman* as the plane dropped over the North Sea, swivelled round Leith, came in low over the rust-red nose-to-tail dinosaurs of the Rail Bridge. He felt the pressure in his ears, swallowed. From the air it looked a small country, small and put-upon but his. It seemed that while he'd been away the value of property had gone up and on the whole that of people had gone down. An economic miracle, some said. Time soon to vote on it.

He walked across the tarmac, looking round and sniffing the air. The airport and the passengers looked smarter, keener and less friendly, like they meant business. Same old weather, smell of diesel, fields and sea, but something in the air had changed or maybe it was him. He hoped it was him. He spotted Alison at the window, waved back, gripped his grip tighter.

'Thanks for the postcards,' she said as she drove. 'In the old days the prescription for broken hearts was big-game hunting in Africa. So now it's floundering about Third World countries trying to start the village's tractor and getting paid in tsetse flies.'

'Developing countries,' he reminded her. 'And mostly water-pumps and generators. It's been an education.'

At least he'd been needed. Not him personally, just his hands and a skill. Still, showing others how to maintain and recondition pumps and engines made a change from gutting the North Sea for the Government and Western Oceanic. And mosquitos and Shagas beetles were a doddle after West Highland midges.

'Anyway,' he added, clutching the door handle as they wheiched down the dual carriageway towards Edinburgh, 'abbing off high buildings in Toronto doing structural inspections wasn't exactly altruistic. I did that because I was skint. And Sweden, even on an archaelogical dig, isn't exactly underdeveloped.'

But really, Lerwick, La Paz, Stockholm, Toronto or Yucatan, it hadn't made much difference. There was no short-cut. He had learned how to wait, that was all.

'So,' she said, taking her hands eloquently but worryingly off the wheel, 'what's the state of the heart? Still radiating?'

'Safely buried in concrete for the next thousand years, if you can believe that.'

'Aye, Chernobyl.' She shook her head. He thought she looked burdened, tense. 'But really?'

'Easy to kid yourself.' He relaxed as she slowed down and the sun came out. 'But the awful bit's over. I can fix cars, radios, scanners and generators, but not myself. Fair enough. But I'm fine. Na, not fine. I'm adequate.'

'I'm so glad,' she said, and with her smile he was home. 'Did you know I cried when you chose Kim?'

He stared at her. He'd thought it had been friendship, and sex a pleasant mistake.

'Thought not,' she said. 'You were a self-absorbed tunnel-visioned offspring of the petit bourgeoisie with little feeling for anyone else except yourself and your idealised notion of her. That exceptions to this can be counted on one hand – and I'm not one – is no excuse.'

'Great to be back in Scotland,' he said. 'The home of constructive criticism. And you're right and I'm sorry. Really awfy sorry.'

She laughed and put her hand on his, squeezed.

'No need. We were what we were, and at least you warned me at the time. I think being unhappy has improved you.'

'I should bloody hope so.'

'Talking of which, you'll have heard about Graeme?'

He held up his hand.

'Please, not today. My head's still full of cities and jungles.'

Alison nodded and drove into the thickening complexity of Edinburgh. He looked around. A lot of sand-blasting, some new repro buildings, building sites, demolition, scaffolding everywhere. The city was being re-conditioned and put up for sale again.

'So,' she asked, 'any new ships on your travels?'

'A couple of short trips round the bay,' he replied in a voice as casual as her own. 'One very nice one. Wasn't ready, though I thought I was.'

'You were still looking for Kim, I suppose?'

'At first. Then someone like her.' He kept staring at Edinburgh's deep stone canyons. So tight-packed, so ordered, no unclaimed space. It's a doss-house compared to Stockholm, a palace after Mexico City. 'Then anyone. Then no one.'

'And now?' Alison asked.

So he told her about a straightforward, well-adjusted woman at the boat-burial dig, who was young and happened to have mid-blue eyes, but she was tall, had that white-blonde northern hair and was not in the least crazy. In fact she saw no insurmountable problem in life, believed in positive thinking. Inge used dangerous words like love, quite easily.

That had amazed him. Who'd dare deploy a word so weighty, so irrevocable? But he'd allowed himself to go with the spirit of the times. Wild offers had been made at the Reykjavik Summit, and she felt like glasnost itself. He'd even used the dangerous word back to her a few times, and though he personally believed positive thinking was a prolonged effort to kid yourself, the world hadn't fallen apart.

'She sounds good for you,' Alison said. 'Sounds like you really liked her.'

'I did. She really liked me. We really liked really liking each other.'

Alison laughed, as he'd meant her to. Something was weighing on her.

'So?'

'So an old boyfriend of hers came back from a year on the oil tankers. She said it would just be considerate to meet him. When she came back she said sorry, she hadn't understood how she really felt, and she had decided to be positive and marry him. She kindly hoped I wouldn't be upset.'

'And were you?'

'My heart's a swinging brick, hen.'

She shook her head.

'James, these young women will be the death of you. You should fall in love with some old Sixties type like me.'

'There'll be no more of that love nonsense. Gonna keep my head below the parapet from now on.'

'It's not nonsense and you know it,' Alison retorted. 'I hope you can do better than cynicism.'

'Christ, so do I.'

He rattled his fingernails on the windscreen, remembering her youth, her optimism, her laughter. Life had not yet laid a finger on that lassie. Their last weekend together had been the trip to Copenhagen when he'd found a British Council exhibition of young Brit sculptors and he looked at Kim's latest and with Inge beside him felt nothing much except proud of Kim that she'd stuck to it.

'Your friend Kim made these?' Inge had asked.

'Yes. She's got better.'

They peered into the little lit display boxes of Kim's last phase before the Golden Triangle. She invited you to be a voyeur then gave so little away it was a reproach. The one of the couple in the bedroom of emerging knives was there, and for a moment he heard her voice again, saw her hunched forward in the attic with a little blade in her hand, and something flickered for a minute then vanished and was gone.

'This is good,' she said, 'but not very happy I think.'

'No, not very.'

He'd touched her white-blonde hair and wanted something very badly. He waited for it to pass, as these things do.

'You want to make love?' she asked, 'or go to the park?'

So far as he remembered, they'd done both and both were very pleasant. Like the city itself, clean and pleasant, healthy. Maybe in time it would have seemed real too. Where had he got this idea there must be pain and grubbiness in anything real? But she'd left before he could find out . . .

He stretched back and yawned. Each familiar street of the

Southside reclaimed him, seemed like each pub had its memory, each bookshop and carry-out, Christ even the phone boxes. Too much history here. His chest feels like scree on the Buchaille Etive Mor, jagged and shattered and pink, dragging him down even as he tries to rise up on it. Perhaps he should have stayed away.

'Anyway,' he said, 'you're looking good but kinda tired.'

Alison smoothed her stomach with her hand.

'Expecting another,' she said. 'Call it a happy accident. We were wondering if you'd be godfather.'

He swallowed and looked out the window. Must be getting soft.

'I know very little about God or children, but I'd be honoured.'

She pulled up outside their flat but didn't move to get out of the car. He waited for it, hoped it wasn't another couple down the tubes.

'About Gerry,' she said quietly with both hands on the wheel. 'Don't know if you noticed he'd been dragging a leg for a while. Then he was having problems with his eyes. Then fumbling things. We went for tests. It looks like he's developing multiple schlerosis.'

He opened his mouth but nothing came out.

'I'm trying to find,' she said, very controlled, like a formal statement, 'a way to reconcile the arbitrary cruelty of life with the joy I feel in being alive.'

He put his arms round her and she cried long enough for him to know it was right to have come back. For better and worse, this was his developing country. He was needed and he owed her. Finally Alison wiped her eyes, he straightened her jacket, gave her the nod then they went inside.

'Not too great,' Gerry admitted when she left them alone. 'Guess I'll never beat Jocky Wilson at the darts now. But how's yourself, man?'

'How can I talk about my wee problems when you – '

'Sod that. Pain is pain. Golden lads and lassies must, eh?' He paused, leaning slightly on the armchair. 'So?'

What could he say.

'Well, I'll no be keeping you up nights again.'

'Thank fuck for that. The twins are bad enough. But you'll still be coming by?'

'Christ, man. Call and I'll come over anytime you need me. Anytime, for anything. You ken that.'

Alison came in from the kitchen carrying three shot glasses and the bottle. She shook her head.

'Now if you guys are through with all this soppy hugging stuff . . .'

He helped Gerry sink back onto the settee. It was like the big man had melted round the edges. Terrifying.

They raised their glasses, Alison assisting Gerry's hand.

'Welcome back. We've missed you.'

What an extraordinary idea.

'Cheers.'

Harsh and burning in his throat at first, smoothing to a glow as it went down. He hadn't touched whisky in two years. The right sort of clouds, the right drizzle and temporary sunshine, the place where you understood the values and the signals, the jokes and the buildings, the love and the anger and the sarcasm. Home. He looked down into the glass, feeling a little weak.

'Have another. I hope you like your lamb chops radioactive.'

Judging by the new estate agent's at the top of the wynd, where people used to have a home, now clients invested in a property. He stood at the window of his home with brother Alec, looking down at the harbour where Charlie the cat prowled watchfully along the wall, reclaiming his old territory.

New boats about, and the old ones repainted. Couple of the inshore fishing boats had the new Decca systems. The old empty Customs House was being converted into flats, with entryphone for God's sake, the greengrocer and centre of essential gossip had been replaced by a new deli, which was handy but he'd miss the crack. The houses looked less shabby and less familiar – a new pantile roof, double-glazing, attic conversions, extensions. Charlie walked delicately over a car roof and plucked warily at its aerial.

He turned away and poured a dram of best duty-free and they toasted the old man, the business. Alec admitted the yard was doing no so bad, which meant it must be booming after nearly going under in the mid '80s. Pick your own election time, eh? Then a dram for Alec's first bairn, Jimmy's first nephew. Turn your back and babies sprout underfoot like mushrooms.

'Good to have you back, loon,' Alec said. 'And a bittie more together, eh?'

'Surely,' he said. 'Sorry I gave you all a hard time. It won't happen again.'

Alec left to go back to his family. He turned at his car and punched the air.

'Get free – Vote SNP!' he yelled.

'Wee free yersel!'

Jimmy sat in the gloamin with the window open wide and poured a last Macallan's. He sipped and flicked idly through the box of mail his mum had put aside. Mostly junk, an awful lot of people wanting him to borrow and spend, then some that looked like Christmas or birthday cards, various expedition cards from friends in the Himalayas. He put aside anything with her writing, and a few from Graeme. A surprise, that. Even in the old days the wee fella wasn't given to writing.

He allowed himself a smoke and laid out their mail on the desk like playing cards, arranged them in chronological order, not sure how much he cared.

Still, he checked out the postmarks. Her first was from Edinburgh. Then from Glasgow, an artcard and a letter. Ho hum. So they gave domestic bliss a whirl? He checked Graeme's small pile – yup, one from him, Glasgow, a few days later. Invitation to a co-habitation party, ho ho. An invite to an exhibition, one of hers. Good on her. A card from Arran, school holiday time of course, her writing, his quick scrawl at the bottom, *Goat Fell good action pal. G.*

He looked away. It really was a bonnie evening, and all the crouched, gabled, dormered houses looking right. Good to be back. Always a few problems, always changes.

What looked like a birthday card, her writing, Glasgow. A wee parcel, same date. A Christmas card. And one from him too, Glasgow again, heartwarming stuff.

Then the surprise – an airmail from Venice, his writing, early in the new year. Then nothing more till six months later, a card from Shetland, postmarked Hillswick, Joan's village. Sent during term-time.

He was almost curious. Looked through Kim's pile. A Chagall card sent the same January from Chartres, then six weeks later another from Avignon. Next Christmas, another card, same postmark.

Well, well. Down the tube like bloody birds.

I hope you can do better than cynicism, he thought. Bloody better.

He held the glass to the last light.

He was not in love with anyone, had no desire to be, could think of nothing more disastrous. It was mostly projection and need, very little to do with the other person. He was nearly sober and without illusion and there wasn't much pain. He'd read the mail and catch up on all the gossip tomorrow, no hurry.

He'd just glance at Graeme's airmail first.

Venice doss, early.
Hey Jim-boy, not much of a one for letters, and who knows where and when you'll ever read this, so I must be writing this for myself. Yet it feels like stretching out my mitt towards you. Take it or knock it away, right?

I can't apologise but it's due. Jesus how stiff these Proddy knees are to bend and say sorry. It's no joke being Glaswegian! Everyone looks to you to be the funny man, fast and hard with the patter, gallus or grim, no quarter given, no apologies. It's in the culture, but like I say to my old man, that daft old Orange bastard, that's no excuse.

You and her, even without me that was bound to end. I hope you accept that now and believe it as I must. But man, I was out of order as a Rangers scarf at an IRA funeral. Never ever sleep with a friend's lover. I'd have killed you if you'd done it with Lesley – you didn't, did you? Did you? (She's writing to me again, instructing in Colorado, says they've fixed one of her tendons, so she's just giving them one finger now.) We should have told you she was bi – guess I felt it was her business, and she was feared Kim wouldn't be the same with her if she knew.

Miss her. Les was my closest friend and I trusted her. Guess we blew it, huh? Sorry, sorry, sorry. Enough of that. Like as not you don't give a shit now anyway – especially if you've stopped living on those beans!

Kim and me. It's a kind of craziness, that kind of affair, like a big amphetamine or coke binge. You need more just to keep going and sooner or later you've got to crash. As soon as she moved in, the only question was who'd be first out the door (yours truly, by a shirt sleeve). Too intense, too difficult, incredibly rewarding – she took me places – but such a low boredom threshold. A forest fire.

Not her fault, but she's got her problems. Been too close to that before – the old dear, you know.

So we've split. She's gone to Avignon – she's got a commission for a big psychiatric institute for fuck's sake! – and I'm sitting up shivering and half-cut still waiting for dawn in this green coffin-sized room in the unreal city, and not feeling very gallus.

Dude, the night's been real bad. Like having the flu as a wean, hell-fire visions and that. I'd gone out on the bevvy to cheer myself up and not think about her or you or Les, came back here and lay down and then –

Mind 'Clockwork Orange' when the kid is shown movies and he has to watch because his head's clamped and his peepers pinned open? Last night was that way inclined. I lay here in my sweating pit and had to watch Hell's judge, the accusers, all that Proddy shite I don't even credit but it must be in there I guess, and they made me watch every shitty thing I've done this last while, every betrayal, broken promise, the cover-ups and the greed, oh man the greedy bastard I am, all the righteous things I say and the crap inside. You, Kim, Les, the old man, even my mum yeah all showed me true movies.

But here's the worst. I was lying there and suddenly it's like Thatcher and her entire fuckin Cabinet are sitting on my chest and looking my way and She points her finger and shrieks 'You think we're the problem but we're YOU!'

That didn't feel too great, I tell you. My life's bad jive, so much Public Relations and such a wee phoney rigging it behind the scenes. It's a dumb joss like the poet says and I'll have no more of it.

So there's going be some changes. I'm leaving Glasgow. The Council can get by without me – some careerists there, pal! I'm leaving teaching. It's been driving me crazy. I mean, what are we about, teaching the weans to obey us?

I've got two hands and a good Scots tongue in my head and it's lowsin time for me. Shetland sounds like the bogging end but seemed to do you good. Gather there's some good routes up there and work if you can turn your hand. Kim's pal Joan says I can stay a while if I don't mind sharing the house with a tortured Chilean priest and a couple of radical nuns . . . I'll take my paints and politics and try to set my head in order.

Between you and me, pal, there's been plenty good and bad. Maybe someday . . .

Ah well, better get some breakfast before I get sentimental. I wonder where you are and how. I don't know what's with Kim, we never did talk much about personal jive. And you, I've loved you more than any other man if that needs said.

Ach well. Don't fall off anything I wouldn't.

     G.

Jimmy stood at the window with the letter in his hand. It was proper dark now, the house felt cold and unresponsive like a guitar unplayed for ages. So things had changed, would change again. There'd be an election soon. In time he might be able to go for his first choice instead of his second, but not yet.

'To absent friends,' he said to Charlie, drained the glass and went to bed ready to start at his father's yard in the morning.

I fold the old blue airmail paper along its worn lines, noticing how Graeme never wrote the way he spoke, any more than I do (we seem to keep a second drawer hidden behind the first). It's one I've come to know by heart. Which, as Ruthie once said, is the only way to know anything worth knowing.

I file it away in the shoe box marked *Graeme*, then sit with my hands at rest on the table. It's so quiet here. I'd got so used to living with Rina. These last few days I keep turning up odds and sods she left behind – a blue shoe, her baseball cap, broken crayons, colouring books, wee things like that.

I'll get them back to her soon enough. No need to drive over this time of night. I can wait.

But back then I was still learning how. To work, eat, sleep, see friends, play with the jug band in the back room of the pub, read another chapter of whatever book before reaching over to turn out the bedside light and think for a moment of all those other solitary sleepers who do the same.

And even when Kim wrote from Avignon during the autumn gales to say she'd had 'a litle blip', meaning her first confessed breakdown, but was getting better now and had met a fella and was working again and it was good we could be friends now – well I kept myself from going out there, wrote to her instead and stayed indoors till the gale died down and the gulls flew back from inland and the barometer rose outside the harbourmaster's office.

Like most folk, I learned to live day to day and wait as if I were not waiting. There were some brief encounters, the odd heady night. I enjoyed them, told the truth and took precautions, knew when to stop. And only once in a while, looking up at a certain colour of sky or turning over her sea-glass in my hand, would I remember there had once been another order of things.

That summer turned slowly into autumn, to winter. The election, well Mrs Thatcher had done us one great service for she was a litmus test. Three times she dipped the UK into her solution and each time the bottom part came out blue and the top pinker than the time before. We had forgotten we were different, and that difference went deeper than a taste for haggis, Murrayfield and Hampden and an inabillity to take seriously anyone called Nigel. What we'd do about it remained to be seen.

The yard was still doing no so bad. In September a card came from Joan to say she and Graeme were (cagily) very happy and she hoped I understood. I sent her an art card of Kim's triangle sculptures, and after some hesitation just wrote on the back *Yeah yeah – Good luck.*

Alison had her next baby, my godson Pete. Gerry's M.S. was in remission but not enough for him to work again, and with the cuts Alison was on part-time and tutoring in the evenings, so I spent a lot of time round there helping with the kids and generally shooting the breeze. It was rumoured the world was warming up, which as MacBeth pointed out would be a right scunner for Scottish winter climbing. Certainly something was changing and melting. The Intermediate Nuclear Weapons treaty actually got signed. We sat in front of the TV stunned – we'd forgotten things could do anything other than get worse, and now something was letting up.

Life local and global went on, and when celibacy left me crabby I took myself off into the hills or along the coast for a day. I was fairly content, I was in neutral.

Then one afternoon in the new year I went down to Coldingham beach, and there was a woman in my private spot among the rocks, sheltering from a snell wind, and she lit a defensive cigarette and said her name was Ruth.

A late entrance but a good one.

I listen to the distant cars on the by-pass and think of the heart and all its little valves opening, closing, opening again, then light a roll-up and think what you should know.

TWENTY-ONE

Intake

SHE WAS SURPRISED and she wasn't. And pleased, she admitted as she cradled the phone to her shoulder and reached for a cigarette. That odd, easy meeting on Coldingham beach on her afternoon off. He'd looked startled, like it was his special spot not hers, said Hi, was ready to leave but she'd blurted something silly and he hadn't.

She lit up, thinking it another foolish reflex, smoking on the phone. As if it was something to be nervous about, with the other person out of sight and a safe distance away. He'd been friendly but detached, leaning slightly to one side as though leaning on something invisible. Not invasive but he'd looked at her as though he was interested in who she was.

She was interested but she wasn't interested in being interested. Not all that again.

'Sure,' she said to the phone, 'how about Sunday?'

She caught the hesitation. No emotional virgins after thirty, she thought. Sunday was fine by him. When?

'After lunch,' she said and groped for the ashtray. She flicked off the ash and added casually, 'My daughter Mary may want to come. We can walk over to St Abbs, if that's okay.'

'Mary,' he said. 'Aye, that would be fine.'

I wonder if he's given it time to heal, she thought. Surely I have. Not that I'm interested.

'Stay for your tea if you want,' she found herself saying. Well, it was company. Not that she needed it. She had her work, her woman friends, Mary. And the occasional fling to keep the wolf from the door. All under control.

'Ta. I'd like that.'

I hope he's not still bleeding. I've had enough of bleeding men.

He put the phone down. He hadn't done anything like that in a long time. She surely wouldn't have given him the number if she hadn't meant him to use it.

An odd meeting, the oddest thing about it was that it had quickly felt natural, having an increasingly personal conversation with a stranger on a deserted beach. She'd said she came here to 'get her head together' but the turn of her mouth had put single quotes round it, so that was alright. So he nodded and said personally he came here to forget his head. And she laughed like she knew that feeling, then looked out at the grey sea beating up the rocks and said something about harmony. He'd said it looked like a right stramash to him, but he knew what she meant.

Now he stood at the kitchen window and looked at the harbour. Surprised and pleased, he had to admit. Alert eyes, roundish face and small, hooked nose, that was all he could remember. Her voice was London, slightly husky – too many Gauloises – and she'd chuckled, the woman actually chuckled. She must have been near his age. Made a change.

The tide was well turned but the boats were still slumped over in the mud. Caa canny, he thought. She's just a person you liked.

And when she had shivered despite her heavy jacket and blue bonnet pulled down over her ears, he'd suggested the café, and she'd said Why not?, just like that.

Now he wanted a cigarette but had deliberately allowed himself to run out. The last addiction. He glanced at the pale space on the wall where the Chagall had once been the loveliest blue in the world. At least Ruth's eyes are brown and that should be safe. Silly how these things matter but we're stuck with them.

Sitting in the café looking out at the sea – they'd been talking about being short of sleep – she'd said that she woke up sometimes in the night terrified of being dead. How could one straight item of personal truth not hold his attention? Yet she seemed assured, very much the modern woman, at ease, independent, in control as she sat side-on to him with her hands jammed deep in the pockets of an old reefer jacket.

And because one confidence deserved another, he'd said there'd been a time when death seemed like a release and he was still grateful to know one day he'd be wheiched away from all this.

All what? she'd asked. He had something against scones and hot Vimto?

Not at all! He'd laughed and changed the subject but for a moment they'd connected.

As they walked out to their cars to go their own way, she'd fumbled in her jacket and handed him a card.

'I enjoyed that,' she said briskly, 'especially the hot Vimto. If you feel like it again, get in touch and we'll have another.'

He turned it over thoughtfully between his fingers while she got into her car.

'I thought social workers drove old Minis.'

'Christ no, I've been promoted off the coal face and I'm only in this for the Polos,' she replied, waved and drove off.

A little repartee, a bit company. Maybe that was why she'd given him her number. Or maybe she was just doing community work overtime.

He wrapped the peppered smoked mackerel (a little cumin, lemon juice) in tinfoil, put it in the oven and watched the water creep in over the mud. The first boat would soon be afloat.

He phoned Alec to say he couldn't make the family meal on Sunday, and then struggled with the urge to run out for tobacco.

She put down the phone and felt pleased. Admit that. Schultz after Reykjavik: 'We must not be afraid to take yes as an answer to our proposal.' But be careful.

'Sprog, I've a friend coming down on Sunday,' she said neutrally. 'We might walk round to St Abbs, would you like to come?'

The child was welded to *EastEnders*.

'Uh huh,' she said.

When they sat down to tea she looked at her mother.

'What's his name?'

Can't fool 'em.

Nibbling her pinkie, she watched them climbing. She would never have let the sprog get so high. They were twenty feet up the sea-stack, making for a ledge connecting it to the St Abbs headland. Christ, she wasn't even seven yet. If Mary wasn't afraid, Ruth was.

But she saw how he had shepherded Mary all the way, just below or all around her, sheltering the child with his body. He seemed leisurely and secure in his movements, very upright, obviously well within his limits.

Mary had been, well, Mary. She'd run out to the car when he arrived. Ruth watched them from the door.

'You're Jimmy,' she said and stared at him.

'And you're Mary.'

She nodded, stuck her hands in the back pockets of her jeans. Here comes the inquisition.

'Where d'you stay?'

'Dunbar.'

'D'you have a dog?'

She was dead set on a dog. Ewan thought she should have one. He wouldn't have to live with it.

'No.'

'Well, do you have a cat?'

'I've a cat called Charlie but he's not very clever.'

'We've two cats and they're both very clever. What do you do?'

'I mend boats and fix engines.'

'My daddy has a boat.' It sounded like an accusation.

Oh dear. Jimmy crouched down till he was head high with the child.

'Tell me about your boat,' he said.

'We have it here but it doesn't go. Can you fix it?'

Good God, child, you're at it already.

'I can try,' he said gravely.

She'd relaxed then, went forward and put her arm round Mary who was already in full flow about all the things they could do when the boat was fixed, touched him lightly on the arm.

'Hi. How you doing?'

'Alright, I think. Yoursel?'

Mary wasn't moving now. She was frozen where the ledge narrowed. Jimmy couldn't get beside or below to protect her. For the next bit she was on her own.

He was bending across, saying something, pointing. Mary shook her head, began to crouch down, one of her legs quivering. Ruth felt the cord that was always between them tighten and twang. Jimmy glanced down quickly, then gestured to Mary to stand up and grip high with her hands. Again. And finally she did it. She shuffled sideways, awkward and stiff, not looking down. Another clumsy step. Another. The cord vibrated, Ruth felt sick. Another trembling shuffle, the ledge widened, she almost ran along it and was scrambling up the steep grassy slope onto the headland. Jimmy followed her quickly. At the top Mary turned and waved, jumping up and down with excitement.

She waved back, trembling slightly and pulled out a cigarette. Jesus.

She sat in the sunlight and calmed down. Men are more bold

with a child, she thought. Ewan's the same. It's not that they care less, they just perceive a different need.

I'd never have taken her up there, no matter how much she'd pleaded.

I can't do it all myself. I can for me, but not for her.

She was still thinking that one over when Mary came running down the hill towards her, windmilling her arms.

'Were you watching us, mummy?'

'All the time,' she said. Christ I love you, sprog, and I don't know what to do for the best.

'Were you scared?'

'I certainly was.'

'So was I! Just a little bit.'

She looked up as he came down the hill.

'You were both very good,' and her voice shook, just a little bit.

They walked back up towards the lighthouse.

'Was that under control?' she said quietly.

'Near as can be,' he said. 'We can't control everything, can we?'

When Mary had got gripped on the ledge, he'd been cursing himself as an irresponsible idiot. At the top he'd hugged her with relief, without thinking, the first entirely natural thing he'd done with her.

'Well, you got off with it,' she muttered.

He stopped, looked at the ground, frowning. Then he looked up at her. She saw hazel eyes, somewhere undecided between brown and green.

'If she was my bairn, I'd do the same if she really wanted to climb.'

'Yeah?'

'You want her to be independent? Sure of herself? Able to do what the wee boys do and better?'

'She got a fright, that's good for her?'

He nodded up ahead where Mary was careering around chasing an imaginary dog.

'Being able to beat it is.' He hesitated. 'But she's not my child, obviously. So I'm sorry.'

'Maybe I've got over-protective. She's different with her dad. She needs – '

She stopped herself in time.

'Maybe she needs hot Vimto and scones back at the Smugglers Hotel,' he said and held out his hand.

She grinned and took it, going up the hill. Bloody hell, she thought, I was going to be sensible in my thirties.

The Smugglers Hotel had a fine Golden Oldie juke. They might share a taste in desolate seascape, but this was testing time.

He let his fingers drift up the keys then punched K7, 'The Great Pretender'. Early teenage afternoons with Bridget, skiving from school.

She retaliated with 'Tell Laura I Love Her'.

'Before my time,' he murmured.

'On yer bike,' she said. 'It was my mum's favourite. Didn't do her much good.'

'No?'

'They separated when I was little. My dad went back to Italy.' She nibbled her finger thoughtfully. 'Not before time, but it hurt.'

'Ha!' He stabbed Barry McGuire, 'Eve Of Destruction'.

'Remember him on *Top of the Pops*?'

'Surely do. My faither was standing behind me, saying nothing, and I wished he'd dematerialise because this was mine. We get on much better, now he's dead.'

'You find that too?'

This is tricky, she thought. There's too much on offer, the sublime and the ridiculous.

She stroked in 'Here Comes The Night'.

'Right, then,' he said, and fed the machine some more.

L8, 'In The Midnight Hour'.

It's nice, she thought, when you can speak in code and someone picks you up and returns it and you don't feel so on your own.

Hm. She retorted with A4, 'The Wind Cries Mary'. Druggy, confused, terrible production, oddly innocent. A long time ago, London adolescence. She felt tearful and didn't know why.

He glanced at her. 'Only one way to top that. Mary!'

Mary ran over.

'Would you like to make the last choice?'

She stood on a chair and looked carefully over the selection.

'Do I only get one?'

'Yes.'

She pressed L11.

'Kylie!' she shouted triumphantly.

Ruth said she cooked well because she liked eating. She also liked drinking, smoking and chocolate. She'd always be a few pounds on the generous side. She'd stopped worrying about that. And she kept on smoking despite her fears, refusing to be intimidated.

Jimmy sat back from the table, she put her feet up on the tiled mantelpiece. Mary was asleep upstairs, the fire had beaten back the damp, and there was peace in the Fifties council house.

He looked into the fire and sipped the wine slowly, he'd still to drive home. It minded him of those evenings in Shetland by the fire with Joan. Joan-and-Graeme now. And why shouldn't we keep it in the family?

He shook his head. Ghosts.

'Yes?' Ruth asked.

'I was just thinking, about Mary. It must be hard. I mean, giving so much care and attention to someone who must eventually leave you.'

She pulled out another cigarette and waited. He cleared his throat.

'I mean, wanting to love and nurture and protect her from everything, while knowing that you can't and that she must leave you if you've done it right. It must be . . . painful.'

She'd been trained to listen as much to the sound of the voice as the words said.

'And was it?' she asked.

'What?'

'Painful?'

She'd been trained to observe too, and read the downward glance, the slight shake of the head before he ran his fingers through his hair and smiled, sortof.

'So when do you go off-duty, Ruth?'

'Alright, I'm asking as me now, just pure nosiness.'

'Ach, it's all by wi now.'

'Really?'

Then one of those quick changes of mood she'd noticed before, as though he'd looked into himself and found something funny.

'No,' he laughed. 'Not really. But you can learn to live with bogles. *Gie them their place, and they'll no hairm ye*, my granny used to say. You?'

'Me?'

'Yup. Ghosts?'

She wiggled her toes on the mantelpiece.

'I've some peace of mind I don't want to lose.'

He nodded, finished his glass.

'Sure, I'll be up the road soon.'

In the hall she kissed him lightly, nothing serious, seeing he wasn't going to do it first.

'G'night,' he said. 'Thanks. A really good day.'

You're losing your touch, she thought as she locked up. In the past you'd have pushed him out earlier or else had him upstairs, no messing. Must be getting wiser. Or just older.

But she was smiling as she padded up the stairs to look in on Mary.

'A right vale of tears,' she muttered to the child sprawled sleeping among her dolls and dogs and telephones. 'Don't hurry to grow up.'

He'd be about Torness by now, driving past the nuclear power station with a big moon rising like radioactivity over the North Sea.

She shook her head and went to bed, feeling like forty going on fourteen.

Nice of you to remember my birthday. Thanks! Sorry I forgot yours – you know me – live on another planet. Restless, bored out here – the wee toy business has folded along with Michel (fun while it lasted, but enough) and I'm waitressing again to stretch the scholarship – which is a joke – I've no new ideas – there's nothing to do that someone else isn't doing better and it all seems forced. The French talk theory brilliantly and I feel like a peasant.

Whinge, whinge. I'm blocked and don't know why. I had to leave Scotland – you understand – so came here and it was good for a while and now it isn't. Maybe I'll come home. Life in our wee colonised country – who are these English? – frustrates me, but I dwindle without it. Glad you liked the Brit Council exhibition, but my past works seem a juvenile fraud.

Had a card from Graeme too. Seems he's living with Joan and painting landscapes! Why not get in touch with him – isn't it time?

It's nice of you to care, about my so-called breakdown. My own fault – just got a bit hyper – lost the place for a while. But for God's sake don't fuss about me – there's only room for one on the cross, so please get down off mine!

Of course I love you too. My friends are dearer to me than my hands.
Kim

He pinned her big Kandinsky card next to Ruth's phone number and a card from MacBeth and Clackmannan on a total death-route in Pakistan, then went for a long walk through the town in the rain, watching what was happening and trying not to get caught up in the familiar, tedious, dirty traffic passing through.

'You look like you're needin a holiday, Jim,' Rita at the fish shop said.

'A heart by-pass operation, more like.'

When it had cleared he went back home, took the card down and re-read it. Kim's notebooks had been an explanation and a dismissal. Severance pay. She really wasn't his responsibility. He put the pin carefully through the original hole and pressed steadily with his thumb. He wanted to phone Ruth and listen to her voice awhile.

Not her problem.

He lay in the bath, just floating. He began thinking about the yard. He was getting bored of engines and the dirtiness of diesel was getting on his nerves and he didn't trust the funny money that was going about. The electronics side was okay but it would be interesting to diverge into something new, something of his own.

He was thinking of his old drilling supervisor. They'd bumped into each other on Lothian Road in Edinburgh the other week. Marshall had left the rigs and moved into building domes. Geodesic domes, radar domes like transparent golfballs. Now he was looking to expand, needed a partner with capital and skill or at least collateral. Better still, someone to tie in the electronic and engineering sides, someone who had no ties and fancied a bit of travel . . .

'But no more bloody games like that twist-off,' he'd said as they parted.

Jimmy had grinned, taken his card, put it somewhere or other.

Interesting structures, domes. Buckminster Fuller, bloody ingenious. The flanges on all the panels must be cut at a slight angle, converging on the hypothetical centre.

He liked that idea. Maximum surface area, pure geometry, and a centre, however hypothetical. Everyone should have one. Travel and a new ploy. So where had he put that card?

'She likes you. You take her climbing and treat her like a small adult. She's also going to be a terrible flirt, unlike her mother.'

'No?'

'I only flirt when it means nothing.'

I considered the implications of this while greasing up the gear-change on her Yamaha outboard. It was several weeks after the climbing at St Abbs because we'd made sure we'd been too busy to meet for a while.

'And she's obsessed with weddings. It's an occupational hazard for single parents. I've never fancied marriage myself, it would make me lazy, or trapped.'

'Mary?'

I worked the handle up and down. Forward, Reverse, Neutral. A bit worn but what do you expect.

'A brilliant mistake. Ewan and I knew we needed a change and neither of us saw marriage as an advance. So we had her. Which was wonderful but it didn't solve things. He – well – it didn't stick.'

I nodded and carefully fitted the new fly-wheel, making sure the teeth meshed properly. That's what had broken the last one – general wear and a bit of impatience. I pulled the starter cord through slowly, checking the return.

'Aye, Bridget and I were together for years till we knew we needed a change. Right idea, wrong change but.'

So I fastened down the engine cover. The water-pump was on its last legs but that was common enough. Sea's terrible for corrosion. Just as well, it kept the yard in business. But it was time to diversify and I was looking into the dome erection business with Marshall. In fact I'd committed us to pitching for a couple of contracts in the UK and Saudi.

'So what happened?' she said eventually.

'Uh? Oh, we got married.'

'You're *married*?'

I looked up.

'Was. Before Kim and that. Anither lifetime. I tend to forget.'

She pushed up her sleeves, the breeze stirred thin brown hairs on her forearms. A bonnie day by the shore, air full of light, still cool but the beginning of Spring. I felt I'd come back to myself for the first time in ages, like there inside my skin instead of a spectator.

'You don't let on much, do you?'

A distant echo of Lesley saying that in Orkney, winding reeds round her fist, trying to tell me, warn me, and me much too obsessed (admit it, dependent) to see what was happening. Not again.

'It's no secret,' I said and lowered the engine onto the transom. 'I just don't blab as much as I used to, or think people should be as close as I once did. But there's no no-go areas. Ask me anything.'

233

The mounting screws were badly corroded. Even greased they'd never turn that well. I screwed them tight as possible and fitted the safety chain.

She lit a cigarette and considered.

'And blow some smoke this way, will you? I'm into passive smoking.'

She laughed, leaned forward and exhaled gently into my face.

'Is this close enough?' she asked in her brownest voice.

'This is fine,' I said. 'This way I can kid myself I've broken the habit.'

She hesitated, but didn't ask. I worked on in the sunlight. Around us the world went about mating and territory and we seemed part of it.

'For a while after I left Ewan,' she said eventually, 'when I was at my worst, I used to light up my next flame from the remains of the old one. I had to have someone, to know I was worth anything.'

'Do any good?'

She shook her head vehemently.

'It's not on.'

'No.'

'And you?'

'Had a few dangerous liaisons. Now I'm into laughter and forgetting.'

She raised her brown Italian eyebrows at me.

'I didn't know you read.'

I sat back on my heels and levelled the pliers at her.

'Ruth. It pisses me off when folk assume because I work wi my hands, I'm thick as two shorts. Like, I'm an engineer so I can only read manuals. I think technically, so Art is wasted on me. Yes? Christ, I lived with one. Don't box me.'

We did a spot of eye-wrestling. At last she nodded.

'Sorry if I sounded patronising.'

'Doesn't matter.' I shrugged. 'Happens aa the time.'

A long silence while I struggled to lever the spring clip off the fuel line. Just how many lovers has she had? Is it better not to remember them, or have each one carved in you forever?

She passed the new valve before I asked. I threw the old one away, it was done.

'This Kim – Government Health Warning stuff?'

'Yup.'

'You going monosyllabic on me?'

I plugged in the fuel line and began to squeeze the bulb till it firmed up.

'Not her fault,' I said. 'The addiction is the addict's. It's not easy for anyone. Especially for her, being an artist, like.'

'Huh. What difference does that make?'

I scratched my head with the pliers. She nibbled her pinkie and looked at me sideways like she was just checking.

'Dunno. Suppose they're like anyone else, but moreso. Man, even when they're sitting having breakfast with you they're partly out to lunch somewhere else. Not easy to live wi.' I checked the few hairs caught in the pivot, a couple were definitely grey. 'Interesting but. I'm kinda lazy so it did me good.'

'End of story?'

'There's not an end of story. Speir awa.'

'Right now it's too nice a day.'

'Then shout on Mary and we'll take a trip round the bay.'

'Hadn't you better check the engine's working?'

'Ruth, I'm doubtful about most things, but I am sure about engines. They're the only thing I'm any damn good at. It'll go.'

'Yeah, but try it.'

'Trust me.'

'You never know. She'd be awfully let down.'

So I tried it. Wouldn't start. It took ten minutes to narrow it down to the fuel jet and fix that.

'If I get cocky again about *anything*, call me on it, huh?'

She lay back laughing in the stern of the wee clinker-built boat. Then held out her hand.

'I could like you,' she said.

I pulled her upright.

'Oh jolly, jolly good,' I said.

'So you may kiss me properly now, if that's not too alarming.'

Dear Jimmy,

Your letter's come as I'm packing up to leave here. It's good to hear you're alive & kicking & heart throbbing (quietly). Me too! I've no short answers to your questions but we can play Passion v. Friendship all night long because due to Unforeseen Developments (ain't they all?) I'm coming back to the booming UK despite the Government, and may stay longer if things work out!

So, you can pick me up as indicated? I'm the tall sassy broad bringing your favourite malt – and a Surprise. And my love, of course.

     Les

He added the card – Aspen, Colorado – to the cork board and, smiling, gathered up the file on domes and radar systems, the pages of rough cost breakdowns and estimates. It seemed like a lot of people were suddenly wanting protective domes over their delicate equipment.

He dumped the papers on the passenger seat and set off for work, still wondering about the Surprise.

Ruth sat on the windowseat and noted the blank spaces on his kitchen wall. She had some of her own. The only photos of Ewan left in her house were the ones in Mary's room. When she went in to say goodnight, they were hard to look at and impossible not to.

'So what goes wrong with these ships of ours, as you call them?'

He kept on stirring the sauce, off the heat. Things had got to a critical stage and she was asking him to say something meaningful.

'Maybe we jump on board and cast off merrily, each hoping the other can navigate.'

'And can you?'

'Scarcely. You?'

She shrugged.

'I can just about manage me and Mary.'

The cream went in fine. Now the redcurrant jelly. She handed him a glass of red and stood nearby in his kitchen waiting to be fed, the first unattached woman to do so in a while.

'Like wi Kim,' he said, swallowed and frowned into the glass. 'In the end I made her, her life, her career, looking after her as I thought it, into the point of my life. I called that devotion. By wee calibrations over the years, I tried to make her my answer, and called that love. Being in love is like eating Fry's Five Boys chocolate in reverse, it starts with Delectation and ends with Desperation.'

'Sounds like you've O.D.'d on sugar.'

'So I'm being too serious.'

'No, I'm being flippant. I'm not used to serious conversation with men. Go on.'

He stirred with his right and drank with his left. His voice still changed when he talked about Kim, which irritated him but there it was. She put her hand on his shoulder and looked down into the pan.

'You see, back then there was a lot about how we men had to, uh, *prioritise* the lady of our lives. And at the same time you were shifting your priorities to careers, women friends, politics, going out on the ran-dan, whatever. We were supposed to be tender and cry while we chopped onions, but still hunky.'

'Ah, the tender hulk,' she murmured, 'Still looking for that one.'

'It fair made my heid birl. I took the prioritising too far because I had nothing better to do.'

She dipped her pinkie in the sauce and sucked it thoughtfully.

'Yessir,' she murmured, 'I remember those days. Apologising for being hetero at intense little meetings. Mind you, it was incredibly exciting. But a beginning, not the end.'

He transferred the contents into the heated dish. Normally of course he just bunged it on the plates but she and the food deserved better.

'In the end,' he concluded, 'for what it's worth I now think we have to carry who we are and not dump it on ships or mountains or sunsets or having babies or anything else.'

'Hm,' she said. 'That sounds hard. Ready?'

'The main course is ready,' he replied.

They sat down to eat.

'And what do you call this philosophy?' she asked.

'Pork and prunes with cream and redcurrant,' he said, 'what else?'

They got stuck in.

'So,' she said later, 'you can cook and you want to talk about feelings. Is this the New Man, then?'

'Christ, no!' The spiced pears with lemon cream were a cinch but always fairly impressive. 'That's glib and phoney. No wonder women don't trust it. There's no such thing as new. Na, Partially-Reconditioned at best.'

She chuckled.

'Meet the Nearly New Woman.'

'Meaning?'

'Meaning these days we're confident enough to suit ourselves. I'm still going that way but not on party lines any more.'

He raised his glass.

'The Nearly New Woman.'

'Partially-Reconditioned Man.'

It was getting late and the question hung between them. She took a deep breath, flicked her cigarette into the fire, and exhaled.

'There's a problem here,' she said. 'It's a nice ride so far, but right now I've one foot on the accelerator, and one on the brake.'

He flipped his first cigarette for ages onto the fire. In truth, it made him feel slightly sick.

'Well, you could always take feet off both pedals and see what happens.'

'What do you want with me, Jimmy?'

Does any woman know what it is to be the man sitting beside her? Knowing – and slightly resenting – that despite everything it's still up to him. He aches to, but he may be out of order. Will she be shocked when he makes that move? Or is she dismayed at his hesitation?

Open your mouth and see what comes out. Trust it.

'I want to open another bottle, but you may be driving back tonight.'

She paused for a long time, then held out her empty glass.

'More, please,' she said. 'I don't think so.'

'And I don't suppose you have AIDS either,' she said as they untangled at the foot of the stairs.

'Tested HIV Negative eight months back. I don't do hard drugs and I loved a man once but I'm boringly straight. You?'

'Since my chain-smoking period there's just been the odd episode.'

'Don't think I fancy being an odd episode.'

'Good. Then I don't think you are.'

He was still figuring that one out when she added, 'There's risk in anything that's worth anything.'

'Tears before nightfall,' he said automatically.

'Christ, don't turn Scottish on me now,' she said. 'I've come to love this place, but your weather and your pessimism – '

'Well then?'

They looked at each other.

'Bloody hell,' she said, 'I spend half my working life telling kids not to do this.'

They went upstairs.

'I'm not sure I remember how to do this, it's been so long.'

'I won't notice because I've forgotten.'

'Just don't mime,' she said huskily, 'and I won't either.'

'Can you just leave me lying in the morning?' he requested, last thing before sleep.

She was twisted on her side, struggling with her portable alarm clock. Without her lenses she was short-sighted as a mole, had to get very close to see much at all. They'd been very close and they'd kept their eyes wide open.

'Oh, I dare say I can tear myself away,' she murmured.

Bloody hell, the women won't let you off with anything these days. But still she rolled towards him and opened up her arms again, and consequently it felt like heaven, in an unexpectedly-arrived sort of way.

'Doing anything next weekend?' he asked sleepily.

She hesitated at the mirror, then popped in her lenses and felt on top of things again. You're a bloody fool, Ruthie, and too old for this sort of carry-on. And there's Mary.

'Is this going to be one of those regular things?' she said.

He watched her from the bed. There are women who fasten a bra at the front then shift it round, and those who hook it straight from the back. She was a back fastener. Either way, a lovely gesture, he thought, personal and inward. Like the cross-armed way she'd peeled off her sweater, something only women do. Women and their way of doing things, it's like irrigation brought to the desert.

'Because I don't know if I've room for it.'

She watched him in the mirror as she buttoned her blouse, thinking of the morning appointments, hoping Ewan could be trusted to get Mary to school on time.

'I'm just asking,' he said slowly, 'if you're doing anything next weekend.'

She buttoned her skirt and hitched it round. Should she be directive in the meeting or let it run itself?

'I've things on my mind,' she said. 'But last night was fun.'

She saw him wince at 'fun'. Fair enough, she thought, but I've spent three years putting together this peace of mind, why should I endanger it now?

He was out of bed like it was on fire and reached for his dressing gown. A flash of Ewan yawning in his old yellow towelling. We loved each other, I wanted his child, our child. I got Mary but left part of me behind. Not again.

'Sure,' he said, 'meaningless as you want.' Then stopped and said more quietly 'But really, I've had enough of meaningless.'

She put on the dark navy jacket she'd brought just in case she was foolish enough to stay the night, buttoned it, checked herself out. Bloody departmental meetings, give me field-work any day. Think of the money, you need it. Mary needs it. Make up? Sod that.

Admit it, if a man was giving you this morning-after line, you'd be furious and you'd have ten thousand righteous sisters behind you.

She turned to look at him directly, brushing her thick hair back, clasping it, brushing out towards her hand again, releasing it again.

'Light,' she said, 'not necessarily meaningless.'

She watched him pull his shirt on over his head as if wrestling with monsters. The way men did things, their utterly foreign gestures, the relief with which they took their clothes off, the abrupt way they pulled them on again. He grabbed his sweater and she felt something flow through her, leaving her weak in the stomach. Too much wine last night.

He emerged tousled and victorious from his fight with the sweater.

'Kindof like a soufflé,' he grinned. 'Light but no entirely pointless.'

She levelled the brush at him.

'Right.'

She checked herself for the meeting, trying to remember the hidden agenda. Every meeting has one.

'How about another soufflé, two weekends from now? My place. I'll have a fair appetite by then. I think,' she said carefully, 'we need to take a break and assess this.'

'Tickety boo,' he said cheerfully. 'And you're right. An internal enquiry is definitely called for.'

She kissed him lightly, friendly-in-a-hurry.

'And now I gotta run.'

Does it show? she wondered. Will they say, oh yeah, Ruth's been getting laid again?

'On the other hand,' he said, 'we could just admit we're scared witless.'

The things he says, she thought as she went into the meeting. Partially-Reconditioned Man is quite encouraging. He's no worse than me, and the Nearly New Woman feels pretty good today.

She opened the door. Watch for the hidden agenda. Here goes.

The way she'd peeled her sweater off, cross-armed, elbows rising and her free heavy breasts falling. And the way she put her watch on in the morning, lying on her back and propping the dial with her chin against her wrist as she fastened the strap. And in between the two, after they'd discovered they still knew how to do this, she'd murmured 'The way people like us live is like trying to grow grapes on the slopes of a volcano,'

Two gestures and her words, they came back to him for days as he guddled about thoughtfully in knackered old engines like clapped-out hearts, trying to find more mileage in them.

'Hi Jim-boy! How's it going, pal? I keep getting this bloody answerphone but this time I'll leave a message.(pause)

Eh, I had a card from you know who the ither day and it got me thinking. I mean, surely it's time we got together again, I mean it's a fair while back, right? (pause)

Joan's well and asks me to send her love and say she saw that otter again. I hope she's not numbered among my crimes against humanity. Against you, I mean. It's no so surprising people fall for people they already know and anyway, you always had great taste in women. (pause)

That wis a joke.

Life's very different up here, suppose you'll mind that. Creepily quiet, except for the wind. Makes you think.

I'm odd-jobbing, and painting again – landscape would you fucking believe. Flogged the odd wan and all. Nae people, jist cliffs and clouds and voes. Actually I'm working on one of Joan on the side. (pause)

Look, why don't we climb the Old Man? Come up and stay with us a few days then we'll go over to Orkney and finally knock off the big yin. Nae sweat and it's about time.

So why not phone, you old fart.

Cheerio.

Oh, and the politics? The industrial proleteriat's a bit thin on the ground here except at Sullom Voe. But I'm still active – we'll give it one more go in the next Election, right? And if we fail, maybe it's time we brought it all back home as the man sung. The struggle continues!

Bye.'

After the message had run through, he hesitated then pressed SAVE and went back to the papers in front of him. *Dear Mr*

Renilson, your outline quotation for the erection of the radadome is
acceptable, subject to the following conditions . . .

'Golly, I had an appetite,' she said. 'That was ace.'

If he'd kept his mouth shut and accepted the ego-massage, likely it wouldn't have gone further than another brief safe trip round the bay.

'Eight out of ten,' he said slowly. 'Jolly good.'

'It beats the solace of two fingers.'

They were lying in her bed with the window open. High tide and a big sea running. She lived even nearer to the water than he did.

'I hate it when you come the woman-of-the-world bit.'

She rolled on her back and looked at the ceiling.

'I *am* a woman of the world,' she said. 'I support myself and my daughter and I take responsibility for my life. I have my work, my friends, the folk club and sometimes I drink and smoke too much. And sometimes I need a little fun.'

It was her litany, it had kept her going.

'Aye, sounds good,' he said. 'It sounds like your life, my life and a whole lot of others. But all this stuff everyone talks about these days, about taking responsibility, taking charge, taking decisions, taking on board – it sounds like too much taking to me. Sounds like our times and I don't like it.'

Silence. Leave it, Jim.

'It was great but I've got this queasy feeling that says you took what you wanted and I feel used.'

'You can feel used?' she said slowly. 'Men? Sexually?'

'Asset-stripped,' he said.

'That's not fair! This is mutual.'

'Sure, it's honest and open and all that, not like the bloody Guinness takeover. But we're still stripping each other's assets for our own gratification and when that runs out, we move on.'

Where had that anger come from?

'It's not right,' he concluded lamely. 'That's not where it's at.'

She rolled on her side and looked at him. Her lenses were beginning to itch.

'Jimmy,' she said, 'you'll never adjust to the Eighties. That's why I live up here – because most of you still believe the dream might just work. You still seem to think we're interdependent.'

'Well of course we are. That's too obvious to need saying.'

'You won't find many still believe that down South. So what is where it's at?'

'I kent once,' he said quietly. He no longer knew what would happen next. This was new territory. 'So did you.'

Even the hard plastic lenses didn't protect her eyes.

'It hurt so much. Losing it,' she said.

'Didn't it.'

'I don't know if I need that again.'

'Me neither, but what's the alternative?'

They looked at each other, helpless it seemed. Soon someone would have to make a move.

Into what? he wondered. Or do we very carefully abseil off this one and walk away from it before someone gets hurt?

If I give up control, she thought, where will it end? She scratched her leg and shivered slightly. It all ends the same, night without end. So?

'I haven't been here before,' he said slowly, wanting to get it right, 'but it might help if two people approached each other thinking less of what they need and more of what they have to give.'

She sat up abruptly and reached for her cigarettes. He wished she wouldn't smoke so much, which was absurd, considering he'd started again. She looked well on it but. Her breasts were full and gravity suited them.

She lit up and looked him over. She could talk to him and he had good ploys and it was good for a girl to fuck her brains out once in a while. But asset-stripping?

'Can we start again?' she said. 'I *was* just sex-starved, and so were you. I don't know the answer to all these questions and I've Mary to consider. It's not fair for her to get used to you and you then disappear.' She made a swirling gesture with her hand, and added to his store of memories. 'Don't do a Guinness on me. Don't give me assurances and win me over, then take it all back.'

'I can't give you any assurances at all. But I'll not lie to you.'

'It's a deal,' she said. 'I'll send round my lawyers tomorrow.'

He got up and made tea, brought it back to bed. She sighed and laid her head on his shoulder, fitting a couple of inches higher than Kim had.

'So, tell me about Kim and the others. The good as well as the bad.'

They talked long past midnight like two old hands comparing yarns of past voyages, of special cargoes, of mates and wrecks.

243

Twinges of jealousy, a little competitiveness, but mostly laughter and recognition. He listened closely to her voice when she talked about Ewan, heard surprise and faint sadness that her feelings could have changed so much. What he heard sounded like finished business. Outside the sea was big and wild and broken on the rocks but kinda wonderful to hear so long as it stayed out there.

'By the way,' he said last thing, 'I have to tell you the tender hulk does not exist,' but maybe she was already asleep.

They woke with Mary bouncing on them.

'Good God, child, can't you sleep in just once? Sorry about this,' Ruth added to him.

'No,' said Mary.

'I kinda like it,' he said. 'really.'

'I'll tell you a story,' Mary announced.

'Let's hear it.'

'It's about a prince and a giant and there's a castle. And the princess. You can be the giant.'

Ruth grinned and pulled on her dressing gown.

'Hm,' he said and looked into the child's eyes. 'Is he a good giant or a bad giant?'

Mary considered while Ruth paused at the door.

'Not bad,' she said, 'just big and clumsy. He keeps falling over and breaking things. Maybe he gets stuck in the castle.'

Ruth went downstairs, shaking her head. The things they come out with.

'Is it scary?'

'Not so very scary,' she said and pushed her hair back. She looked nothing like Ruth. Her father's child, Jimmy thought. Fair enough. 'More exciting, especially for the princess!'

The things they say. In all innocence. Well, maybe.

'And is there a happy ending?'

'I don't know – I'm just making it up now.'

She sprawled on the bed and danced around the room, acting out a story of princes, giants, castles and princesses, full of contradictions and dead-ends, irrelevances, sudden changes of tack, tense and point of view, what Alison called narrational self-reference and suchlike. Really, a child could do it, he thought. Finally she drew it to a close with an improbable wedding, jumped onto the bed and stood looking down at him.

'My dad really likes my stories,' she said, and waited.

'It's a great story, hairy Mary.'

244

'I'm not hairy Mary,' she said indignantly.

'And I'm not your dad.'

'Of course not,' she said. 'He lives with Catherine and Billy and Luke.'

Ruth called them down. Breakfast was on the table, bacon and eggs, tattie scones, coffee and rolls.

'The Nearly-New Woman strikes again,' she said. 'How was the story?'

'Confusing,' he said, 'but lots of fun.'

They sat down to eat. Outside, the sea was glittering and calm. They'd take the boat out and go wherever they felt like, within reason.

The card was of Chagall's stained glass windows, postmarked Paris. She was getting closer.

Got to go where the money is! Artist in residence in Glasgow. Help ma boab – but consider the alternative. So I'm coming home – see you soon? Love.

ps These windows are everything I want to do but can't. Pack it in? Not on yr nellie.

Kim xx

He pinned the card next to the others, noticed his heart running a bit faster than usual. Paris, he thought, I remember that. Ach, might as well see her and get it over with.

After all, there was Ruth. Maybe they could carefully cultivate grapes on the slopes of the volcano and drink the wine, and celebrate modestly without getting guttered.

I snap the elastic band back round the stack of cards, automatically lining up the pin-holes, then put them back in the shoe box labelled CARDS 85–89.

Once this is over, there'll be a clearing-out, I promise you. This attic is stuffed with slumped bin bags and boxes, tools and notebooks, photos, sleeping bags, tents and skis and climbing gear and exhibits I haven't had time to sort through since. No wonder Les finds Kim's flat empty and a bit creepy.

The later and quieter it gets, the better I can lean into the lamplight and hear the wind and sea and distant cars, and feel my heart, that engine, pumping into the night.

TWENTY-TWO

Compression

AN OIL LAMP was burning on her kitchen table as she was cooking. It must have been over-filled, because she turned to see flames overflowing and flickering on the surface of the table. She hurriedly damped them out with a wet towel before any damage had been done to the surface. She turned down the lamp and went back to the stove. Again the lamp overflowed and again, though it was a nuisance, the flames left no mark. She continued stirring the pans on the stove, the meal was a large and complicated one for several people and she thought it would have been better to keep it simple and for one. Then she smelled the smoke. She turned to see the lamp overflowing like a fountain. Flames poured over the table and cascaded onto the floor and now the wooden floorboards were on fire.

Ruth stood with a stirring spoon in her hand. My God, this time the flames are real.

They were hunkered down on the pre-dawn Pentland hills, looking back where the windy city was about to emerge from the grey.

They had been silent for some time, since she'd finished telling him her dream. Now she took a deep drag and passed him the joint. He took it, said nothing, waited for whatever was coming. A green light shimmered just above the horizon, another summer solstice coming.

'So it seems I love you,' she said.

He looked at her. His mouth opened but the word was stuck crosswise in his throat like a bone.

'I know,' she said briskly, 'but I've decided to take the risk. I don't say it so you'll say it back. This is a unilateral declaration, right?'

He looked away at the smaller shadowy hump of Arthur's Seat and felt inadequate. That word.

He coughed and passed her the smoke but held on to her hand. The bone was still stuck, he just couldn't cough it up.

246

'Don't worry about it,' she said. 'I just thought you ought to know.'

Anything he could say seemed so much haivering. The red stain haemmorrhaged, the sun edged up over Leith, he took a photo and the lights of the city began to look tiny and ridiculous.

'These hills of yours are alright,' she puffed as they hurried across the summit plateau. 'Once in a while, if there's food, a hot bath, and a bottle of wine at the end of it. Too healthy a lifestyle would be the death of me.'

'So let's do it more often,' he said and swerved downhill towards the artifical ski slope. She glanced at him as she struggled to keep up. He seemed at home here, moving at ease, in place in a way she'd never be. A small-town boy, he'd said, a cheuchter at heart with a few modern tastes, such as soft drugs, pushy women, and hard Rhythm and Blues. Was this man serious?

'But you must miss it.'

'Miss what?'

'You know. The climbing world, your friend Graeme – her. It's not my kind of scene.'

'Ach, suppose I do. But on the whole I'd be happy just to hill-walk with you.'

'On the whole.'

'Aye, on the whole. Why not?'

Head down, she awkwardly picked her way down. He did it at a run, zig-zagging to ease the angle and for the fun of it, feeling the world change direction under his feet.

She caught up with him at the car, limping slightly. She stood square in front of him, her hands jammed deep in her coat pocket, her long mouth set.

'I don't want to be something you just settle for,' she announced.

'Who said anything about settling?'

She punched him on the arm.

'Don't get funny with me, mate.'

'That hurt! Anyway, I've virtually no sense of humour.'

'I hate it when you're glib.'

'And I hate it when you push too bloody hard.'

They glared at each other for a while, then she looked over at the city while he studied the hills. She kicked the turf, hating it but there it was. Engineers. He nibbled his fingernail. Social workers, he should have known better.

Absolute beginners, he thought.

Absolute dick-heads, she thought.

She got into her car and slammed the door. He sat in the passenger seat, glanced at her unyielding profile.

'What are you waiting for?'

'No bloody key,' she hissed, 'you've got it.'

'Really?'

He fumbled through his pockets, losing his hands in them among the bits of heather, shells and stones. That dope had been rather strong.

'You're right,' he mumbled, handed her the key. 'Defensive posture and that.'

She hesitated with the key in the ignition.

'And I'm a right bossy-boots sometimes. Mary says so.'

'Well . . . yeah, you are.'

'And I get scared, you know that.'

'I know that.'

'It's still her, isn't it?'

He stared at her.

'I'm not jealous,' she said quickly. 'I accept her like you accept Ewan. We're not kids any more. I just want to know where I stand.'

He looked down at the city, then up to the hills, wondering where indeed.

'I loved her, of course. Very much, well, totally.' He listened to the resonance. For a moment he was stooped beside the well in the broch of Gurness, trailing fingers in the water. 'And, for accuracy's sake, I probably do still love her.' Hashish always made him pedantic. 'But I don't want her,' he said, and it sounded possible.

'Do you want anyone?'

'Ah,' he said. 'And you can mak a kirk or a mill of that.'

'She sounds a right pain in the neck. Just like me,' she added.

'Not like you. Quite a different sort of pain.'

This time he protected his arm.

'She's probably a very ordinary person.'

'Very probably. Ewan's not the monster slime-bag I was led to expect.'

'I'd like to meet her someday.'

He took a deep breath.

'You can.'

'What?'

'She's back in the country. I'll be seeing her soon enough.'

248

'Ah,' she said. 'Is that a big deal?'

'Not so very big.'

She started the car and tried to remember how to do this. Move up slowly through the gears.

'Well, keep me posted.'

'I'm licking the stamp already, babe.'

'Glib!' they chorused.

That photo from the Pentlands, Ruth kept it in her office through her promotions. Just the strong curve of her shoulder and head against the growing light. A hopeful time. Angola, Namibia, Iran-Iraq, the Soviets out of Afghanistan, the IMF treaty signed: a time of peace and negotiation between exhausted parties.

And that word love beginning to be used again. Heady stuff, and worrying to someone convinced he was a loving spoonful short of the whole canteen.

He walked slowly up and down the platform of Dunbar station, clicking his heels on the concrete, counting paces in and out of the sunlight. The rails were shining and empty, converging on some mirage to the South.

He wheeled sharply at the end of the platform. Imagine waiting for Lenin coming off his sealed train. Here comes trouble. Here comes the past. Remember meeting her off the train back from Morocco, waking in that room with an almost holy sense . . .

He pivoted at the other end of the platform. That time wouldn't come again. There were consolations, like Ruth and Mary, like not confusing anxiety with passion, like a human warmth that wasn't a forest fire.

He'd probably never know how she lived now, not intimately. That had been the hardest, accepting her thoughts and daily life would always be turned away from him, like the dark side of the moon.

The dark side. He thought again of her father's end, her breaking in on the echo of the shotgun blast, what she must have seen left lying across the bed. He'd seen the sketches erupting from harmless doodles in her notebooks, then furiously scored over as though one side of her brain was cancelling what the other had done.

It was a kind of arrogance, thinking he could help her. It was a useless pity.

The rails began to zing. The train came in and she got off it, wearing a peaked cap but otherwise not the least like Lenin. She was an awkward wee figure at the far end of the platform, looking uncertainly about her, carrying no obvious baggage.

She waved and smiled. As he walked towards her, the sun was in the sky where it should be, not shining out of her mouth. And pale blue eyes are just pale blue eyes. A dream is only a fine example of a dream.

'Christ it's good to see you.'

She hesitated, then put her arms round him. For a moment he felt her lips brush his cheek.

'Full circle,' she said.

He woke in the darkness and knew she wasn't there.

He groped for her watch. 2.30, the graveyard shift. Thanks be he wasn't still on the rigs. Jesus, what a way to go.

The house was silent. She could be anywhere. Not his business. He squeezed the watch she always removed at night or before making love. She said it was like having a time-bomb strapped to your wrist.

It was his business. He put on her dressing gown and went to find her.

She was at the window in Mary's room. The child was sleeping sprawled behind a rampart of assorted furry toys. Ruth was leaning on the frame in the moonlight, her head bent on her forearm as though weeping but there was no sound.

'Ruthie?'

Her head moved slightly from side to side.

'Night fears,' she whispered. 'I was dead and buried and the darkness will go on forever.'

He tightened his arm round her, and stroked her sweating hair with his other hand. Forever, yes, it could seem like a long time.

'Then I wake up, and it's still true. Soon I'm going to cease to exist. I'll be ashes like those poor men on that platform! Forever!'

Her voice shook. He couldn't tell her it wasn't true. All he could do was be there.

'I'm *not* going to cry,' she said firmly, then he felt the moisture on his shoulder. 'All this beauty, then nothing till the end of time. Oh, how can anyone not find it unbearable!'

This tearing feeling, he hadn't had it for years. She was right beside him but she was on her own and this time he had to accept that.

She dried her face with the back of her hand. He said what he could, held her and listened to the sound of her voice and the kick it made inside, and wondered if this painful caring made the difference between mutual gratification and something better.

He listened till the shivering of the naked woman beside him was natural and then took her back to bed. She was asleep in seconds but he lay awake a long time, listening to the incoming tide.

'Sorry about last night.'

They were sitting on her doorstep in bright sunlight, all night terrors gone and unlikely as having made love to someone five hundred times.

'Dinna be daft. Wish I could carry it for you but I can't.'

'I know the boundaries,' she said and studied her cigarette. 'Only children are entitled to depend. But it helped you being there.'

'I love you,' he said. He'd had half the night to check on it. 'At this moment,' he added, to be accurate.

'Christ, you sound raw. Take it easy, huh?'

The word was rusty in his throat, he hadn't used it in a long time. It sounded different from before, but not untrue.

'No hurry,' she said.

They leaned lightly against against each other and watched the world go about.

'I expect it's just lust speaking.'

Her long mouth creased.

'I expect it is.'

On the shore Mary was playing with her wee friends. She stood ankle-deep at the centre of her universe, waving back to them.

The card was of the Old Man of Hoy, taken from the landward side. He could pick out the exact point where he'd fallen, a lifetime ago. Re-incarnation is true in that way.

Hi youth!

Time we got together and knocked this one off.

Down in a couple of weeks to see my old man. Let's meet and talk about it, huh? And anything else.

Miss ya.

    G

And underneath, in a more regular hand:

Jimmy, he still feels badly about the whole thing, he's brooding and drinking too much. Give him a chance. You owe me that much.

God bless — Joan.

He pinned the card below the others and studied the line of his fall.

She took the curling Borders back road fast, propelled by Talking Heads up loud on the cassette, somehow managing to watch the road, the countryside, Mary in the back seat, think to herself and talk to Jimmy at the same time. Mother, lover, herself – there were times it all seemed possible.

She came to a fork, took the left one, hoping she still remembered. Maybe she did make up her mind too quickly, but she was pretty sure.

In the passenger seat he admired her forceful driving but felt slightly sea-sick as she swept the car into the Duns valley. It was an exhilarating ride but he wished she'd slow down a bit.

She wished he'd have a little more faith.

To be in charge was a burden. To not be in charge was worrying. There had to be another way, but Ruth said it had to be negotiated every day. Which sounded like social worker speak and a lot of hard work. Jollification was important too. Mary had a clear grasp of the importance of having fun. She was able to spend hours blowing bubbles and then running round bursting them without regret.

Ruth turned into the Mony Nut valley and pulled up by a low wall.

'Everybody out. It's over here.'

He lay on the bank by the flickering water, keeping an eye on Mary leaning over the pool as she tried to catch tiddlers with her hands. Ruth lay sunbathing, mother-naked on the warm stones. She and Mary took their clothes off at the slightest opportunity. As one made sceptical by the vagaries of his country's weather, he'd gone so far as to roll up his shirt sleeves.

The deep pool, the hidden bank – she'd taken them straight to the spot. She must have been here before, probably with Ewan. He didn't ask, she'd talk about it if it mattered.

He closed his eyes. It was good to see Kim once in a while, each time more normal than the last. He'd watch her while she talked, noticing the new phrases she used, the assurance, the first few lines around her eyes. Good to feel the distance as well as the closeness. They gossiped, talked about her work, friends, present ships, about everything but the past.

Except the last time, at his house, when she'd hesitated then asked for her notebooks back. Thought she might need them. If she fell under a bus or something, of course they were his, along with her unsold works and any other junk. No, really. It was all his, he'd know what best to do with it. For her part, she'd probably burn the lot.

Nothing he could say to that but: look out for them buses.

She'd stood in the empty attic, looked at the bare table, the kettle gathering dust, everything just as she'd left it. Shook her head. That irritated him for days. She could still wind him up like no one else. Nice to see her, but not too often.

She'd tucked the notebooks under her arm. He turned to go back downstairs, but she reached out and touched his arm. Gripped it quite hard at the elbow, lifted her eyes.

'I didn't want you to make allowances for me. I cannae bear that. That's why I couldn't tell you.'

He saw himself take hold of her, demand just what she'd meant by 'Full circle', wildly offer anything just like Reagan at Reykjavik, say he loved her but better than before, would ask nothing except that she lived with him when and as she wanted, let her use the house, the security – he saw the whole disaster in slow motion, like a man sliding into a car-crash of his own making.

'About your dad,' he said. Her hand dropped from his elbow. 'There's no reason to think that you – '

She stepped back. In her eyes the old familiar *Trespassers Will Be Shot On Sight* signs went up.

'Leave it,' she said, and pushed past him down the stairs.

Now he looked up into the eye-blue Borders sky. Somewhere in it a laverock was endlessly burbling as its wee heart pumped.

Ruth stirred and sat up. She looked at him then padded carefully to the edge of the pool and checked it for depth.

'What say we jump in?'

'I say you English are crazy. It'll be bloody freezing.'

She called on Mary. They held hands and hesitated on the edge, the one skinny and tanned, the other all rosy fullness, dark-haired, full-bellied. Mary glanced back at him, looking for his approval. He felt himself standing on the brink of something new of unknown depth.

Mary and Ruth counted down then jumped, shrieking. The splash soaked him. He lay back on the bank, wiping his face.

'Spud asleep?'

Jimmy glanced in the back. It's hard not to be sentimental about children, especially sleeping. Utterly unmarked, at least on the outside. Beautiful, really. Waiting to be scarred.

'She's awa.'

'She's really happy about you now, so long as she's clear you're not replacing her dad.'

'She's told me.'

Nowadays Mary insisted on Jimmy last thing before sleep. He'd sit on the end of her bed and they'd talk. It had become his second favourite time of the weekends.

'So how do you feel about her?'

'She's a joy.' He checked himself. 'I mean, she can be a right pain, but still. You know. I mean, she's not mine but when she rushes out to see me, or puts the wee paw in mine. Ach, y'know. She's alright.'

'You lot,' Ruth shook her head. 'You think sentimental is the worst charge could ever be levelled against you. There's worse things.'

'You should meet Graeme, I'm a marshmallow in comparison.'

She was right, of course, and he could change up to a point. Men had to. He knew there was a problem. But he also knew he could never fully explain his culture to her, nor why you could no more extract it than you could fillet the backbone and expect the fish to swim.

He was silent as she cornered intricately home. There was no unsentimental way of saying what he felt at times.

'I'm not pushing you at her,' she said eventually. 'I hate seeing single parents do that.'

'No pushing required.'

'Mind you, you're seeing her at her best. She's at a lovely age and she tends to behave better when you're there. The first four years were pretty bloody and we still have big stand-offs.' She nodded, then said quickly 'Last week I hit her.'

Jimmy looked at her. She stared at the road ahead, her mouth tight.

'That's not in the manual.'

'It certainly ain't. She was more shocked than hurt. I felt terrible, a monster. It's a bloody power struggle sometimes, and I hate that,

254

and she uses that. Maybe there's too much pressure, just the two of us, you know?'

She drove on towards dusk and the first star. The colours drained from the land, the skyline walls and trees and farms were becoming clearer by the minute. At such times the edges of everything, the boundaries, were mysterious yet absolutely precise.

'Ever thought of having one yourself?' she asked.

In Orkney, the second time with Lesley and Graeme, holding the baby in the lit kitchen. Maybe again when they first moved to Dunbar. Or maybe every time they'd made love, who knows. That ruddy diaphragm, what was that about? He must have been half crazed. Was. Probably the lowest thing he'd ever done. God knows what she must have thought when she chucked it out.

'Once or twice maybe, a while back.'

The trees and houses were simple now, all outline and no depth. She flicked the lights on. Each bend of the road in the right order took them nearer to home.

'Well,' she said carefully, casually, the way she'd approached the edge of the pool, 'purely hypothetically, the best possible scenario, the big dream, an outline draft of the hidden agenda . . .'

'Get on wi it, woman.'

She jumped in.

'I wouldn't mind a strong reason for stopping smoking. Not right now, but some time in the not too distant.'

She turned down the back lane to the row of houses by the sea. He got out and opened the gate. She drove through. He closed it then got back in.

'Giving up smoking,' he said. 'Yon's a big decision.'

'I am aware of that.'

'I suppose you'd need some support?'

'I wouldn't try it otherwise, sailor. Not again.'

She stopped the car quietly by the back door. He scooped up Mary, her head rolled sleepily into his oxter. Christ, bairns, he thought, they could break your heart.

'I just thought I should let you know,' she said.

He nodded in the dark.

'Jolly decent of you. You English, you're so damn roundabout. Hey, you can't hit a man carrying a sleeping child!'

'Put down that sleeping child.'

'You've got to be kidding.'

She opened the door, switched on the light and glanced

back at him. He thought she looked flushed and uncommonly bonnie.

'Not really,' she said.

'Thought not.'

He came in and shut the door behind him for the night.

Through plate-glass windows and steady drizzle he watched Lesley lope across the tarmac, moving on the balls of her feet, looking eagerly around, bright and erect.

Upper-middle English, he thought, they even walk differently. Even the most critical look around as if the world was theirs and ready to be made something of. And us lot, we walk and keek about as if it's something we maun thole.

He hugged her when she came through the door. They grinned and hugged and grinned again, comrades through the old campaigns.

'Same ol shit weather. Jeez, it's good to be back in Jocko Land.'

Her American drawl had got stronger. England no longer existed for her beyond a mother weeping at the piano and the garden she played in as a child.

'How's the hand?'

She waggled it at him, drummed her fingers lightly on his cheek.

'Got some movement back in one finger. The other's only good for sticking up your ass.'

'So what's this surprise you've to show me?'

A slight dark figure came through the door, hesitated then held out her hand. Horn-rimmed glasses, lick of hair falling into her eyebrows, jeans. For a moment he had a whaft of the Bruntsfield flat, Alison, Kim saying 'I've decided I'm not a lesbian.'

He shook her hand, confused by his response to her as an attractive adolescent boy. Another stone he must look under sometime. Lesley put her arm round Tess and they stood grinning at him, delighted, and he had to laugh at the economy of it.

'Well, you two took your time getting it together!' he said.

'I know,' Lesley replied, 'but we're making up for it now.'

'We're very happy,' she added. 'Aren't we?'

They watched while Tess hovered by the carousel for the luggage.

'Tense and difficult,' he said. 'Just your fatal type.'

'Don't I know it. I've always been interested, I'm amazed none of you saw it. But when she broke up with her long-term lover, she came over to the States. We fell in love on a Greyhound to Atlanta. Booked into the nearest hotel and never came out for a week. I've decided to chance it again.'

'Heaven and hell?'

She nodded.

'The usual. I get so bloody insecure, you can't imagine what I'm like with her.'

'So the men have had their chance?'

She squeezed my arm.

'Reckon so, bub. Like a lot of bi people I was probably hedging my bets.'

'Good luck to you both. Even if it goes wrong, it won't kill you and at least you'll have had it.'

'You've changed. I'm glad. Last time I saw you, you were near the edge. I was worried.'

'You weren't a picture of health yourself, Les.'

She laughed.

'Things change, sometimes for the better. You look different. A fine hardening or something.'

'Or something, I hope.'

'I'm dying for the gossip,' she said, 'but we can't stay long. Tess wants us to move back to London. Trouble is, I hate London and anyway I'm happier in the States and I've a green card but she doesn't. God knows how it'll end.'

'Must it end?'

'Hey, we're mortal, y'know?'

'Speak for yourself.'

They watched Tess lean and yank a case off the carousel, then stand frowning, hands in her jeans, looking into the tunnel.

'How's her ceramics doing?'

'Now she's decided she's a craftswoman, not an artist, a lot better. And happier. She says she just got tired pulling everything out of her guts.'

Tess bent to pick out the second case, lugged it awkwardly off the carousel. He noticed Lesley lean forward, as though she could help across the distance. Look out, it must be love.

'Can't it just be good and equal between people?' she said to him.

He squeezed her arm back.

'In friendship – yes. As far as romance goes, the jury's still out. Probably the Scottish verdict.'

'Pardon?'

'No, Not Proven.'

'Meaning Guilty?'

He smiled and let go her arm as Tess wheeled the trolley across.

'Meaning just what it says.'

'Joan? Is she counted among ma crimes?'

The first personal question he'd asked all day. We were sitting at the top of a route on Traprain Law, the big whale-backed volcanic hump surfacing among the level fields of East Lothian. I glanced at him, the anxious eyes set deep in their boney sockets.

'Na. It wasn't thataway wi us. If she's happy, I'm dead pleased. Really.'

He looked me over then nodded. The taut face had filled out, slightly slack and puffy now. The bevvy, maybe, or just time jabbing away at us.

'And Kim?'

I looked over to the coast, the Bass Rock sinking in the haze of evening. End of summer, the wheat fields tablet-white before harvesting, jingle-jangle of climbers packing away their gear, distant voices rising from below, Ruth and Mary two specks on a travelling rug. A sense of gathering-in, like everything was coming back home.

I wanted to be friendly but he wanted the truth. So I said nothing.

'Jim, it had to end some way.'

'No that one.'

I stretched my stiffening legs. I clicked a karabiner, open, closed. Such a simple thing.

'Face facts, she's long gone. That wan will no be back.'

Open, release, close. Click-click.

'I ken that. I don't even fantasise it. So I wish I could say it's forgiven, but it's not.'

He hunched in on himself. Then relaxed. He always knew how to receive the bad news, he never expected any other.

'Gie it time.'

'Sure.'

He nodded to himself, then shook his head and a rare grin came out.

'Golden Triangle, for fuck's sake. Ye had tae admire her nerve.'

'I still do. How much did you know?'

He grimaced.

'Only recently. Joan's been filling me in a bittie about Kim and her auld man. Pair lassie. Times she wis aa ower the place, like a compass needle in the Cuillin. What would you call it?'

I shrugged. I'd checked it out through friends of Ruth. Hypomania, manic-depressive, latent schizophrenia, or a sane person traumatised by the past, take your pick, as though a name could tame the beast. Pair lassie indeed.

'She seems a lot more settled now,' I said. 'She thinks she's winning. One more route before we pack it in?'

He had to pick the hardest route left on the crag. Gnarly bastard, a long thin crack that whispered up the face into an overhanging roof.

I led the first pitch, and struggled. I hadn't climbed regularly since the Old Man fiasco, and I was certainly less strong than before, and much more aware of my limitations. Which meant having to look a little closer, think a bittie harder, use my head to figure out other ways to do this.

I set up a belay some ways below the roof and waited for him to come up. Just a boy's game, I thought, though some girls play it too. To be very good at anything takes tunnel-vision, a slight craziness.

I thought of Kim in Glasgow, and her endless struggle to pull herself upwards through her work.

Graeme climbed steadily towards me, Ruth waved from below. I waved back and felt connected. He was humming 'In The Mood', his theme tune on better days. My tunnel-vision, my wee brush with craziness, had been Kim and that was done wi. Sure there was an ache, something like my knee on cold days, but I could carry it even if I hirpled a little. Not the tragic type at all.

'Good value, eh youth?'

He stood alongside me, grinning broadly.

'No so youthful,' he said. 'I felt that.'

I started passing him the gear for leading.

'Some great climbing to be done in Shetland,' he said. 'You should come up some time and we'll knock off a bunch.'

'Let's see you finish this one first.'

'Aye, okay.'

He jammed his fingers into the crack, set his feet wide on nothing special, and cautiously eased up.

I watched him go as the sun melted away. Below, the mist settled like silt on the fields. It was a good route, but I was looking forward to the pub, then home with Ruth and Mary. Maybe you just grow out of some intensities. Or just lose your bottle?

The kind of folk that talked about bottle were not those I much cared to drink with. The time for hard men – blustering angry boys, really – was long past. Give Graeme his due, he'd known that from the start.

The ropes had stopped moving and there was no humming or whistling from above. Graeme was spread-eagled, groping around under the roof. He finally got in a runner then groped some more, sliding his hand over the rock like a blind man. We both knew the true line of the route went straight over that roof, not a big one but hard.

He stretched full out, got a hand onto the lip of the overhang. I heard the grunt, then saw the belay twitch out and come sliding down the rope to me.

'Shit!'

He lowered himself back under the roof and crouched there awhile, put in another runner. Faint muttering descended to me. He faffed around some more, his movements cramped and tentative now, he didn't look sure at all. I reckoned he'd go for it and peel off, and tightened myself to hold him.

'Hey, Jim!'

'Yeah?'

'Reckon I must have the wrong line. Must be round this roof.'

It wasn't. We'd both checked out the guide book. I thought I could see a move he couldn't, but that's not the kind of advice you want from a second.

'Whatever you think,' I yelled up.

He nodded, then slowly sidled off onto an easier line, round the corner of the roof, then came across onto the top of it and continued as though that counted. No shame in that, but it wasn't the man I'd known.

When my turn came, I stretched back out over the roof, got the one good hold I'd seen from below, and lifted myself up and over on a wave of adrenalin. No competing? Aye, sure. Then again, I had the bigger reach and I was seconding, so it didn't really count.

'Tricky wan,' he said when I arrived.

'Enjoyed that.'

He nodded but didn't look at me.

We coiled the ropes, split the gear and sauntered down the easy way towards Ruth and Mary.

'That's the last time I watch you climb,' she said. 'Mary was bored because she wanted to do it herself, and I couldn't bear to watch you.'

'Ach, it's safer than it looks,' Graeme said.

'It had bloody better be,' she replied, but took my arm and Mary grabbed my hand as we brushed through the knee-high fields towards the car.

'Enjoying the instant family, then?' he asked while we waited at Dunbar station next morning. I looked at him. It sounded like a straight question.

'Yeah, I am. Any thoughts that way yoursel?'

'Question disnae arise, pal. Joan cannae.'

'Whit?'

'You didni know? She had an abortion wance – Kim knows. Now she cannae.'

'That's a bloody shame.'

He looked off down the tracks.

'Ach, it's no world to bring kids intae.'

'That's a terrible thing to say. Really.' I heard a rare conviction in my voice, wondered where its resonance came from. 'Seems to me it's getting better.'

'Don't kid yersel.'

'You'd be lost without it, wouldn't you?'

He ducked his head like riding a gentle clout.

'These days I've a better idea where the anger comes fae. Disnae mean I'm no still angry.'

'And the politics?'

He straightened up and looked off across the fields where an invisible combine was droning.

'I'm still a political man, Jim. Been re-reading Scottish history. There wis no Golden Age. We've nuthin to go back to, you and me.'

'So?'

A sudden smile and he looked much younger.

'So we make it new.'

The train chuntered in. We said our rushed cheerios. He got on, pulled down the window.

261

'So you'll do the Old Man wi me?'

'Ancient history,' I said. 'It's no big deal. Dinnae be a stranger.'

'Nivver.'

He smiled, held out his hand. We shook on it as the train began to move. Our hands loosened, parted, first the palms then the fingers. He waved once then ducked inside and I turned and went my way.

It was a day full of things that were going to be. That was somewhere between them, unseen and unstated.

They plugged on up the hill above Abbey St Bathans, Mary running and stumbling up ahead. It was a fair hike at her age but she'd announced she was a climber and didn't need any help.

Ruth was puffed and claimed a scenic break. She sat down and lit up.

He stood and looked back the way they'd come. It was late autumn now and the hardwood trees were shedding their poisonous wastes. He thought of his scattered friends and lovers and wondered what all the fuss had been about when nothing really disappears, it just gets re-arranged.

Ruth got to her feet.

'Ready when you are.'

They passed a young couple hurrying down. The girl said 'Hi' to Mary, who was starting to flag, and he realised he was now old enough to think of some couples as young. He'd assumed his life was a try-out and tomorrow he could start for real. Now he was nearly halfway through and each day went quicker than the last.

At the top they sat out of the wind inside the remains of the old stone fort, while Mary played houses among the blocks.

'So are you going to climb the Old Man with him or not?'

'I kinda indicated he might as well do it on his own.'

'But you hope he doesn't?'

He scratched his head, but there was no certainty there.

'You know sometimes you want something real bad, but you're no sure if it's a decoy?'

She closed her eyes and listened to the wind straining through the stones, snatches of Mary singing to herself.

'Yes,' she said quietly.

He stretched out on the grass and looked at the sky. Orkney, Shetland, there was nowhere better to be than here. He reached out in her direction, found a foot. Stroked it, felt good.

'Tell you what I do think. I think the harmony between a woman, a man and a child – when it's there! – is quite different from that between a man and a woman.'

'It's certainly more . . . stable,' she said.

'Better distibututution,' he said. 'It's the difference between weight distributed on two legs, like on stilts, which are unstable though kinda intense vectors, and something based on a tripod. Tripods are very stable, even if one leg's shorter than the others.' He grinned at her. 'I could draw it for you, if you like.'

'Romantic types, engineers.'

'I could colour it in, if that helps.'

Her other foot tapped his shoulder.

'Men need friends of their own sex too. Christ, can't you see he's begging you to forgive him?'

'But I can't feel to order. We're getting there. Maybe next Spring.'

She nodded towards Mary who had wound down like a toy.

'That one's puggled, we'd better get back. Tears before nightfall, I think.'

'I could draw you the curve for that, too.'

On the way down, Mary lagged behind. She allowed them to lift her over the fences but that was all. Children are so transparent, he thought. He could see the stubborn pride that kept her going and the tiredness that made her whinge. It was the same whenever she was up too late or needed to eat – she didn't know why she felt what she did, only that she felt it.

All the same, watching her stumble grumpily along in her wee red wellies, he wondered if he or any of them had ever understood any better what they were about.

The evening light was uncertain now. He had no idea what was coming to him and Ruth or the others. Probably the same old blundering in the dark, the same needy confusions as they ricocheted from ship to shore. How could anyone seriously consider having a child in the face of that? He wasn't ready, never would be.

Ruth had drifted away. The evening was full of things that were going to be but he suddenly didn't feel up to them.

Then, behind, Mary was shouting.

'I'm sinking! Mummy, I'm sinking!'

He turned and ran back. She'd wandered disconsolately into a boggy bit that deepened into a pool. The water was over her boots but no more. Even as he approached she dragged herself out onto solid ground.

He emptied the water from her wellies and put them back on.

'Are you alright, Mary?' Ruth asked.

Mary nodded.

'Come on then,' Ruth said briskly, 'we want to get back to the car before dark. It's not far now.'

They set off then realised Mary wasn't following. She stood flapping her arms, then the first tears, then working herself up into a full-scale psychodrama.

'Come on, Mary!'

'I can't' she wailed. 'I'm stuck!'

'Come on.'

'I can't move! I can't move and you don't care!'

She was jumping up and down in her rage, utterly unstuck, whirling her arms like a chicken trying to take off. Ruth glanced at Jimmy.

'You're laughing at me!' Mary screamed.

'No we're not, darling.'

Ruth put her hand over her mouth and shook silently.

'I hate you both! I hate everyone! I'll be stuck here *forever!*'

'The wean's had a fright,' Jimmy said and went back to get her, that farcical *forever* hanging in his head.

He picked her up and put her on his shoulders. The cries stopped, she tried to prolong the heart-rending sobs but soon lost interest. By the time they'd reached the path through the woods she was singing *I should be so lucky*.

He felt his head clear from a long and confused dream. The outline of the trees was clear and sharp, each overlap, each boundary precise. Then in under the cool piney woods. Ruth took his free arm and said nothing. The other was hanging onto the child's feet and her wet plastic boot was slippy on his palm. He remembered that exactly, wet wellies, his father's shoulders, being carried half-asleep through the darkness, his mother nearby, knowing that food and bed would be there for him. Children have a right to expect that of us. Funny how good it feels to give it . . .

He adjusted his grip on the child and thought: we took it all so seriously.

Ruth was humming 'Wild Mountain Thyme' under her breath. *And round her I will lay/ All the flowers of the mountain*. Kim in peach-coloured pajamas lying by the shore in the Orkney Simmerdim.

Ruth hunched against the wind on the Pentland hills. *And we'll all go together*. Seconding Graeme that first afternoon on the Etive Slabs, Lesley working out in the gym or bent in tears over her bandaged hand. Gutsy Alison, shy, angry Tess. Gerry hanging in there, trying to put the twins to bed. Joan laughing at the Shetland dance, or standing by the lightswitch in her bedroom telling him to look up.

And that otter, rising to the surface, peering and disappearing into the depths yet never fully leaving him.

And if I should lose my love. Mary lowping up and down, screaming she was stuck when she wasn't, and we had to smile though we loved her. The pain is real, but our attachment to it is so touching. *I would surely find another*. And this burden I think I carry, this guddled past and unkent future, it's as real as the monster hanging on a feverish child's door which in the morning is just a dressing gown again.

The child was drooping now, her hands slack on his shoulders. Ruth was silent but he sensed at peace. It was nearly dark now among the trees, the birds were mute and the wind had dropped. Everything was in place.

That's what happened at the end of a comedy, everyone ended up in their proper place. Graeme and Joan in Shetland, Lesley with Tess in London, Kim in Glasgow just round the corner from Graeme's old flat with a new bloke and new work, Alison and Gerry closer than ever it seemed, Mick DeTerre still driving on the road to somewhere with guns under his feet. And himself walking through a forest with a friend and lover and her sleeping child on his shoulders.

Only Kim's father's death could never seem comic. The name called, roar of the shotgun, the girl at the door staring at the bloody aftermath – something too cruel to ever fit in a comedy.

They came out of the wood. The first stars were out, the sky was blue-black with a few pale lochs with impossible shores over the western horizon. An illusion and he knew it so well.

They leant on the car in the last of the light, shoulders touching. He felt himself finally arrived. A comedy. That, if anything, was what it was.

'So what now, big boy?'

He tipped back an invisible cap.

'Let's go home and make babies – what d'ya say, doll?'

265

'I say Hello, sailor!' she said, turned the key in the ignition and they drove away.

And that should have been the ending.

I file letters archaeologically, of course, the latest layer on top. So it's easy to dip into the shoe box and pick out Kim's last letter, the one Lesley wordlessly returned to me a few nights back. For the time being I put the letter itself aside and shake a few small dry leaves from the envelope. Bog myrtle, the scent of the Scottish moors, she knew what it meant to me.

It's too late to phone Lesley. Some nights you have to finish things alone.

So is love, Ruth used to ask, miracle or psychosis? (always one for the tight formulation). Then I still wasn't sure. What do I think now? You, you're asking me to think, to come clean at this hour in the morning, with three hundred close-hearted, tight-lipped Protestant years sitting on my neck?

For what it's worth, I think what I can't say out loud, not yet, not in this country with our terror of sentiment and high words. Maybe only the Gaelic poet can say it, in another language with eyes shut, in the language I'm still struggling to learn, that passionate love is a wild deer on the hills, and some stalk it for days and years on end till they finally come on it in a high corrie. And they fix the cross-hairs on it, squeeze the trigger, and if their aim is true . . .

It's deid, you fuil, I hear the old man mutter.

Tonight I say lay your vehement gun aside, and watch till it moves on, as it will. Then go home and lift a glass with an old friend, content to know it's out there, somewhere, living.

I crinkle the leaves in a sweaty palm, lift it to my face. *To sweeten your thoughts of the world when they grow bitter*, she wrote at the end. The rest all went down so fast.

TWENTY-THREE

Explosion

'CAN I COME and see you?'

She was using her casual voice.

'Sure. When?'

'Friday evening?'

I stood in my kitchen and glanced at the small photo of us in a café in Chora, Patmos. These days I allowed myself only one, which I changed from time to time. A long time ago and it caused no pain.

'Yeah, that's fine.'

I'd have to put off going down to Ruth's.

'Can you put me up if necessary?'

In the photo we looked happy, though she had refused to look directly at the camera and her eyes were in shadow.

'I've finished decorating the other bedroom.'

She laughed.

'Got the message.'

'It's not in doubt, is it?'

'I've decided to settle with Keith,' she replied.

'Good,' I said.

I wondered if she'd ever tell him the whole truth about her father. About as likely as her head turning in the photograph and her eyes coming into the brilliant light that splashed all around us.

I waited for her off the train at Waverley Station. Even the forecourt had changed, bright plastic surfaces, electronic destination boards.

My coffee and burger came quicker than before but tasted of even less. I could actually make out the P.A. system; her train was late but the voice apologised three times. I glanced at myself in the glass of the non-burger stall. With hair shorter now (Ruth's advice, 'after a certain age, Jimmy . . .') and meeting-the-bank-manager jacket, what I saw looked like an adult member of society rather than a free man.

Dad would have jeered and secretly approved. I rolled a smoke for old times' sake, then went to meet what we'd become, heartened that behind the diesel there still lingered a whiff of coal and steam, the old dirty way.

Her black hair was brushed back and permed, kinda Forties, she was wearing a tweed suit, coat and flat shoes. She looked older, almost staid. I guessed she was dressing for the forthcoming role as settled, responsible woman. I'd met Keith at her last opening. He had shaken my hand but not mangled it, said he was pleased to meet me but didn't overdo it, and he didn't touch her in my presence. For this I liked him.

We hugged and looked at each other, as though we hadn't already reached our conclusions.

'You finally look older,' I said, tactful to the last.

'I feel it.' She pushed her fingers through my hair. 'And you've got grey bits. You'll be quite distinguished. Quite fanciable. All these women I've heard about from Alison . . .'

'Listen,' I said, 'in this town any single heterosexual man in his late thirties who is not hideously scarred is in demand.'

'It must be interesting.'

'It was. In a numb kinda way. I don't do that any more.'

We got into the car.

'Where to?'

'I've got you a present,' she said, 'but you'll get it later. Can you afford to take me out to eat? A bad case of not not while the giro.'

'I feel like red meat, red wine and some provocative conversation. Suit you?'

She laughed. It was a relief, feeling safe to flirt a little.

'Apart from the meat. Och, I'm tired of having no money.'

I nodded and concentrated on negotiating Leith Walk traffic in the belting winter rain.

'I hear Lesley's gone back to work in the States.'

'Alison told me. She says Les can't cope with the security. Because she's scared she'll lose it. So she leaves it first.'

'You still analyse things too much. Les just has fun.'

'Tough on her partner. Tess is miserable.'

Kim shrugged, and we abandoned that line of conversation.

'I liked Ruth.'

'Me too.'

'It must be difficult with the wee girl.'

'No. It's dead interesting.'

She laughed as though that was unlikely, or maybe I imagined it.

'So this one is serious?'

'Getting that way. Aye, things are pretty good.'

She put her hand on mine on the wheel.

'I'm glad. It's taken a long time.'

To feel pretty good again? I wondered. Or to be able to talk like old friends? She removed her hand. We waited for the lights.

'Trendy Leith then, is it?'

'Ach, apart from the restaurants on the waterfront, most of it's still the same. Still lots of poor folk in poor folk's clothes living in ratty housing. Humour's the same too. I used to live down here with Bridget.'

She sat back and sighed.

'I'll soon be the age you were when we met. Makes you think.'

I didn't know what it made me think. The signals changed.

'Yeah,' I said, 'all that yearning and getting and losing. Being wildly happy, then quietly happy, then stagnating – we were stagnating, you were right there – then splitting up and dragging our carcasses about the place until we meet someone else and do this waltz of unwinding bandages and call it love. Sure, it makes you think.'

She looked at me like she hadn't seen me in a while.

'Christ, you've changed,' she said.

'You never used to swear.'

She was still examining me like I was of some interest.

'It's like you've come into focus,' she said eventually. 'You used to be easy-going.'

I was feeling oddly free and giggly.

'Passive, anxious and repressed, more like. Loving somebody too much can be very debilitating.'

'Would I know?'

'What d'you mean?'

She stared straight ahead, then it came out in a rush.

'D'you think I'm heartless, Jimmy? That I cannae love?'

The question wasn't rhetorical.

'You had a terrible gliff once,' I said carefully, 'and maybe you went into deep-freeze. No one would blame you.'

Her mouth tightened but she nodded.

'I loved my dad,' she said. 'In his right mind, he was a wonderful man. No problem there. Just most of the time I feel nothing much about anything.'

She switched off and tugged vaguely at her hair till I stopped the car outside the Waterfront Wine Bar and we sat for a while listening to the rain stott off the roof.

'I haven't been here for ages,' she said at last, in something like her normal voice.

'Me neither.'

Not since the hot afternoon we'd drunk wine on the floating pontoon and I'd blurted 'I love you' and she replied 'I know – but why not spread it around a bit?' And I had, a bit, at home and abroad. I'd had my second HIV test, I'd got off with it. So had Ruth. Enough.

'Let's go for it,' I said. Her changes of mood bothered me.

We ran through the rain over the cobbles. I opened the door for her. She suddenly stopped half-in.

'But do you regret it?' she asked.

Her perm was dripping and she looked younger for a moment but that bloom which had been mostly in my eyes anyway wouldn't be coming back.

'Is this going to be one of those retrospective evenings?' I said.

Now she really looked at me, that sharp blue-eyed rap.

'You *have* changed,' she said. 'You lived so much with the past. I couldn't understand it.'

'You didn't have so much past to live in, then. I've had quite enough.' I motioned her in. 'After you.'

She made for the corner table, back to the wall.

'But do you?' she insisted.

'Nah.' I could see more was expected. 'The good was good and the bad was the beginning of wisdom. What's yours?'

The wine went down, we caught up with each other, and I tried to hold her at the distance that wine in time dissolves.

She'd decided to move in with Keith, commit herself, she said that was a relief. I agreed. She glanced at me, continued. She was tired of struggling on her own, tired of no money, of no home worth the name. Celibacy was a good idea but made her crabbit. Fooling around seemed exciting but was a scunner in the end. Without a man around she had more time for work but couldn't settle to it so what good was that? Keith was a good man: warm, secure in himself, was of sound mind apart from the fact he loved her, asked little of her other than she be herself. He didn't *probe*. Another glance at me.

Uh-huh. I briefly wondered how she made love now, stamped on that one. Did she give more, had she learned to talk? Not my affair. Better the mugs of tea in bed with Ruth and no no-go areas, however difficult that could be, better that than passion and silence.

She respected his work – our Keith was a Senior Registrar in Paediatrics – it had more value than hers in the end. She shouldn't say it but he was very well paid and didn't regard his income as his own but as there to be used, shared and enjoyed. An end to the endless, wearing worry about money. What did I think?

I could understand it. Yes, it could well work.

'Someone interesting, but older and stable,' she said. 'Someone like you were for me.'

'Ah.' I said. 'I never really was that.'

A big commitment, she went on, and she was nervous about it. She'd only tried it once before, with me, and that hadn't lasted. She'd been too young, that was it. But we had been good for each other, for a long time.

She stopped abruptly, looked at me over her glass. I felt again that ripple of disturbance, of significance out of her. I don't know how she did that.

'I know you don't think you're strong,' she said. 'Or good. But you were always there for me. And for your friends. We value you.'

'Gosh, a testimonial.'

She wafted the back of her hand at me.

'Haud yer wheesht,' she said. 'It's a shame we're not meeting now for the first time. We might be right.'

Not on your nellie, I thought.

She put down her glass carefully, dribbled a ring of salt round the base, then lifted the glass and left the circle behind. She studied it then looked up at me.

'I want to be good,' she said. 'I want to be warm and loving and lovable. I know I'm not but I really . . . do . . . want.'

I wished she wouldn't get vulnerable and direct on me. She put her hand on mine and I flinched.

'I am sorry,' she said. 'About . . . everything. I couldn't say that before.'

'Forget it,' I said. 'It's understood.'

'But forgiven?'

'Forgotten.'

'Oh yeah.'

271

'Oh yeah, yourself.'

I rescued my hand to pour more wine. She put down her glass and began to make another white circle, just touching the last.

Keith hoped they'd get married but wouldn't pressure her. He was a good man, she repeated. Of course she was a bit feart. All the things she'd have to give up, like attractive men, like being answerable to no one. Maybe in time they'd go for everything but the babies.

'I seem to be thinking about having bairns.'

'With Ruth?'

'I guess.'

She laughed.

'Must be your age. Getting broody, huh?'

'It's not that abnormal. Or that funny.'

She looked down.

'I was too young,' she whispered, 'we both knew that.'

We glanced at each other, remembering. It had been years since we'd mentioned it. She was weaving a little raft of toothpicks with her clever scarred hands.

'You know why I mustn't hae bairns.'

'Look, Kim – '

She held up her hand like she was stopping traffic.

'*Please.*'

Things came to a halt for a while. She finished her raft and balanced it on the carafe.

'So what's this then?' I asked.

'A raft that swimmers reach and share,' she replied. She looked up. 'It's all I've ever tried to make.'

I swallowed, got my eyes away from hers. Dabbed my finger in the salt and licked it once or twice. A taste of the big sea.

'I think,' she said eventually, 'if you climbed the Old Man with Graeme, you might feel free of something. Sure in yourself. Ready to go on. Whatever.'

For a moment I was there, bridging up the last few feet of the summit blocks, emerging, slowly standing up . . . Free?

'So you've seen him? Is that what he wants?'

'Once or twice when he's been down from Shetland,' she said and dropped the raft into my hand. 'I've missed the last train back to Glasgow. Can you put me up?'

We sat by my fire and she was talking about Keith, what she needed and everything she'd have to give up. Freedom against security, we were still trying to rig that one. I was talking about Ruth, who'd said she knew it was a risk but she wanted the whole bloody lot with me.

Commitment. It's a bonnie word. It made the heart beat a little faster.

'But I've tried that. The first time was a terrible mistake, the second, well . . .'

Kim looked at her hands, nodded, accepting that.

'Conclusion?' I wagged my finger in the air. 'Either commitment is a mistake, or I am.'

'Or your time is yet to come. There's always a third possibility.'

I glanced over at Kim. I didn't want her, it was great. I briefly pictured falling asleep with her head on my shoulder but on the whole I wanted her less than any other clever young woman in my house late at night.

Maybe I love you, I thought, but I'm over you at last.

She'd taken off her jacket and was kneeling by the fire, looking middle-aged, scratching patterns on the carpet with her nail. Lamb dressed as mutton. Talent apart, she was what she'd always been, an ordinary, struggling mortal. Free, I thought. Who needs to climb anything to prove it?

I spoke without thinking, in the way of old friends late at night.

'It's so good not having you. I can't lose you.'

'You said something like that to me years ago. That the only way to keep me was not to hold on to me.'

'I did? Anyway,' I laughed, 'it didn't turn out to be true.'

'Didn't it?'

I looked at her. Sometimes she baffled me. She leaned across and kissed me lightly on the cheek.

I sat back and grinned, foolishly pleased.

She kissed me lightly on the lips, just a touch.

Then she sat back on her heels and opened her eyes wide and unblinking, like a shutter rolling up, like a curtain opening.

I stared at her. She leaned forward and kissed me again, very light, soft and dry, then sucked my lower lip, bit gently and slipped her tongue behind my teeth. It was like no one else and I felt myself splintering like an axe was tearing through a rickety fence.

I gently pushed her away.

'No,' I said.

273

She stared at me and her eyes slowly enlarged, blue and white-flecked like a breaking wave.

'Just tonight. I don't know why.'

I shook my head but couldn't move back.

'*I need you*,' she said, and I was washed away.

There was clumsiness, slight embarrassment, absolute need. I re-entered a world I never thought to know again.

And I was angry. She'd broken into the near peace of heart that had taken me years to build.

And it was too fast and lustful, she'd scarcely changed at all. As she lay on the duvet and reached for me, I was being asset-stripped again.

'No,' I said. 'Not like the last time.'

She opened her eyes.

'If we're going to do this,' I said, 'it'll be my way.'

'What's that?' She was hoarse. 'Kinky?'

'*Personal*. All you do is open your eyes and make love with me like I'm me and not a stand-in.'

'You've changed.'

'I've used and been used for sex often enough to know when it's happening and I hate it.' I was throttled by anger out of nowhere. I must be crazy to refuse her. 'If you can't do this looking at me, you shouldn't be doing it at all.'

'You should have been like this more often.'

'It doesn't matter now.'

'I like it when you're dominant.'

'Shut it!' I held her face between my hands. 'I don't want your fantasies, Kim.'

She tried to struggle free. I gripped her hard, wouldn't give way.

'Let me go!'

'Look at me!'

She lashed out and caught me on the mouth with her chunky ring.

I let her go.

She sat up. 'I just wanted . . .' she panted. 'Just wanted.'

She was unguarded, half-naked, beautiful. I was ready to betray anything and anyone for her.

'Go away,' I said. 'Don't just want wi me.'

'I will then!'

She was off the bed and out the door in a pale flash. Then a squeal, a crash, her cry, then silence.

I was crouched holding her halfway down the stair.

'Christ, you alright?'

She nodded, dried her eyes on my shoulder.

'I trod on Charlie, I was in too much of a hurry.'

'You can say that again. Apologise to him in the morning. He's got no balls so he won't understand.'

She giggled. We were crouched on the stairs naked in the dark, and we were fairly preposterous. She was starting to shiver.

'I *was* in too much hurry, wasn't I?'

'Yes.'

She considered it then kissed my lip where she'd bust it.

'Shall we try again or just call it off?'

'Yes.'

I carried her back to bed. She'd sprained her ankle and anyway she liked that sort of thing.

'My way.'

'I want you.'

'Me?'

I hadn't forgotten the last time, when I'd been a stand-in for old pal Graeme, a test-bed to see if she still wanted me enough.

'You.' She paused. Her face flickered between now and then. She said it quickly but clearly.

'I do love you.'

I was almost embarrassed. Even in fantasy, she hadn't said that to me in years.

'It doesn't mean . . . you know . . .'

'I know,' I said gently, and I did, as she began to suck my nipples. Probably she didn't hear me. Her hands were moving lightly, unhurriedly this time over my body and we began to learn each other again. Lord she was a skinny wee thing after Ruth. This was a terrible mistake and I'd make it only once so it might as well be good.

'One more thing,' I said as she came up for air.

'Yes?'

'You might look into my eyes when you come.'

'Wild,' she said. 'Where did you learn that?'

I put my finger to her lips. She began to nibble it. She was terribly oral.

'None of your business,' I said. 'Alright?'

'Yes,' she mumbled.

And she did, the longest, hardest, most desperate look short of death.

I sniff the crumpled bog myrtle leaves in my sweaty palm, and to my surprise after all this time they still smell faintly, of a hillside where we once made love, of summer childhood, of my country, of everything that is most real to me.

I shake my head. Strangest of all, I'm smiling.

She left in the morning after a quick breakfast, friendly but that was all.

'Will you tell Keith?'

She looked at me like I was daft.

'Of course not. It would just hurt him to no point.'

I was already dreading telling Ruth. Perhaps she was right.

'You think I've no conscience, don't you?'

I shrugged. Not my business.

'At least I don't do what I want and then agonise about it afterwards.'

I had to laugh, and suddenly felt strangely well and free. Or maybe it was just that she was sitting across the breakfast table. The repercussions would come later. Maybe there wouldn't be any.

'Why should I tell Keith, it's only once before I settle down.'

'I know that,' I said.

She still believed there could be acts without consequences. I cleared the table and fed the martyred Charlie while she packed her overnight bag.

We kissed at the door – lightly, friendly, old friends. Former lovers.

'Thanks, Jimmy.'

'Any time.'

'Really?'

'No, not really. But it was . . . nice. A lot better than last time.'

She laughed, hugged me briefly.

'The earth doesn't move often and become a spiritual thing,' she said, 'but it did with us a few times and we should settle for that. Be seeing you.'

I watched her set off down the street, limping slightly and looking eagerly around her. Tweed suit, green coat over her arm, fragile and undefeated, slightly absurd, human.

'Hey! That present you mentioned?'

She turned at the foot of the wynd.

'Was it good for you too?'

'Cheeky bisom!'

She laughed and disappeared. I closed the door, ignoring the look from my next door neighbour. I went upstairs and sat on the bed we'd shared. Her pussy-cat brooch was lying on the floor, winking at me. I clenched it in my hand and closed my eyes for a while.

Then I went downstairs and phoned Ruth.

'Sorry about last night,' I said. 'I'll get down sometime this evening.'

'Can you make it Sunday morning instead?' she said, 'I'm kinda busy down here.'

I changed the sheets, put the brooch in a drawer and carefully made up the bed. I felt I'd blown something very precious, like an egg, the only one of its kind.

I spread butter and jam on the scone and put it into Gerry's hand. With great concentration he got it to his mouth.

'Wipe ma beard, will ya?'

I wiped jam off his beard. His voice was only slightly slurred, under better control than the rest of his body.

'You daft bugger,' he said. 'Could you not just have said No?'

Alison passed through the sittingroom.

'No,' she said. 'That's just it. Where she's concerned, he can't.'

'Why can't he? She's not that fuckin devastatin.'

She waved her finger at him.

'You bugger, I'll not have language in this house.' Gerry grunted and made an effort with his tea. 'He can't because he loves her, anybody can see that. Including Ruth, I'd guess.'

I held the mug to his lips, timed the tilt of it to his Adam's apple jerk as he swallowed.

'He's the cat's father,' I said. 'I didn't say No because I didn't want to, and I can't do anything about that yet. Anyhow, it'll no happen again.'

'Sure?'

'Sure, sure.'

I stared her out. She raised her eyebrows and went back into her study, left the door open. She was hanging on to her job by a fingernail, and the strain showed round her mouth.

'Fag, pal?'

'Na. Still hetero, but thanks,' I replied, but started to roll him one anyway.

'Get tae fuck,' he grunted.

'Language!' from the study.

I lit up for him, passed it over. Since he'd been confined to the wheelchair, he'd started smoking. Said he didn't see why not.

I stirred the fire and sat looking into it for a while, remembering that night, feeling it. It had been a much better last time than our previous last time.

We both sat smoking and there was peace in the house. There usually was. Its storms were fairly spectacular but brief. Maybe that was their secret. Maybe there really was more to human solidarity than convenience.

'Question is,' Gerry slurred, made a great effort and straightened his neck, 'are you going to tell Ruthie tomorrow?'

I grimaced at the fire. I'd been wondering that myself. We told each other the truth wherever we could find it. But then again, she'd said more than once that in her work she had to balance truth with reponsibility. Would telling her about something that would never be repeated, that was bound to hurt her, be honest or just indulging my guilt? Would not telling her be responsible, or saving my own skin? I'd lapped this circuit more often than a Grand Prix driver, and I still hadn't come to the chequered flag.

'What d'you think?' I said.

'Yes,' from Gerry.

'No!' from the study.

'Tell her straight but don't grovel,' he added.

'Haivers!'

Alison stood in the doorway, hands on her hips.

'Don't you listen to that blethering skite,' she said. 'If you care for Ruth and want to keep her, then keep your mouth shut.'

'Thin end of the wedge,' Gerry muttered.

Alison sighed and leaned against the doorframe. She looked knackered.

'Men,' she said. 'You try so hard but you don't understand. Sometimes it's friendlier not to tell the person you love everything.'

A glance flicked between them, like a very fast rugby pass. Looking at them, I wasn't quite sure who now held the ball.

'I'll awa hame and sleep on it,' I said.

I looked in on my godson Pete the Neat, blew on his whispy pale hair. He looked positively edible, like a sugar mouse. 'Sentimental jeelie-bag,' I whispered.

'It's a small step,' Alison said behind me.

'What?'

'It's a small step from fear of sentimentality to fear of sentiment, of feeling itself.'

'Who are you telling – me or yourself?'

She looked deeply unhappy.

'Are you two alright? Or am I being nosy?'

'No,' she said. 'You're not being nosy. But please don't ask right now.'

So I kissed her goodnight and hit the road.

'I'm worried about Ewan,' Ruth was saying. 'He came over the last couple of evenings when you didn't come down. He stayed the night – on the settee,' she added.

'Should I be worried?'

'You know I don't fancy him any more. But he's in a bit of a state – very withdrawn, isn't sleeping well, talks about leaving his job and Catherine. He misses Mary so much, and me, he says. Christmas always makes that worse.'

In his place, I'd miss her and Mary like hell. Though from everything she'd said, his repentance was kinda late in the day. I watched her curled up in her Orkney chair. Yes, she was precious to me.

'He finally asked me . . . if I thought he was cracking up.'

'Do you?'

'Could be.' Her mouth was down, she looked tired. Even her hair had lost its bounce. I wondered just how late they'd been up.

'Every so often I'm reminded that his happiness matters more to me than – more than I'd like it to. Can you understand that?'

'I can understand it.'

We looked at each other. Eventually she stretched out her hand. I took it, stroked it, couldn't help noticing the difference. Bigger, softer than Kim's.

'So – did you tell him that? He could crack up?'

Her fingers curled back onto mine.

'No,' she said. 'The truth doesn't always help – does it?'

She squeezed my hand and looked me in the eye. I had that old feeling of being out of my depth.

'C'mon,' she said finally. 'The moon's full and I've the new J.J. Cale album. Let's go upstairs and screw our lights out.'

The scent in the bedroom was salty, sweaty, an adult perfume with just a hint of desperation.

I was avalanched once, in the 'Gorms. I was out with MacBeth, we called him that because most of his challengers in the climbing world were dead. We were traversing an easy-angled slope on our way back to the van, probably taking a short-cut of sorts.

A crack line opened silently across the slope, just above my feet. The upper wind-slab snow broke away and I started sliding with it, like on a moving walkway, slowly, almost comical. I remember looking back round towards MacBeth who was standing still as I slid away from him, and I held my arms out part in appeal, part to say isn't this ridiculous? I tried to step off the moving slab and was whipped off my feet, then spun over, snow filling eyes and throat, my axe thumping off my skull as I thrashed away, trying to stay near the surface, part laughter and part terror as I grasped I really was going down in an avalanche.

It's the acceleration I remember still, the way it gathered speed, from the first gentle tug underfoot to the white wind all around me.

Two months later, Kim at my door in the February morning, wrapped to the eyes in coat, scarf, hat, gloves.

'Come for a drive,' she said. 'Please. Now.'

Behind her, Keith's green MG with the hood down. Frost glittered on the harbour wall. What I could see of her face was white and stiff, and her eyes had been streaming.

That *please* did it. I phoned Alec at the yard, then Marshall at his cubby-hole office in Leith, grabbed my winter climbing duvet, balaclava, mitts. Wallet, camera, tobacco.

I put out food for Charlie and followed her down the garden path.

'He's no needing it for the day,' she said over her shoulder.

'Trusting fellow.'

'Yeah.'

We hopped in. The sun was just rising, dark clouds like bruises over Fife. Snow later.

'You must have been up early to get over from Glasgow.'

'Didn't go to bed,' she said.

She revved the engine and we slewed away.

'Where are we going?' I asked, clinging to the door-strap.

'Anywhere.'

She really was terribly pale, or maybe it was the cold.

'Ah,' I said, and clung on tighter.

We were coming onto the curved slip-road joining the A1 heading North. I didn't like the colour of the surface as she glanced back over her shoulder. An articulated lorry was booming up the inner lane of the dual carriageway. She accelerated to enter in front of it, the speedo swung to 80.

'I'm pregnant,' she said.

Then her foot came off the accelerator, switched to the brake. I've wondered so often but I'm sure of this: she didn't touch the brake pedal – she stamped on it.

Next thing I was looking straight at the artic coming down on us, then across fields, a flash of the sea, a petrol station whirling by. Kim's gloved hands rising off the wheel then on our second spin we were out on the carriageway, the artic on top of us like a whailing wall. I saw a face, an open mouth, a hand held up as though commanding us to stop this madness, then my last glimpse of fields, grey sea, petrol station as she was turning towards me to have her final say.

A monstrous darkness shot by screaming its Doppler scream, then our tyres gripped. I leant across her, grabbed the wheel and steered us zig-zag across the road, onto the verge till we ploughed into the banking, stalled.

'You stupid bitch!'

Her head came forward, bumped lightly against the windscreen.

'Ouch,' she said quietly. She leant her head on the wheel and began to howl.

In the service station the coffee tastes terrible but that's better than not tasting it at all. A baby whimpers restlessly, is reassured, abruptly falls asleep again. A young man in a sharp suit takes out a portable phone and murmurs to it something about Pindar printing schedules.

She sits opposite me, cradling her mug. There seems to have been a cosmic TV repairman at work. Everything looks sharper, brighter, more in focus. I see the articulated lorry crash down on us and begin the first of a series of shivers that will recur for days. As I wait for her – she has, after all, promised to tell me the truth – the dreamy woman behind the counter rocks from one foot to the other, humming 'Hey Jude' as the sun tangles in her cigarette smoke. Chimes, a blue ice-cream van pulls up outside and though it's freezing out, I suddenly want one, an ice-cream cone with a jaunty chocolate flake. I want everything.

'So, is Keith fair chuffed?'

Her gloved hands grip her mug.

'He doesn't know yet.' She looks up, flicks hair away from her face. 'You see, it's not his. Can't be. I still keep a journal, I can count. So can he.'

Some extraordinary radiance is coming from somewhere. I look away, dazzled. Outside, a pane of glass on the ice-cream van throws the sun into our faces.

I clear my throat.

'Are you going to have it?'

'What do you think I've been up all night for?' she whispers. We stare at each other, speechless for a while.

'Of course I can't have it,' she says eventually. The van moves off, the radiance departs. 'You know why. Anyhow, do I look like a fit mother? But I'm too old to kill anything again. So I can't not have it. But I can't . . .'

For once she's not fiddling or looking away or anything, just helpless and scared with her back to a yellow wall.

'If you have it,' I say, 'there's no way I'll run away. I'll do . . . everything.'

She nods, as though that was obvious.

'There's a slight complication,' she says. Shakes her head. 'Christ, I should have stuck with the Pill. Never trusted the diaphragm.'

My voice comes from the bottom of the pit.

'What is it?'

She puts her hand over her eyes. It slides down over her mouth, and though what she says next is muffled, there's no mistaking it.

'Graeme,' she says.

And then she spells it out.

'The afternoon before the night you and me . . . Yes, I know it sounds terrible and hoorish but it wasn't like that. He'd been down seeing you, came by . . . I wanted one last time with the men I loved most before settling with Keith.'

She spreads her gloved hand on the red plastic table top. I take it and feel a terrible headache coming on as she twines her fingers round mine.

'It could be either of you,' she says, squeezes convulsively and it hurts like hell. I'd forgotten how strong she was, in her way.

The baby begins to girn, the young man glances our way and tells his device he'll be a little late but no he hasn't forgotten and yes he loves her. She begins to cry quietly into her coffee.

'Get me out of here,' she whispers, 'I'm so embarrassed.'

We wandered for hours along the shore, talking and not talking. She cried some more, my eyes filled with painful water and the headache eased. In the end we sat hunched in our coats, holding hands like troubled teenagers, with nothing left to say.

It started snowing as we stumbled back towards Keith's car. I insisted on driving her back to Glasgow. I could still see her foot hesitate above the brake then stamp down hard. She wasn't going to kill herself or anyone else, not that day. Beyond that, I couldn't protect or police her.

Most of the way back she sat silently in the passenger seat, her scarf keeping her mouth well hid.

'I didn't mean -' she said once, then stopped.

I still wonder exactly what she didn't mean.

Early dark. Keith's car hadn't been badly damaged, just a buckled wing and a busted headlight. We chanced it and drove on, one-eyed into the West, towards the dark and Graeme's town. As we went down the Great Western Road she agreed Graeme had to be told. She'd write to him tomorrow. Promise? She nodded. I never knew her break a promise, she made so few of them. And Keith? Long silence. Only the tremble of her shoulders told me she was crying again and for the first time I realised how much she stood to lose.

If she was going to have the baby, she'd have to tell him the truth. He could bloody count. What would happen then? She shook her head. And if not?

We turned into the broad quiet street where Keith lived. She shivered and hugged herself. If not, if she didn't have the baby, he might never have to know. It could stay a secret. In time we'd all forget it. She still cared for him, very much. Loved. Anyway, she wasn't going to break up what Graeme and I both had now. It wasn't fair, she wasn't worth it.

'Balls,' I whispered. 'I prefer you in egomaniac mode.'

But that was it, far as she was concerned. Have the baby and disrupt all our lives. Or not have it and we all went on as before as if nothing had happened.

I shook my head. Sometimes she defied disbelief.

'You have any better ideas?' she snapped.

'You know what I think. And want.'

She stared back at me, long nose and deep eyes shadowed in the streetlight. Finally she nodded, looked away.

'But I'll be behind you, whatever.'

I didn't dare say more. She put her hand on mine, quickly, impersonally, like someone touching wood for luck. Then she straightened her hat, her scarf, and got out of the car.

'I'll let you know,' she said, 'soon as I know.'

'Kim?'

'Yeah?'

'No more stunts like today's.'

She shook her head. I think that meant Yes, and I walked off to catch a train home.

When I got off at Dunbar the night was very still. The stars were spattered all over the sky like an exploded diamante brooch, and I had a criminal headache.

My answerphone was blinking. A message from Ruth. She had to see me, soon.

That avalanche, it carried me a long way. Maybe 800 feet and over a couple of small cliffs, MacBeth said later. After the acceleration and the confusion, I remember the dense silence when it all suddenly stopped, creaked – then bundled me away again. Then was there time to be truly frightened before I was falling through space, trailing snow and ice like some minor comet.

'Thanks for coming down,' Ruth said. 'This is hard.'

She was sitting apart from me, Mary in bed, the house quiet. Between my seat and hers slept the recent arrival tentatively known as *us*. I nodded, still wondering how to tell her.

'Listen, there's something I have to say,' she said. 'It's serious. Well it's not that serious. No, it is.'

She's pregnant, I thought.

'Ewan and me have had another long talk, the other night. And, well, he proposed to me.'

'Good God!'

I sounded like my father, who didn't believe in a good God either.

'That's wild,' I added. 'After the way you parted and all this time.'

'Maybe,' she said and stared at her hands. 'But it's changed everything.' She glanced up. 'That's why I had to see you. I'd no idea, honest. You still there?'

'Yes.'

I sat on the edge of the chair looking at her carpet, my insides starting to go down like those wee plastic divers you used to get in cereal packets.

'We'd been talking,' she said hurredly. 'I was saying I only wanted monogamy now, that being single and having the odd fling to keep the wolf from the door seemed sterile for me. I told him how it was with you, that we might commit ourselves and have children. Then he said he'd finally come round to that too, life-long commitment to somebody, but the only person he'd ever wanted that with was me, and Mary. And then I started crying. You are still there?'

The orange maze pattern on the carpet was ugly but interesting.

'More or less.'

'As soon as he said that, I knew I'd got everything wrong. It had always been him.'

'You mean,' I said carefully, just to get it clear, 'you're seriously considering it? This proposal? You said you'd no interest in marriage, nor in him.'

'Yes, I am seriously considering it.'

'I believed you when you said that was over.'

'So did I.'

I'd seen the two of them together, listened very carefully when she'd said she didn't fancy him at all, that it was hard to credit she'd loved him for ten years. Her tone of faint surprise and sadness that feelings can change so had convinced me. She was a woman, so she was naturally more in touch with her true feelings than I was, everyone agreed on that.

'Please believe me now. I wasn't lying to you. I really believed it too. But all this has been me running away and hoping he'd leave Catherine and come back. Can you understand that?'

I dragged myself out of the interesting maze and looked at her pleading, resolute face. The night was very still as we stared each other out.

'I believe you. I just feel . . . foolish.'

I listened so carefully, I thought, and still got it wrong.

'We didn't do anything definite. I mean, didn't sleep with him. But I'm pretty sure. I do love him. He's been part of me for so long. And he's Mary's dad, you must have some idea what that means.'

'Sure do,' I said. 'We are talking about the same Ewan, aren't we? The one you couldn't imagine you'd ever fancied, the one who drank too much, spent your money, slept with your friends and colleagues, the one you feel sorry for and hope he'll finally commit himself to his girlfriend?'

'You *are* angry.'

'Course I'm fuckin angry.'

She looked down.

'It's been lovely,' she said. 'I'd be angry too.'

She was hunched forward, sucking her pinkie. I wanted to put my arms round her and say it was alright, but it wasn't. And I still hadn't told her. There was no point now, except a little revenge.

'I know all this – ' she gestured to include me, herself, the fast-disappearing shade of *us* – 'has really been Ewan and me working it out. I'm just sorry you got caught in the middle. I've been happy, you've given me back so much worth I'd lost, and now I'm ready to be with Ewan again, on my own terms this time . . .'

Her low voice faltered.

'It's kindof ironic,' I said. More than she'd ever know. 'After me and all my unfinished business you've had to put up with.'

'I know,' she said, and laughed a little. 'I guess the strong, loving, self-knowing woman doesn't exist either.'

The carpet and its tacky maze – all those orange and green whorls – could be considered comic, if only I could escape from it. Looked at from high enough up I'm sure we were funny, running around in circles at the foot of our wee hill of beans, but I couldn't get that high up any more.

And then there was nothing more to be said, though we said it half the night. There was no point in pleading or persuading, even less in being angry though I said some bitter things and held others back. She bowed her head, didn't disagree, didn't budge.

And though she didn't know about my night with Kim, I felt a superstitious connection, that I'd lost Ruth and deserved to because of it. How very nearly it could have been.

I slept downstairs on the settee for what was left of that night. I saw Graeme turning to me at the bottom of the Old Man of Hoy, Ruth and Mary waving from the cliff-top, Kim blown out to sea with her arms outstretched like holding an invisible sail. I stood on the shore with a coiled rope in my hand, unsure which way the wind would blow it, and who if anyone could be saved.

Ten days later I was walking down the same road from the station on my way back from a trip checking out a dome site in the Pennines. A complete waste of time, my concentration was shot. The evening was very mild, Spring a possibility again. Re-birth and that. I was hurrying back to the house to see if Kim had left a message. If she hadn't, I'd phone her anyway. Couldn't wait any longer, I needed something definite.

The chip shop invited in the half-dark. There'd be no scran in the house, so I went in and stood in the queue. Glanced at the *Six O'Clock News* on the TV above the frier, seemed like nothing much was happening.

I ordered my fish supper and looked at myself in the glass – jeans, tweed jacket, briefcase, ear-ring, brogues – pretty mixed-up character. Didn't look like my idea of anyone's dad. What man does, compared to his father?

'Salt 'n sauce, Jim?'

'Salt, Ada.'

I remember feeling a squirm of sympathy for Joan as I left the chipper. She wanted a child but couldn't, Kim didn't but could. An obvious solution there, but nothing's that neat. And Graeme, fifty-fifty he's helped bring life into this world he's so down on. I almost smiled, trying to picture his face when he'd got Kim's letter. Had to talk to him.

I wandered down the brae to the harbour, tearing off strips of hot fish, blowing and licking my fingers. In the Electrical Repair shop, a couple of screens flickered in the dark interior. I went past, stopped, went back and looked again.

Bloody hell, the Old Man of Hoy, from the land side. Good to see, like an old friend with whom one's had a long flirtation. I couldn't hear the commentary, but the camera zoomed in on the long overhanging crack then panned smoothly up past where I'd fallen in another life. A back rope had been left fixed in position.

That would save a bit of hassle. I wondered if Graeme was watching the programme, he might be tempted to nip over there and do it himself. Watching, I rather hoped he didn't. We were always meant to do it together.

The camera slid up to the summit, and I shook my head in disbelief. It must be a bleeding model – and they'd got it wrong. Typical. Instead of the familiar lop-sided two summit blocks, there was only one, sticking up alone.

I laughed and began to move off, stopped and stared, a chip half-way to my mouth. The camera had cut to interviewing two men with ropes and gear who looked like part of a rescue team. Behind them was a group of people standing on top of the Hoy cliffs. Behind them was the Old Man. It couldn't be a model. But it had to be. There was only one summit block left.

Some kind of film, I thought.

The TV screens cut back to the studio presenter's face. It was the Scottish News alright, not a mock-up or a reconstruction but something recent, something that had happened today, some newsworthy accident –

I dropped the fish supper and sprinted for the house, but even as I ran, I knew. The answerphone light was blinking like mad, a stack of messages. And even as I pressed *Play*, I knew what I was going to hear.

Only the darkness, and the sound of blood pounding in my snow-stopped ears.

This is what you do when the avalanche comes to rest and you are buried not knowing which way to get out: bring up some saliva. It dribbled across my right cheek. I began scraping in the opposite direction, the one that had to be up.

TWENTY-FOUR

Exhaust

QUIET HERE NOW, like after a pin has dropped. If distant motors have gone by, I haven't noticed them. There are none now. But this empty room is full of voices shaking the moonlight on the climbing ropes, glinting dully on the tangled web of pitons, slings, friends and karabiners. And in the darkness over the harbour, those faces still turn my way as they once did.

I roll a final cigarette, exhale the light dry tobacco of Virginia and look into the space that's been closing, these last nights, between now and then.

I find the hotel where Ayr shades into Prestwick, near the long curved beach I remembered. Kim and I stayed here one night during the Golden Triangle on a week of driving and screwing. We were being dense again.

A distant scream as somewhere in the clouds a Jumbo makes its approach. I'd forgotten the sound of the planes through our night here. All those scenes of passion and exhaustion, they must have suited us.

A muffled roar as the engines slam into reverse thrust. I wait for the sound of the smash but there's none. I pick up my wee overnight case and go inside to check in.

The hotel is off-season, half-empty, smells of wood polish and generations of potted geraniums. The receptionist puts down her book, changes faces from dark to sunny. She asks if it's just for one night. Probably, I say, but can I leave that open? You never know. She agrees and I sign the register.

'It was a double room, Mr Renilson?' she asks.

'No,' I say.

'I'm terribly sorry, I must have written it down wrong. My memory . . .'

'Stick with the double. You never know.'

'You never know,' she says and smiles. Nice toothy uncalculated smile. She's about ages with me and has a few lines to her face, just as I do these days. We smile and shake our heads over the unknowability of things for a minute.

'You're here on business, Mr Renilson?' she asks.

'No. Funeral.'

Something flickers behind her eyes.

'Thanks,' I say, pick up my case and key and head upstairs to my room.

I run the bath deep and hot and lie out in it with a cigarette, cup of tea, and my feet up between the taps. It doesn't take long to go coast to coast in this country, and I've hours to kill before the others arrive. I sip and smoke and stare into the wallpaper.

The receptionist looks up from her book.

'Everything alright, Mr Renilson?'

'Jimmy,' I say. 'Hunky-dory. Can't sit in that room any more – thought I'd take a daunder on the beach.'

'It's going to rain.'

'That's the West for you. Rains for fifteen minutes every quarter of an hour.'

She grins though it's an old crack.

'Have fun,' she says.

She picks up her book again. *Grieving and Healing.* Our eyes meet for a moment. You're not the only one, son. Always remember that.

Down to the sand and start walking fast, anywhere.

At low tide the Prestwick sands go on and on. Mostly about emigration and absence. The wind wheichs in from the West and bends the whippy marram grasses that fringe the dunes. It's good to wear a coat, lean into the belts of rain and endure.

Graeme was crazy to consider climbing in this. He might have put it off. He might have waited for me. He might have checked a rusting Sixties cable round the summit blocks, before abseiling from it. Idiot.

I throw stones at the sea for a while as the waves accelerate towards the shore. It seems to me they mount like grief and break only when shallowest. In the last three days, the only things that brought tears to my eyes were a raggedy child staring into a shop window and an episode of *The Archers.*

A hill of beans, Jim, I hear him say.

I drop the stone into my coat pocket and wander on.

The sea spreads grey fans onto the sand, then folds them away again. A chunk of pale blue sea-glass. I pick it up, turn it over. Nothing special about it, just a piece of old bottle. You'd need some kind of vision to make anything more of it.

I drop it into my other pocket and walk on, pressing it slippy into my palm. So this is what the ultimate triumph feels like, Kim, if we'd known it, long time ago.

I watch the crest of the wave unzip itself from two ends and the breaking ends rush towards each other and meet and all the white foam-feathers fly out. I like the big blank noise, the long gritty sook, the big blow. It's a half gale on the beach now. Think of the poor fishermen at sea, mum used to say. Think of all the fragile ships.

His stone in one fist, her glass in the other, it balances like a funeral and a woman pregnant. And me stuck between them as I come to a stop.

A haar's come in, the sea's trauchled and gull-grey, but what I see over and over when I look out there is the Old Man breaking up, and my friend falling without a word – I'm sure of that, the best ones go that way.

Again he is striving upwards, bridging up the gap between the rough red summit blocks. His face is set, determined, concentrating hard. Left foot, right foot, hands and elbows pushing out, held in place by sandstone's resistance. The wind moans through the gap, there is air all round, gulls and the distant sea glittering through between the blocks. I see him climbing, and then falling, but nothing in-between. I cannot see him on the summit as I turn back to retrace the way I came.

Wind over the Prestwick sand dunes and wind through the Dunbar pines sound much the same. I lean on my windowsill at four in the morning, still listening and talking with people who are not there. It's a hard habit to break. Perhaps that's why I've not loved, not really, anyone since – except Rina. And then I wave my hand irritably and say Na, na, don't give me pop songs, spare me the Country and Western. I'm not finished yet.

I lean on the windowsill, I squeeze the sea-glass on Prestwick sands, and let myself merge. They say anything fully experienced needn't be repeated. I'm neither washed up nor dried out, I'm not dessicated coconut! This stint is almost done and I want you to know that when I've met my responsibility to you, I will go downstairs, pick up the grip that's waiting there, and go on.

The woman at reception looks up from her book and smiles.

'Good walk?'

'Such quantities of sand,' says I.

'You wept?'

I nod and smile back. 'Like anything. Must have been the wind in my eye.'

'I'll bet,' she says. 'That kind of wind.'

Though she's smiling there's something around her eyes that says Yes, she knows that kind of wind.

'I could go tea and scones and raspberry jam.'

'With or without cream, Jimmy?'

She leans forward on the counter, propping her chin on her left fist. She's married, or was. Her mouth's broad and humorous and she's really rather lovely, but her eyes are dark and her hair is brown so it's okay.

Her badge says *Laura*. Something demeaning about those badges. Kim hated having to wear one when she worked in the café.

'Kill me with kindness and cholesterol, Laura.'

'Might as well go out in style,' she says, but her voice catches and I wonder about the wedding ring.

I sit in the lounge in a faded chintz armchair by the window and wait for my tea. The light's poor and it's coming on rain and there's an empty feeling gathering like a wave that's still to break. I sit watching raindrops hit the glass, hesitate then streak downwards.

'I'm sorry that took a while,' Laura says and puts the tray of tea and scones down on my table. 'A guest came to Reception and I completely forgot.'

'I was in a dwam, I didn't notice.'

When she smiles the lines at the corner of her mouth are like litle brackets, as though she smiles as an aside.

'Me too,' she says. 'My husband Peter -'.

She stops. I can see it go through her, brief as lightning.

'Sorry,' I say, not knowing for what but that I am sorry.

She looks away, out the window. When she turns back there's a slight smile.

'My husband used to say I was the only person who could serve lunch while being completely out to it.'

'Are you the manager, then?'

'Not yet. Assistant manageress, receptionist, tea lady and chatterer-in-chief. Used to be in insurance but there isn't any, is there? Enjoy your cholesterol.'

She goes through the swing doors with a slight bounce in her step. I look out the window for a while, then slit open the scone which is hot as it should be, spread the butter, pile on the red jam and the smell of warmth and raspberries brings back summers in Blairgowrie with Bridget. I'd planned on going there in summer with Ruth and Mary, the wean would have had a great time. I can see her red bike, the one I'd stripped and re-painted, left lying in the long grass above the shore, and hope someone – Ewan, perhaps – tells her to bring it in.

I sit in the empty lounge in an off-season hotel run by a young widow with a cheese-grater for a memory, with scones I've suddenly lost desire for what with that bright pulpy jam, and something stuck in my throat that no amount of tea will wash away.

'Phone for you,' Laura says. 'Transatlantic. From America. She does sound in a state.'

I'm ready now to face this bit, brush the myrtle leaves from my hands and pick up Kim's last letter. The pages blur, become transparent, like the dawn breaking outside my window.

Kim's breakdowns, crack-ups, 'episodes' they call them, like some malign soap-opera, the first one you see is the worst. It is watching someone you love die over and over. It starts with the early morning jumbled phone call, then the drive through the dark with a vision of her drowning, going down flailing in her mind. Then the pleading at her door, elaborate tests to establish who you really are, reduced to pushing your credit card under the door (she's sealed the letter-flap) and it comes back shredded. Her sobs and rages, muffled speech like she's talking through a towel, the terrible silences. And eventually she lets you in and her hands and eyes and words whirr like disconnected piston-rods.

There is no way to describe how that feels, other than say she is dying, over and over. For a bit she comes to life, she speaks normally, and then she starts to die again.

And Lesley comes, or Alison, whichever friend is in reach to help bear it. And you let them in and she says you have betrayed her, you will kill her, she will kill you with her thoughts. And you grab her. She goes rigid. You sit her down, you let her go, she belts you in the mouth and makes for the kitchen drawers.

At that point you admit it's over. Lesley holds her and you make two phone calls. And in the hospital car park – limp as laundry all the way – her hands strike for Lesley's eyes, a blur and you see her face snap back, then she collapses into Les' chest, a shaking damaged hand stroking her dark head.

She looks up at us, returned for a moment. 'Please,' she says. 'Yes?' Long pause, she looks away to somewhere you can never follow her. 'Please.'

And at Reception where the 'episodes' are received, she is led away, passive, unresisting. And she turns once to look back and you know you have betrayed her. She looks back, her white face, shock of black hair, the shocked stripped eyes. Then they help her round the corner and she's gone though her eyes linger, and all that's left to do is find out about visiting times and the two of you crawl home with what's left of your humanity.

The first time is the worst, the shock of it. But the second time is the worst too, because then you must accept there will be other times.

I smooth out her last letter and lay it in the lamplight one more time.

Don't get me wrong – I'm grateful beyond words but still wish you hadn't seen me like that and I resent it – Can you understand? – It comes between us when I'm well, when you must treat me like anyone else – please humour me in this.

But thank you for holding on, for getting me to the hospital whatever I said and did. For me, I felt like Eurydyce (spelling?) being drawn out of the Underworld and I nearly came to the surface but at the last minute you looked round, didn't you, you doubted me. Perhaps if you had no doubt I could always be in my right mind – so I let go and slipped away again.

Dearie me. Dearie dearie me.

It could happen again, it probably will if I don't keep taking the sweets.

I don't know if I can live with that.

It's early evening here, after visiting time, between tea and the night trolley and medication. No therapy groups, no assessments, no nothing. Two of the anorexic girls are whispering, Paul's slip-slopping around in slippers singing *Mama We're All Crazee Now*, which was funny at first but is getting on my nerves. The three women and that poor man with the stammer, the ones who had ECT this morning, are staring into space and suddenly I miss my mum. The card school are hard at it. I'm getting edgy and bored now. Apparently this is a good sign: I'm 'stabilised' – would to God the Orkney ferry was! I'd love to get there again . . .

I'm bored and it's on my mind to try for once to tell you how it is with me.

My work's my lifeline, you've always understood that. It's also my noose. When I'm hard at it, patterns and meanings are offered everywhere, days and weeks when everything fits. I get excited and the excitement feeds the meaning which feeds back into the excitement – it all intensifies – and then the pattern of leaves in the gutter, words on the background radio, the depths of the afternoon, all speak to me alone. Numbers, angles, the room across the street and the blade in my hand, the child's balloon, the creak of the garden gate before dawn, they all speak to me alone. They all *mean*. Sleep's impossible when patterns of light are messages from the Absolute – voices in the street outside ventriloquise my dad, his hand guides mine as I work. If I concentrate hard enough, all will be explained and redeemed and I'll never again have to open that door and see him spread there and his blood still gobbing –

Sorry. But all these significances they enter like whispers into the things I make. If my stuff moves anyone, that's why. And without them – this is it – I'm not even adequate.

I'm tired and lyrical and brain's running away with me a bittie despite the medication. Now day by day I can feel it retreating, the weirdness, the beauty, and the world becoming mute and ordinary again – words mean only what they say, the branches in the trees outside the ward are only branches after all, and the Beautiful – the Absolute – World does not exist. It's gone.

Maybe you felt like that when I left. That the light and its madness had gone. I used to be angry with you, feeling you were over-reacting, but now accept you were right. Because I too know that sober emptiness. Level-headed and in my right mind, it's so flat and banal and I'm so hateful it seems there's nothing for me here. On medication I can cope alright, but deep down I'd rather be dead.

There, I've written it. Dearie me. But that's why sooner or later I'll stop taking the medication again, because I need my Beautiful World and its meanings and my toys . . .

My noose is my lifeline. And now I want to sleep until the world is over –

That's all I can take for now. I'm laying aside her letter. Only the last page remains, her scrawled postscript added a few days later, the last thing she wrote me. It makes sense when you know the rest, as you will.

Laura puts her hand on my shoulder, and firmly sits me down.

'I'm sure this is really unprofessional,' she says, 'but I once needed someone to talk to, and it helped.'

I look at her and I can see she's been there. She has the authority and I'm just a beginner in these things. In telling Lesley about Graeme's death, I have just passed through kindergarten. There was no gentle way to tell it. She'll not make the funeral, she'll be over when she can. Please notify Tess, she says. I already have. And what about Kim? And I have to explain about that, and listen to the silence washing over the distance until she speaks again and gives her instructions.

'How long have you got, Laura?' I ask.

She takes out a cigarette and swings her legs over the arm of the chair.

'As long as you give. Or until the lunches start.'

I look at my hands, my jailers somehow. There has to be some sense in these things.

'Only if you'll tell me about your man.'

TWENTY-FIVE

The Equations

THE TABLE'S ALMOST clear, there are no motors running, the game's near done. I pick up the last piece of Kim's Game, the Prestwick hotel business card with three scrawled equations on the back. I wait, holding it carefully at a distance.

He wakes, dazed and distant. Lunchtime sleep after a couple of drinks on an empty stomach. Already he can hear the voices downstairs. He swings his legs down and notices the hotel's business card on the bedside table. His own writing.

He frowns, pushing away an oncoming headache. He can't quite remember what he and Laura said, his mind wasn't functioning right. But eventually he'd come upstairs and scrawled a set of equations that resolved everything.

He peers at them again.

Painting – is Archaeology.

Hill of Beans = slopes of volcano.

Ships sail through the Aquarium.

Just what he needs, a message from himself to himself in gibberish. At the back of his mind a fourth equation is whispering. *The Plane of Severance* . . . Then silence. He sticks the card in an inside pocket. Maybe it'll make sense when he finally comes to. But for now he's overloaded. In clouds.

He takes two aspirin and changes into his dark graduation suit. He checks himself in the mirror. Yup, that's him alright. Maybe he'll come to, in time. Time to go downstairs and face them.

It's difficult to hug a man in a wheelchair, especially when that man is a Scot of the old school with a blasted face and nicotine-stained grey quiff who swaps his cigarette to his left hand, holds out his right and croaks.

'I aye said the laddie would make his mark – jist didnae think he'd re-arrange the geography of Scotland. He'll no be forgot noo, eh?'

'No,' Jimmy agrees. 'He made the headlines alright – and made a lot of tourist guides and postcards out of date.'

The old man inhales, coughs.

'Aye, that's the way of it. Noo, Mary, will ye gie us a push into the kirk – bloody freezin oot here.'

Jimmy watches him go, the old Ayrshire Eagle, head erect, having a last defiant drag before the church door. A climber in his day.

He's clutched from behind. Joan puts a cold hand on his cheek then they hold each other up awhile.

'Let's go inside,' she whispers eventually. 'Please sit beside me. I've got some of his climbing things for you.'

Over her shoulder he sees the others starting to arrive. Relatives, some of the climbers, Tess and Alison holding on to Kim, who's chalk-white in a long grey coat. He's scarcely been off the phone the last three days – now all that remains are the handshakes, hugs, fleeting touches on the arm, the service and the drinks, all the assurances of the living that they really are alive and the long cheerio has begun.

Joan kneels in the church. As a former stiff-necked Protestant, Jimmy inclines his head slightly towards the Almighty then sits upright. He is not impressed by God's will, and Joan's prayers make him angry. His father mutters that Graeme is dead not because of God but on account of rust and metal fatigue.

Joan sits up beside him, dry-eyed.

'I suppose Jesus wanted him for a sunbeam,' he mutters.

And regrets his cruelty as she takes his hand and squeezes hard into the pulp between thumb and forefinger.

'So you loved him too, but don't take it out on me.'

The burning pain up his forearm brings tears to his eyes. She relents, lets off the pressure, smoothes out her long black skirt. A snuffling sound. He awkwardly puts his arm round her, then realises she's stifling a giggle.

'Hey, I bet he's already organising the angels for better pay and conditions.'

(It wasn't that great a joke but they laughed. Muffled and stifled, but a laugh. I think now of those times when we were most tormented – with Kim in the Waterfront Wine Bar, with Lesley bent over her bandaged hand, even with Graeme after Disappearing Gully – and suddenly we'd laughed. Not harsh laughter, nor just because we were ridiculous – though we were – but because for a moment we accepted and we were still alive. If I could hand you one spark of radium from this heap of dross, it would be that laughter.)

Across the aisle Kim sits flanked between Tess and Alison like guards. She's taken off her coat. She's in white. She's cut her hair savagely, a devastated version of the jaunty quiff from ten years back. Her neck and ears look terribly vulnerable. She's wearing white flannels, white sweater, white wool jacket with a black velvet border. Her face is blank, her eyes dead – Keith's likely loaded her up with Valium – but she looks like she's about to walk onto a cricket field and flip a coin.

As they get to their feet, he sees Ruth bending over him and for the moment feels the warm drag of her breasts on his face. He must take that as meaning never again. And then the coughing and the first hymn, 'All Things Bright And Beautiful', for pity's sake.

When he next sees properly, Kim is standing on the very lip of the grave. He must be imagining the bump of her belly. He is on her right, slightly behind, balanced by Joan on her left. Fanning out and further back, as though ranked in rows, come the others. Alison and Tess, Graeme's dad and his aunt May. Then the relatives, mostly elderly. Then the climbers, who've been through this before – the Sheffield crowd in their best jeans, a sombre MacBeth, Gypsy and Fairer and Slide. At the end of the line, whispering to the bald Clackmannan, the poet in a cute blue beret. Behind them, Cathy and Shonagh scarcely recognisable in dresses but their fingers flexing involuntarily for the day is dry now, the wind not too cold – it's the beginning of another rock climbing season.

I look down tonight and see them: a frozen echelon, a loose V like a flight of geese. At the leading edge, a pregnant young woman poised over a grave, the rest of the living ranged on either side behind her, supporting, flanking, following her direction. Only the minister is on the other side. The wind is blowing but nothing else moves.

An engine revs and cuts out. Jimmy looks round and sees Mick DeTerre jump down from his jeep, feels no surprise. The group breaks up and straggles back to the hotel for the reception.

Everything happens at a distance. He is strung between Kim and the Old Man, walking the wire. He is frozen, in clouds.

He can't get to Kim. People keep way-laying him. He has to see her alone, talk about the baby. But she's always on the other side of the room, talking with other people. She's in among the climbers, now flushed in a way he's seen before. Her hands and features won't stay still, keep flickering.

'So it could be you or Graeme and she really doesn't know?'

Jimmy sips orange juice, nods, keeping his eye on Kim.

'What about Keith?'

'She's told him. He's asked her to move out. Enough's enough, can't blame him. That's the latest update.'

'Bisom. I could kill her. How dare she!'

He looks at Joan and realises she's half-cut already.

'That's not very Christian.'

'Graeme got her letter at breakfast. By afternoon he was on his way to Orkney to climb your stupid Old Man. Do you think I don't make a connection?'

'There's no telling if she's going to have it,' Jimmy blurts.

Joan's mouth tightens.

'We'll see about that.'

She gulps the rest of her whisky and heads across the hotel lounge towards Kim.

'Hi, comrade. Bad joss this.'

For all the dumb things he says, DeTerre's eyes are alert and curiously gentle. Jimmy decides not to hit him after all.

'Aye,' he says, watching Joan detach Kim from her group. 'No too smairt.'

Mick's re-appearance makes him uneasy, though he can't place why.

'How did you hear about this?'

'Jungle telegraph,' Mick grins. Shakes his big bull's head. 'Na, saw it on the telly, made a couple of calls. He was living with Joanie?'

Jimmy fills him in, Mick nods thoughtfully, lowers his face into his pint. They lean against the bar in silence for a moment. Too many possibilities, Jimmy thinks. I've got to see her.

He pours himself another orange juice – he feels sick and cloudy enough without adding to it. Anyway, he may have to drive somewhere this evening, but where and with whom he can no longer predict. Mick asks about the woman in Perth. Jimmy finally gets his mind back that far, shakes his head. Is he with anyone right now? He says he really doesn't know. And Mick? Snap, he says. Check.

They both look across the room where Joan's got Kim backed against the wall. Looks like she's giving her a right talking to. Kim's hands are in her blazer pockets, her head and shoulders twist from side to side like she's deflecting blows.

'Uh huh,' DeTerre murmurs. 'As the Cold War starts ending, the little hot ones begin. Gotta talk to some people.'

'Try Joan. This is awful for her.'

Mick looks away, scratching his head.

'Yeah,' he says. 'Yeah yeah. I'll miss him. Awkward cuss but on the right side. Catch ya later.'

He heads for the climbers round the far side of the bar. Now surely it's time to get Kim alone.

'I never got on with him, but I'm sorry for your sake, and Lesley's,' Tess says, blocking the way between him and Kim. This is like bloody musical chairs. 'She couldn't make it over in time – but you'll know that, she phoned you before me.'

'Christ, loosen up will you, Tess? Nobody's going to pinch Lesley from you, least of all me.'

Tess scowls, he stares back till she looks down and shakes her head. She folds her glasses and sticks them in her pocket. A brief smile.

'I'm so jealous and she's so popular.'

'That's what she says about you.'

'Then we're daft as each other.'

'She's crazy about you, she just gets scared.'

'Is that what she says?'

'That's what she said.'

Tess almost blushes. It's true, he thinks. Gay or straight, it's the same old heaven and hell.

'She's told me about Kim. We've discussed it.'

'Oh,' he says.

'We'll do whatever's necessary. If she has it. I want to move back North anyway. You understand?'

'I understand. Thanks.'

She nods and slips away. Now surely he can get to Kim. He looks around, sees her going out the door with DeTerre. He's gesturing earnestly, she's laughing. Her coat's still over the chair, so she'll be back.

He goes over to the climbers who are mourning in their own way. The bullshitting yarns are in full flow, tales of Graeme's epics and escapades, shared days and nights with him up and down the country. Already he's becoming myth. Only MacBeth is frowning at the floor, knee jogging restlessly.

'Anither one bites the dust,' he mutters. 'Makes you think, eh? Still, he never should have abbed off that cable. Bad judgement trusting anything from the Sixties.'

He shakes his head again. Jimmy has seen this before. The hard climbers have to persuade themselves every casualty made a mistake. How else can they carry on? Gypsy leans over.

'Hey MacBeth, there's a new finish to the Old Man now – I reckon that counts as a new route.'

MacBeth nods thoughtfully, gets the point.

'So we'd better get up there before some other bugger does.'

'Right,' says MacBeth. 'We'll call it McGlashan's Finish. Can you get away next weekend?'

Jimmy drifts as the plans are made, and overhears Cathy and Shonagh plotting to get in first on the Old Man by flying up mid-week. Shonagh takes his arm and gently pulls him down beside them.

'Tha mi cho duilich, Jimmy.'

'Aye, I'm sorry too.'

'Ciamar a tha Kim?'

He shrugs. There is no language adequate for how Kim is.

'Want to come with us?' Cathy whispers.

He looks from one to the other, sees the excitement in their eyes and finally accepts how ruthless true obsession is.

'No thanks,' he says. 'Truth to tell, the whole thing makes me feel kinda sick.' He fumbles in his pocket, takes out the stone he'd picked off the beach the day before. 'But throw this off the top for me, will you, a ghràidh?'

'Aidh. Ni mise sin, m'eudail.'

'Thanks. And good luck.'

'How's it going?' Laura asks.

Jimmy leans on the Reception desk and can only shake his head. Behind him in the Lounge, a fair party is developing. Graeme's dad, smoking like a lum, has got in amongst the climbers. Tess is talking intently with Alison, who looks up and raises a theatrical eyebrow at him. DeTerre is back, in a corner with Joan, their heads close together. Her hand's on his shoulder, hard to say whether she's holding on to him or holding him away. Outside, Kim is awkwardly climbing out of the jeep, hand in a pocket. As she jumps down, he feels again Graeme part company with rock. Did he say anything? Did he mutter 'Christ', did he fight thin air, cursing, all the way down? Did he finally accept?

Laura's hand on his arm, he opens his eyes again.

'It does get better,' she says. 'At Peter's funeral all I could think of was whether my new black hat was going to blow off and affront me.' She smiles at him almost apologetically. 'It only becomes real later, and that's when it starts hurting.'

Jimmy sits down heavily in the chair beside her. It sounds like the first sensible thing he's heard all day.

'He was part of me,' he says. 'He was my partner. I should have been there.'

Laura pushes her hair away from her mouth and leans towards him.

'Anyone for tennis?' Kim says. She is standing at the front door in her whites, her hands working furiously inside her blazer pockets.

'In that case, can I borrow your room key for a while?'

Her eyes won't hold on his, she is sending out ripples. Maybe DeTerre's been giving her coke.

'*Please*. I just need – a break from all this.'

Laura reaches behind her and silently hands Jimmy his room key, then sits back and picks up her book.

'You alright, Kim? We've got to – '

'I know,' she hisses. 'Later. Leave me alone and I'll sort myself out first.'

Still he hesitates. She is so pale again, she seems to be upright only by an effort of will.

He hands her the key.

'Thanks. Thanks so much.'

She kisses his cheek, then backs away, glances through the glass doors into the lounge, grimaces.

'Don't worry,' she laughs. 'I'm not going anywhere. Promise.'

She hurries up the stairs. A little wave at the top, then disappears.

'So that's Kim Ruslawska,' Laura says eventually. Seeing his expression, she puts down the book. 'I recognised her from a magazine article. Also you told me about her when we were drinking this morning.'

'Did I? Oh God.'

'And I've got something of hers, Peter bought it me. A clear perspex half-hitch, with these little forget-me-not flowers set in it and from just one angle they make a question mark. It's called "Knot".'

He nods, just remembering it. A time of light-hearted puns, and light, pretty things made for money and her amusement. Rain on the attic roof, drinking coffee, reading to her as she worked.

'I can see she must be difficult,' Laura says as he looks away. 'But it's always meant a lot to me. It . . . helped.'

He nods, unable to speak.

'Do you think I should tell her that?'

'Do that. It might help her. She tends to forget she's ever done anything worthwhile.'

He goes outside. Soft, damp West Coast air, sweetest in the world but Graeme won't be smelling it. The Old Man of Hoy makes one hell of a tombstone.

He walks round the garden a few times. He must come to, he must register what's happening. There's a nagging feeling of urgency, like he's missing something important.

He stands outside the French windows and looks in on the life inside. They're all framed there, all the clearer for being inaudible. Graeme's dad leaning forward in his wheelchair, glass in one hand and fag in the other, talking vigorously with Shonagh who seems to be miming a lay-back move. The climbers are bunched in small head-to-head groups. MacBeth sees him, waves him in. Jimmy shakes his head, struck by how grizzled his friend has become.

A lot of scars, visible and invisible, on the people he holds most dear. Alison for instance, now laughing and flirting with Gypsy, living with Gerry's inexorable decline. Joan inclining her head to listen to Graeme's aunt May. Through the other door, Laura staring into space, Laura with her wedding ring and darkness round her eyes, yet her mouth quick to smile. Tess is sitting knee to knee with Cathy, locked in intense discussion. Cathy nods, her hand rests lightly on Tess' arm, the two women lean towards each other and laugh. And DeTerre, who knows where he's been the last three years or why he's re-appeared again to hand the reluctant poet her mandolin.

And the three most important are not there. Graeme no longer anywhere, Lesley getting packed up in the States, and Kim upstairs resting in his room with the future in her if she can bear it.

The end of a rough decade. How can he be an optimist without being an idiot? How can he tell up from down without Graeme around to contradict him? And the missing fourth equation is still out of reach.

He goes back inside. A sequence of departures. He says goodbye to Graeme's dad, aunt May, Joan's going with them. They hug, slightly awkwardly as always.

'I'll not disturb Kim,' she says, 'but one thing's on my conscience. I implied to her that Graeme went for the Old Man because of her letter. That's not really true. He'd already decided to go anyway. I was just really angry – will you tell her that?'

Alison comes through with Tess.

'We've got to get back to Gerry and the bairns,' she says. 'Where's Kim?'

'Gone upstairs for a rest. Best not disturb her.'

'Give her my love and say to come and see us soon. She told me she's split up with Keith – what's going on?'

'I'll tell you later when I know.'

'I see,' she says, and gives him her most old-fashioned look. 'Joan's talking of leaving Shetland and going to South America, sounds like a good idea to me. She tries so hard and she just gets shat on. Come and see us soon.'

They hug goodbye. Tess hesitates then squeezes his arm.

'Don't worry. We'll work something out.'

Inside the Lounge, the remaining climbers are becoming riotous. Their unharmonious voices sing that time is short but the days are sweet. Outside, Mick DeTerre is climbing into his jeep. Jimmy shakes his head and takes a deep breath, about to go in and join them in a session, maybe shake off these clouds that surround him, give Kim a bit more time before going up to see her. He daren't think any more about the possibilities.

Then DeTerre hurries in the front door, grabs him by the arm, hisses in his ear.

'Hey man, one of my guns is gone. The automatic. You know anything about that?'

Kim climbing down from the jeep with her hand in her pocket, Joan's lie to her earlier, Kim's last little wave at the turning of the stair.

It comes clear, and for the first time in hours he comes back to himself.

I used the pass-key and came in fast.

She was huddled in the corner under the window, knees drawn up, one arm across her belly, the other held the gun across her chest like a crucifix to ward off evil. She looked up and I saw she'd come to the end.

'Leave me be,' she whispered. 'Leave me.'

I swung the door shut and took another step forward, watching her hand.

'Leave me alone!'

The gun was pointing at me so I stopped. I didn't know if

she could shoot straight but she looked ready to kill some-one.

The barrel moved up, down, across me as though she was trying to sketch. Her other hand came up and clasped her wrist. I looked at that little black hole, had my hand out as though that would protect me. Nothing in life can prepare you for standing on the wrong end of a gun.

'Why don't you . . . fucking . . . leave me in peace.'

Whoever she was talking to, she hated him.

My stomach felt terribly exposed and soft. I wondered how likely she'd be to miss and if I could get to her in time. It looks easy in the movies but with a loaded weapon pointing now at my face and that look in her eyes, between me and her was too far.

I lowered my hand, slowly, and said the first thing that came into my head.

'For Christ's sake Kim, be original.'

Her eyes closed for a moment, then opened. I stopped mid-step.

'I killed him.'

I made a guess.

'You didn't kill Graeme. He'd knocked off the Old Man and it was an accident. Joan lied, he was already going to do it before he got your letter.'

'He called my name,' she whispered.

Wrong guess.

'Your dad was dead before you opened the door! You didn't do it and you couldn't have stopped it. He must have been out of his mind but you're not.'

'It runs in families,' she said. 'He was right to do it.'

She slowly bent her wrist and looked down at the gun like she hadn't really seen it before.

I put all the conviction I'd never felt into what I said.

'You are not schizophrenic, Kim. You are saner than anyone could expect. We can manage.'

She pressed the gun gently to her chest as though comforting it.

'Kim!'

Her head slumped and shook slowly from side to side.

'Christ, give the bairn a chance! We can do better than the past. Got tae!'

Her head came up then. Her lips opened. Her voice was tiny, puzzled.

'If I'm not schizophrenic, the baby won't be?'

'That's right,' I said and tried to smile. 'All its fathers are certifiably sane.'

She didn't seem to hear me. She lifted the gun and stared into the barrel.

'How could you do that to me?' she said. She wasn't talking to me.

'I'll no do it,' she said, and her hand dropped to the floor.

I grabbed the gun from her before she changed her mind. Found the safety catch, pushed – it had been off alright. I put it on the bedside table and turned to her to do what I could.

She wept and wailed the whole aquarium empty. I just held her and made inarticulate noises.

Finally we helped each other to our feet. Her face was stripped bare, but human again.

'I must look a fright,' she said shakily and almost smiled. 'I'd better wash my face.'

'Marry me.'

'Should I?'

We stared at each other, astonished. Then a banging on the door. She fled into the bathroom. I picked up the gun and went to answer.

'Don't ask,' I said to Mick.

He took it, checked the safety and thrust the gun into his camouflage jacket.

'No problems, comrade?'

'None we can't face.'

He nodded. 'See you at the christening, then.'

He grinned and left, made his way slowly down the stairs. At the turn he waved before disappearing, our catalyst, our dark angel. When I turned back she was standing there.

'Well?' she said quietly. 'Shall we?'

I looked into her face, into her eyes looking steadily back into mine, and it was clear as day.

'No,' I said. 'It's owre late for that.'

She checked my face and nodded like I'd made sense for once.

'Sorry about the melodrama.'

'Ach.'

'Joan must hate me. I'll have to explain . . .'

'He was already going. My guess is he was really chuffed at you being pregnant.'

'You think so?'

307

'I'm sure,' I said, fibbing again. 'We'd talked about that kind of thing before.'

She took a few deep breaths and absently stroked her stomach.

'I'll have to have it, then.'

'Yes.'

'I'm scared,' she said, and looked it. 'I mightn't be completely nuts, but I'm no exactly getting any better. I don't think a baby would always be safe with me. And I need to work, I have to travel for commissions, and my mum's too old to look after it.'

She always knew how to ask.

'Les and me have talked on the phone. She's still not ready to commit herself to Tess, and I'll be away a fair bit with these domes, but if it comes to it, one of us will aye be there.'

'We could do tests,' she said then hesitated. 'Keith told me. To find out if it's yours.'

'Doesna matter a damn to me,' I said. 'Far as I'm concerned, we all made this wean.'

She considered it almost absent-mindedly, as though her attention was already drifting.

'Fair enough,' she said quietly. 'I had only two parents, and it didn't do me much good. We could surely do better than that. What will Ruth say?'

'She's offski. Back to Ewan.'

'I'm sorry,' she said.

'Me too.' I looked down at my hands, remembering. There'd be plenty of nights for that. 'And money, don't worry about that.'

'Thanks,' she said. 'Money doesn't matter but it's important, eh?' She dropped onto the bed and sniffed a couple of times like she was about to greit again. Then she straightened her back, pushed her small, broad hands through her hair and looked at me.

'Weel, I'd better get into some work before the wean arrives,' she said. 'Perhaps this has all been my apprenticeship and one day I'll do something fantastic. That's the only thing that counts in the end.'

'And this. Love. Y'know.'

She laughed.

'You're so sentimental.'

'Everybody's got to be someone,' I said, 'and that's who I am.'

She looked at me hard.

'Congratulations,' she said. 'Ruth's been better for you than I ever was.'

She looked away, out the window. Me, I was cried out for

the day. I packed my bag, there was no reason to stay any longer.

We said our goodbyes. Keith was coming to pick her up later, he was always a decent man, she said. She'd probably move back to Edinburgh, find a flat. Dunbar wasn't far, but far enough. Did I understand? I understood.

At the door, I looked back at her sitting small and distant and almost demure on the edge of the bed, staring into the middle distance. I wanted to hug and hold and protect her always, but that was my need, not hers.

'Makes no odds who the dad is,' I repeated. The rest came out in a rush. 'We all made the bairn and I'll aye be there. So will Les, I know. Graeme's in us, we're all part of each other. You and me, we've aye kent that.'

The longest look from deep inside the aquarium. The monsters were out and named now. Her mouth opened but nothing more came out.

'Love you too,' I said quickly. 'Dinna be a stranger.'

I closed the door and slowly went down the narrow stair. Though we'd be connected till one of us buried the other, in a way that had been our final interview, the one that completed our first conversation. She knew her work now. And the question of who I was – that was haivers. I've aye known who I am. I'm the child of my mother and my father and my country. And now I was a parent of the child-to-be. That's the centre. That's where the compass point digs in. The circumference is as wide as you care to make it.

The climbers had gone, suddenly as migrating birds. I paid the bill to Laura for a night I'd never had, explained Kim would be down later. She looked at me but didn't ask.

'Maybe see you again, on some happier occasion,' she said, and added her easy, slightly lop-sided smile.

'I hope so,' I said, 'though there's a way to go before I'm any use to man nor beast. Good luck to you.'

'Make your luck, Jimmy. Keep in touch.'

We hesitated then shook hands. She went back to her book and I felt oddly free to be the man walking across the car park, smiling to himself, on a mild March afternoon.

I slung my bag in the back, turned the key and drove away from that little seaside town.

For a while I thought about Kim sitting alone but not alone in the upstairs room, then I thought about Graeme, then Lesley and Ruth and Joan, and then I forgot. Lanark came and went. On the car radio the Corries were singing 'Sally Free and Easy' as I drove and central Scotland went by inside, outside, all around me, the shadows on the windows and the things themselves.

TWENTY-SIX

I LEAN FORWARD and turn down the lamp.

Until this moment I've believed the best of my life was in the time spent with her, and all that intensity and joy which will not come again. As long as I believed that, there would always be buried anger and reproach in this telling. But now I look out the window and it's so clear that the most valuable part began when she left. Only then did I begin to learn. The best gift she ever gave was leaving.

Hell's teeth, I believe that.

And I sit back from the table open-mouthed.

The table is clear now. I have tried to tell you, Irina, the things you should know when you're old enough. Anything more, just ask. No no-go areas, right?

All that remains is the last page of her letter.

Yes, come and see me next week. I do want to see you, and by then I'll no be a daftie! My hands will be quiet – I'll be your old friend, walking and talking like I used to, just a little less sparky – till the next time – and yes there probably will be a next time because I won't keep taking the medication.

So there likely will be more 'episodes' and more Art – who knows how it will end, but everything outside the Beautiful World ends.

And what you did, you bastard, with my diaphragm – well I can forgive, for it has given us Irina. The lowest thing you ever did was the best. We'll work something out, the trust is there and the past like a rope has bound us together. Thank you all so much, thank you for taking care of her. Thank Lesley for her kindness in coming back to stay.

Yes, come next Thursday unless you hear from me. Come early and alone – I can't face the others yet, not even Rina – and please make no fuss, accept me and don't ask too much more. Must stop – they're bringing the squeaky trolley with tea and sticky buns and the pill buckets. Come early and bring flowers that have no secret messages

> *but love*
> *K.*

*

I fold the letter back into the envelope, brush in the myrtle leaves, put it away in its place on top of the pile, methodical to the last.

I lean on the windowsill, yawning, not used to these all-nighters any more. Soon it will be time to wash, pick up the grip I've packed for Kim and drive to the hospital. Buy flowers on the way, as she requested. Take her to her mum's in Plean till she's ready to go back to her flat and Rina, and from there on we live it day by day. Lesley has committed herself to staying, Tess is already looking for a house and studio in Musselburgh. The new extended family, you might say, and I hope it's suited you.

The hardest is knowing that once in a while we'll have to fetch Kim from the shades. This last crack-up decided us – and thank God she'd packed Rina away to Plean when she saw it coming – but if she can find the strength to live with that, so must we. Psychosis and miracle, you might say.

I turn over the hotel card and glance at the equations again, thinking about her and me, and Rina sprawled restlessly in her T-shirt, that precious mongrel who will in time become independent as any of us can be. And finally that elusive fourth equation comes to me from some old engineering text book. I lean over and carefully add it to the others.

The plane of severance is also the plane of connection.

I put the hotel card in my pocket, maybe I'm ready to use it soon. Downstairs, Laura's latest postcard is pinned to my cork board. She wrote *Healing over – how about you? Forget knot . . .*

The light rises over the harbour where the small ships bob. The shadows on the windowpane reflect back the room I'm in, and in them I see Jimmy driving home from Graeme's funeral at the end of a rough decade, watching Scotland slide by his windscreen.

And through all these shadows a man, bridging hard but confidently up the final moves, sets his hands on the sandstone lip and pulls. One knee up onto the coarse, sweet-smelling grass of the summit, then the other. Wary, exultant, he slowly gets up off his knees. The wind whips his clothes, the sea is shining grey. He stands up straight and looks to the south.

On a better day you can see Scotland clear.

I lean forward and blow out the lamp.